THE Dating Ban

FINDING MYSELF...
ONE CLAY GNOME AT A TIME

Copyright © 2025 by Dani Elias

All rights reserved. No part of this publication may be reproduced, stored or transmitted in any form or by any means, electronic, mechanical, photocopying, recording, scanning, or otherwise without written permission from the publisher. It is illegal to copy this book, post it to a website, or distribute it by any other means without permission. This novel is entirely a work of fiction. The names, characters and incidents portrayed in it are the work of the author's imagination. Any resemblance to actual persons, living or dead, events or localities is entirely coincidental.

© Copyright Dani Elias. All Rights Reserved.

Copyright Protected with www.ProtectMyWork.com

Editor: Sofia Artola Diaz
Proofreader: Stephanie Savu / Happily Booked PR
Beta Reader: Nina Harris

PA Support: Happily Booked PR & Nina Harris

Contents

Content Warning		VII
Dedication		IX
1.	Three Boners	1
2.	Pee-Pee	7
3.	Marketing Genius	21
4.	Sun Salutation	31
5.	Attack of the Ladybug	39
6.	Bendy Yoga Friends	49
7.	Dazzled by the Warrior	59
8.	I like Brunch	69
9.	Just Friends	77
10.	The Frozen Hulk	91
11.	Collapsed Star	101
12.	Massive G and Wonky I	109
13.	Chicken Soup for the Army of Gnomes	117

14.	SOS from Kent	131
15.	Quack and Other Treatments	143
16.	The Wettest Dry Hump in History	155
17.	Being Human	163
18.	Lost, Soaked, Frozen, or Eaten by Foxes	171
19.	Indoor Survival Queen	181
20.	Austrian Baking Logic	191
21.	Victory to the Loser	201
22.	Peanut Butter Laundry Fraud	209
23.	Crazy Frog Secrets	219
24.	Somewhere in Dorset	225
25.	Hopalong and the Queen	233
26.	Emergency Jammie Dodgers	241
27.	Exile in the Shower Shed	249
28.	Great Survival Adventure	259
29.	Someone's Packing	267
30.	Unbalanced	273
31.	Level Up	283
32.	Overthinking Drama Queen	291
33.	The Green Lamp Conspiracy	301

34.	The Siege of Vienna	311
35.	Austen-esque	319
36.	Three Tubs of Ice Cream	329
37.	Most Handsome Channel Islander	335
38.	Cuddles, Kisses & Ice Cream	351
39.	Bracing for Impact	359
40.	Nervous Bugs in my Tummy	367
More from Dani Elias		385

Content Warning

This book contains all of the following:
> Strong language
> Scenes of sexual nature
> Adult content
> Infertility

If any of this serves as a trigger for you, please decide if this is the book for you.

Finally, the book is set in England and British English spelling is used throughout. That means a lot of times you'll find an "S" where you may expect a "Z". And our ass has an extra Rrrrr to it ;-). Also get ready to learn new words like knobhead and numpty.

Dedication

To everyone who thought, "This isn't how my life was meant to go" and somehow ended up somewhere better, stranger, or wearing significantly less clothing. Enjoy every second!

THE Dating Ban

FINDING MYSELF...
ONE CLAY GNOME AT A TIME

DANI ELIAS

1
Three Boners

Ivy

THERE THEY ARE. ONE... two... three. Three boners pointing straight at me. It's like a dirty version of Goldilocks. One cock that's too long (seriously not sure where Michael wants to put that but my mouth is a no, because, hello gag reflex!); one dick that is definitely too thick (Harry does have a bit of a mini barrel there); and then there is the one that looks just right, not too long not too thick. Maybe I should have stuck with just Graham.

Ivy, what did you get yourself into this time?

One minute I am flirting with three guys in a bar, next I am kneeling naked on Harry's bed, ready for my first foursome. Well, ready might be a bit of an exaggeration. To be honest, when Harry—or was it Michael—first suggested a bit of group fun, it sounded incredibly exciting. I imagined them all three worshipping my body, hands and mouths everywhere. Reality was slightly different. Graham kissed me and undressed me whilst the others stripped off. Michael led me to the bed and then they just lined up and looked at me. I was almost expecting them to go, "Rock, paper, scissors!" to decide on who gets to fuck me first.

"I'm not one for the big girls normally, but your big arse is mighty fine," Michael chuckles as he crawls behind me and strokes over my bum. *Excuse me? This big girl might punch you right where it hurts in a minute.*

"Baby girl, open up for me," Harry groans and stabs at my lips with his dick like when you try to get a key into a keyhole in the dark. I almost swat him away and not just because it is annoying but because he called me *baby girl*. I hate that. I mean, to each their own, but I never really did go for the whole baby-daddy thing.

Before I can say something wrong, I open my mouth and he pushes his girthy cock in. He tastes... not great, but I just get on with it hoping that my sacrifice will be rewarded with an orgasm or two... for me, that is.

"Great, and what do I do?" Graham asks before I can feel his fingers on my bum hole. *Absolutely not!*

I pull away from Mr Barrell-dick and shout, "No!"

"Calm down, baby girl," Harry coos before trying to push back into my mouth.

"No, nope," I protest. "Nothing in my bum and frankly, not too keen on your cock in my mouth either."

"Woman, what did you think would happen at a foursome," Harry laughs and pulls on his stiff dick a few times. *Yeah, what was I thinking?*

Michael, clearly bored of the conversation, pushes in me without much formality.

"Fuck!" I exclaim.

"That's the idea, baby girl. Let Daddy back in your mouth," Harry laughs and pokes at my lips again.

"Okay, stop," I groan. All three freeze, Michael with his dick half in my vajajay. "Happy to sleep with all three of you. But no bum sex, no fucking baby and daddy talk and no poking at my lips," I say.

"That's bollocks," Graham protests, and gets off the bed. "Call me when it's my turn!"

Michael starts moving again and Harry seems to have gotten the message. He slides under me and sucks on my nipples whilst rubbing my clit. *Oh, okay, now that's nice.*

In the other room, I can hear the sound of loud commentators, the roar of a crowd, and the occasional outburst from Graham.

"Shit, that's the Champions League final. Hurry up, mate," Harry moans, his eyes wondering to the open door, my clit completely forgotten. On command, Michael starts moving faster.

"It's a penalty," Graham shouts out. "Penalty for Arsenal."

"Shit," Harry groans, slides out from under me and runs out of the room.

I try to laugh it off. "I guess football is more exciting than my pussy, huh?"

Michael flips me over and then grins down on me. "To be fair, it's a big game."

I don't know what answer I was expecting, but it wasn't that.

"Baby girl, I'm so close," he moans in my ear. *Another baby girl.*

Michael moves faster but somehow, I've lost all interest in being banged. I try to squeeze my muscles to speed this whole thing up a bit and that seems to do the trick.

"Oh yes, yes, that's it," he yells as he comes.

Harry calls out "Game's going into overtime!" just as Michael collapses on top of me, his skin damp with sweat. He stays there for a few moments, catching his breath, before finally rolling off with a satisfied sigh.

"I'll send in the next one," he chuckles, stretching before striding out of the bedroom like this is a fast-food drive-through and I'm just an order they're taking turns on.

But I have had enough.

My face burns with embarrassment as I sit up, my hands fumbling to gather my clothes. My heart is pounding, not from excitement but from the crushing weight of realisation—this wasn't what I thought it would be. It wasn't thrilling or empowering. It was just... disappointing.

I pull on my tights and slide into my glitzy dress. I don't even bother fixing my hair. I just need to get out before one of the others strolls in for their turn.

But I needn't have rushed. Nobody comes.

I'm not even that quiet when I walk past them in the living room but they only have eyes for the football match.

I glance at them and wonder if I should say anything. All three of them are sitting naked on the sofa, eyes glued to the TV, utterly enthralled by whatever match is on.

It's such an absurd sight that for a split second, I almost laugh. Three grown men, dicks out, not even bothering to put on clothes, completely uninterested in the very thing they were supposed to be excited about... me.

But the laughter never comes.

Instead, a dull ache settles in my stomach, a quiet humiliation that makes my throat tighten. I don't say anything. I don't even bother with a sarcastic remark.

I just slip out the door and leave.

It's still early. Normally, I don't go home before midnight, but it can't be later than ten. I walk down the street, my coat pulled tight around me like it can shield me from the humiliation clinging to my skin. London is alive; people laughing outside pubs, a group of friends singing off-key as they stumble down the pavement, couples pressed close in the glow of streetlights. London on a Saturday night in its usual chaotic, romantic mess.

Meanwhile, I just got ditched for football.

I let out a sigh and make my way to the bus stop. No point wasting money on an Uber when I can stew in my own bad decisions for £1.75. The bus arrives in minutes, and I flop into a seat by the window, hugging my bag to my chest.

As the bus pulls away, I stare out at the blur of neon signs and moving shadows, my brain running an autopsy on the night.

What had I expected exactly? That this would be sexy? That I'd leave feeling thoroughly satisfied, drenched in the glow of a scandalous, unforgettable night? That Michael, Harry, and Graham, the trio of disappointment, would somehow make me feel like the centre of their universe rather than an extra in their night? That this would turn into an MMMF romance where I am the goddess in our happily-ever-after?

I snort. *Fuck, I'm an idiot.*

The worst part? I didn't even consider how this would play out before I agreed to it. Not really. I jumped straight from *Ooh, this could be exciting* to *well, this is happening* without stopping to think if I even wanted it.

Spoiler alert: I didn't. Or at least, not like that.

I blame Pee-Pee. She told me not to think, so I just went for it. Epic fail.

The bus slows at a stop, and a couple stumbles on, giggling, clinging to each other like they've just fallen in love at first sight—or at least over their third round of tequila shots. They collapse into the seats in front of me, whispering and grinning as if nobody else exists.

I look away and try to block them out.

I don't regret leaving. But I do regret going in the first place.

By the time we reach Shoreditch, I feel a little less like I need to disappear into a hole and a little more like I just need a shower, a cup of tea, and to never speak of this again.

2
Pee-Pee

Ivy

I AM IN PURGATORY.

Alright, technically, I am in the waiting room of my therapist's office, but the difference is negligible.

The walls are a bland shade of beige, the kind that aspires to be "calming" but just looks like old porridge. There's a sad little fish tank in the corner with one lonely goldfish who always seems to be glaring at me. I swear it knows. It knows I am a walking disaster.

I glance at the clock. Ten minutes to go. Ten minutes before I have to sit opposite Phyllis Philpott, aka Pee-Pee (let's not tell her I call her that behind her back) and admit that my most recent attempt at "living adventurously" resulted in feeling utterly humiliated.

I check my phone for any last-minute emergencies that might get me out of this, but of course, there's nothing. Not a single text, not even a train delay I could exploit. Just my own impending doom.

I let out a long sigh and sink further into the uncomfortable chair.

I've been seeing Pee-Pee since my divorce three years ago. Back then, my biggest problem was figuring out how to rebuild my life after my husband left me for a woman he met on a meditation retreat. (She "taught him how to breathe," apparently. I hope she's still coaching him through it while he chokes on his own spit.)

Back then, therapy was about healing, rediscovering myself, and coming to terms with the fact that love isn't always enough. Honestly, I should've started sooner. It might've saved my marriage if I'd had Pee-Pee to help me process the fact I can't have children.

Instead, I dragged Barry into every alternative therapy going, hoping one might magically conjure up a baby. He got fed up and went looking for fun elsewhere, rather than just talking to me.

But if I've learned anything over the past three years, it's this: Barry and I were never really suited to each other. Still, just because we're not compatible doesn't mean I don't despise him for cheating. *Knobhead.*

Nowadays, therapy is about... well, kind of still the same. I still don't know who I am and what I want. Apparently, I am a slow learner. Yet again I am sitting in the waiting room, trying to figure out how to explain my latest life choice without making it sound too tragic.

For a brief, fleeting moment, I wonder if I should just... lie. I could make something up—talk about work stress, pretend I've taken up gambling, literally anything else.

But lying to a therapist seems like a whole new league of issues. And besides, Pee-Pee would know. She has that unsettling, all-seeing quality, like a wise old owl wrapped in a pastel cardigan. I'd get maybe three words in before she'd tilt her head, hum thoughtfully, and somehow extract the truth from my soul.

The receptionist, who has the enthusiasm of a woman who is counting the seconds until she can go home, peeks her head out from behind the desk.

"Ivy? Phyllis is ready for you."

I plaster on a tight-lipped smile, shove my phone in my bag, and stand up like a woman being led to an interrogation.

Here we go. Time to tell my therapist that I got downgraded from a wild, reckless woman of passion to a mildly inconvenient speed bump on the way to Match of the Day.

I step into Pee-Pee's office, which is just as beige and aggressively soothing as the waiting room. The walls are a soft eggshell-y colour, the armchairs are that expensive kind of beige that rich people put in rooms they never actually sit in, and there's a small tray of herbal teas that I have never once seen anyone take.

Pee-Pee herself is perched in her usual spot, dressed in her signature cardigan-and-sensible-trousers combo. Today, the cardigan is a gentle mint green, which I suspect is meant to lull me into a false sense of security.

"Hello, Ivy," she says, with that calm, knowing smile. "How are you this week?"

Oh, we're starting with that, are we?

I sink into the chair opposite her, already feeling the walls close in. "Oh, you know," I say breezily, waving a hand. "Can't complain."

She nods, waiting. She knows I am going to complain. It's just a matter of when.

There's a long pause. She looks at me. I look at the tiny wooden figurine of a tree on her coffee table, like maybe I can will myself into becoming one with it.

Pee-Pee tilts her head slightly.

I panic. "Actually, I've been thinking about getting into clay."

She blinks. "Clay?"

"Yes. You know. Crafting sculptures, making mugs, all that." I make a vaguely circular motion with my hands, as if this will somehow prove my deep and genuine passion for ceramics.

She nods again, but now with mild amusement. "That's lovely, Ivy. What's brought this on?"

Oh no. I have not prepared for follow-up questions. "Uh... mindfulness?"

Her lips twitch, as if she's trying not to smile.

Damn it. She knows. *Of course she does, Ivy, you sound like you've lost your marbles.*

Pee-Pee waits again, giving me the opportunity to dig myself out of my nonsense, but I am committed now.

"It's very therapeutic, apparently," I continue, grasping at straws. "You know, the whole... earthy, grounding thing. I thought I might try it."

"Hm," she says. The dreaded *hm*.

She picks up her notebook and taps her pen against it lightly. I know this move. This is her version of a master-class interrogator.

I need to change the subject before she calls my bluff. "Anyway, how's your week been?"

She raises an eyebrow, ever so slightly. "Ivy."

I swallow. "Yes?"

She leans forward a fraction. "Would you like to tell me what's actually on your mind?"

No. No, I would not. I would like to sit here, sip an imaginary cup of tea, and pretend I am a well-adjusted person who did not get left mid-orgy for a football match.

I force a laugh. "It's nothing, really."

She just looks at me.

"It's silly," I add.

More looking.

I sigh, slump back into the chair, and blurt out, "I had a foursome."

A beat of silence.

Then, in the calmest, most composed voice, she asks, "Would you like to elaborate?"

I groan, rubbing my hands over my face. "Not really, but I suppose I have to."

She gives me that therapist nod that means yes, you do.

So, I tell her. The whole ridiculous, humiliating story—how I thought it would be exciting, how it was, in fact, not exciting at all. How, instead, Graham and Harry abandoned ship to watch football, and how I ended the night sitting on a bus, contemplating my own poor life choices.

Pee-Pee listens without interrupting, nodding occasionally, her expression unreadable. When I finish, she does something truly terrible.

She hmms.

It's the deep, thoughtful hmm that lets me know that my entire existence is about to be psychoanalysed to pieces.

I brace myself.

She adjusts her glasses slightly. "And how did that make you feel?"

I blink. "Like a discarded takeaway container?"

She tilts her head again. "And why do you think that is?"

"Oh, I don't know, Phyllis," I say dramatically, throwing my hands up. "Maybe because two out of three men literally walked out halfway through and didn't come back?!"

"Hm."

I groan. "You're loving this, aren't you?"

She smiles... just the smallest, knowing smile. "Not loving it, no. But I do think this experience has left you with some feelings worth unpacking."

Ugh. Of course it has.

I cross my arms. "I was just trying to have fun. Be spontaneous. Isn't that supposed to be good for me?"

"Fun is good," she agrees. "But I wonder if you were looking for something more than just fun."

I open my mouth to argue, but nothing comes out. Because the annoying part? She's probably right.

I sigh. "So, what you're saying is, I didn't just make a bad decision—I made a psychologically bad decision?"

"I think you made a decision that didn't give you what you were really looking for," she says gently.

I huff. "Which was what, exactly?"

She shrugs. "That's something only you can answer."

Oh, brilliant. A therapy riddle. Just what I needed.

Pee-Pee writes something in her notebook. I imagine it's just a slow, tired scribble that says *Here we go again*.

"I blame you," I say, arms folded like a toddler who's just been denied pudding.

She doesn't look up. "Of course you do. What am I responsible for this time?"

"You told me not to think."

Now she looks up. Tilts her head slightly, the way people do when trying not to look directly at a car crash. "I told you not to *overthink*. That's not the same as switching your brain off entirely and mistaking chaos for spontaneity."

"Well," I mutter, "you could've been clearer."

There's a pause. Then she says, very gently, "You've had a pattern, Ivy. Of meeting someone and immediately imagining a future with them. Why do you think that is?"

I roll my eyes so hard it nearly counts as cardio. "I don't *always* do that."

Her silence says, *Go on then. Prove it.*

"Okay," I say, holding up a hand. "Exhibit A: the fitness coach. Remember him?"

"I do."

"Mr Abs-for-Days who told me I'd 'blossom' if I stopped eating bread. I left with the food, not the man."

Pee-Pee nods, neutral.

"And Exhibit B: the one who said—on date *one*, mind you—that he wanted a woman who cooks, cleans, and doesn't argue."

"And you tried to cook for him," she says softly, not accusing, just... reminding.

"Almost burnt the kitchen down, yes. But the point is, I don't always go full Jane Austen. Sometimes I meet absolute clowns and *still* try to be normal."

Pee-Pee sits back, watching me. Not with judgement, but with that therapisty stillness that makes you feel like you've walked straight into a trap made of your own logic.

"So why didn't you walk away from him?" she asks.

I hesitate. "Because he talked about marriage. Not in a creepy 'let's name our kids' way. Just... like it was on the table. And I thought maybe, for once..."

She lets the silence settle for a moment, careful, like she's stepping over broken glass.

"I know you've had a lot taken from you," she says, voice calm but warm. "And that sometimes, a promise—even a flimsy one—feels like something to cling to."

I swallow. Look away. "It wasn't just about him. It was about the idea. That there might still be a version of a future where I'm... enough."

Pee-Pee nods. "You are."

I roll my eyes again, but it's weaker this time. "Don't go full Hallmark on me, Phyllis. You'll ruin your image."

She smiles, just slightly. "I wouldn't dare."

Pee-Pee lets the silence settle, then lifts her pen again. "So," she says, "tell me more about the other night. The foursome."

"Nothing else to say, really. It was a disaster. Let's move on," I shrug.

She gives me the look. The *I am patient, but you know I will outlast you* look.

I sigh and drop my head back against the chair, staring at the ceiling as if the meaning of life might be written up there between the eggshell paint and a suspiciously flickering lightbulb.

Phyllis waits. She's good at that—waiting me out until the silence gets too unbearable and I start talking just to fill it.

I try to fight it, but the weight of her stare is too much.

"Alright, fine," I grumble, rubbing my hands over my face. "What do I want to take away from this? Maybe that I should stop making decisions purely because I think they'll make me feel desired?"

She nods, encouraging. "That's a start."

I frown. "But also... I did think it would be fun. And maybe it should have been? But it wasn't, and I don't know why."

Pee-Pee tilts her head slightly, her cardigan sleeves bunching at the wrists as she folds her hands in her lap. "Well, what did you really think would happen after a foursome?"

I open my mouth to answer quickly, but I hesitate. Because honestly? Yeah, I don't think I can tell her about my MMMF fantasy right after she's accused me of conjuring up imaginary futures.

"I suppose... a connection with someone," I say slowly, testing the words as they come out of my mouth. "Excitement? Confidence? Like I'm a person who does fun, spontaneous things instead of just..."

I trail off, not really sure how to finish that sentence.

Pee-Pee watches me for a moment before gently prompting, "Instead of what?"

Instead of being alone.

The thought flashes through my brain so quickly I barely catch it before it disappears.

I shift uncomfortably in my seat. "I don't know," I say, avoiding her gaze. "Instead of just sitting at home watching telly, I suppose."

"Hm," she says. The worst possible thing.

I give her a wary look. "What's that *hm* for?"

She taps her pen lightly against her notebook. "Ivy, would you say you've spent much time on your own since your divorce?"

I blink. "What do you mean? Of course I have. I live alone."

Pee-Pee smiles kindly, as if I've just confirmed something she already knew. "I meant emotionally. Have you given yourself time to be by yourself, without looking for the next person to fill that space?"

I let out a breathy laugh. "I'm not looking for someone to 'fill a space.'"

She arches a brow.

I shift again. "I mean... okay, yes, I've dated a lot. But I like dating. It's fun."

"And when you're not dating?" she asks, tilting her head again.

The room feels suddenly warmer, like I'm under a spotlight. "I... I don't know."

Phyllis hums again, scribbling something down.

I groan, slumping further into the chair. "Fine. Maybe I haven't spent much time alone. But isn't that normal? People like being with other people. It's human nature."

"Of course," she agrees. "But there's a difference between enjoying other people's company and needing it to avoid being with yourself."

I open my mouth to protest, then snap it shut. Because I don't have a counterargument.

I think about the past three years—about the string of dates, flings, and relationships that barely lasted long enough for me to learn their middle names. About the times I've thrown myself into something just because it was something, without stopping to ask if it was what I actually wanted.

And the worst part? I don't know if I've ever really asked myself that. Instead, my brain hijacks the moment and fills it with fairytales and happily-ever-afters I didn't ask for but secretly dream of.

Phyllis watches as the realisation sinks in. "I think," she says gently, "that you're still figuring out who you are on your own."

I exhale sharply, running a hand through my hair. "So, what are you saying, I should just... stop dating? Go on some kind of romantic detox?"

Pee-Pee smiles. "I'm saying it might be worth exploring what life looks like when you're not focused on the next relationship. What do you like? What excites you? Not in relation to someone else, but just for yourself?"

I blink. That is a horrifyingly big question.

"I mean... I like brunch?" I offer weakly.

Pee-Pee laughs, the first proper laugh of the session. "That's a start." She smiles at me, the kind of smile that therapists use when they know they've led you right into a trap of your own making.

"I think you need a break," she says gently.

I squint at her. "From therapy?"

"From dating."

I physically recoil. "What? No. Absolutely not. What am I supposed to do with all that free time?"

She gives me a patient look. "I don't know, Ivy. That's kind of the point."

I cross my arms. "This feels extreme."

Pee-Pee tilts her head, which is never a good sign for me. "Let's look at the facts. You've been dating almost non-stop since your divorce—"

"Not non-stop," I interrupt. "I had that two-week gap last summer when I went on holiday."

"Which, if I recall correctly, you described as 'the worst fourteen days of your life because you had to eat alone and no one was there to take Instagram photos of you'?"

I open my mouth, then close it. "That doesn't sound like me."

She gives me a look.

I sigh. "Okay, fine, but what if I just... slow down? You know, only go on, like, one or two dates a month? A gentle, leisurely pace."

"I think you need a proper reset."

I narrow my eyes. "You're really going to make me go cold turkey?"

Pee-Pee smiles. "I'm not making you do anything. I'm simply suggesting that if you really want to figure out who you are outside of dating, you must take it off the table entirely."

I groan and let my head fall back against the chair again.

"Three months," she says.

I snap my head back up. "Three?"

She nods, entirely too calm about this nightmare of a suggestion. "No dating, no relationships, no flings—just time to focus on you. Tomorrow is the first of June, so let's say until the first of September."

I gape at her. "You do realise what you're saying, right? Three whole months?" *That's a lot of days without a dick. I need to buy more batteries on the way home.*

She nods again, completely unbothered by my horror. "I think it'll be good for you."

"Define 'good'."

"You'll have space to figure out what you actually enjoy, what makes you happy when you're not trying to impress someone, and what you want your life to look like outside of a relationship."

I huff. "Sounds boring."

She chuckles. "And yet, I think you know I'm right."

Ugh. Of course she's right. But that doesn't mean I have to like it.

"Alright," I grumble. "Fine. Three months."

Phyllis nods approvingly, like she just convinced me to save the world instead of banning me from my entire social life.

I squint at her. "What happens if I cheat?"

She shrugs. "You're only cheating yourself."

That is the most therapist answer I have ever heard in my life.

I groan and drag my hands down my face. "Three months," I mutter again, as if saying it out loud will help me process the tragedy that has just befallen me.

"Until the first of September," Pee-Pee confirms.

No dating. No flirting. No falling into yet another doomed situationship because I got bored on a Sunday afternoon.

I take a deep breath. "Fine. I'm in."

"Good," Phyllis says with a smile. "I'm looking forward to hearing what you do with all your extra time."

I stare at her, horrified. "Oh my god, I'm going to have so much extra time."

Pee-Pee laughs. "I think that's exactly what you need."

I groan again, standing up and grabbing my coat. "If I become one of those people who suddenly gets really into candle-making or hiking, it will be your fault."

She grins. "I'll take full responsibility."

I mutter something about emotional sabotage under my breath as I head for the door.

Three months.

That's not that long, right?

... Right?

3
Marketing Genius

Theo

I HAVE CLEANED THIS counter four times.

Not because it needs it... oh no, it is already spotless. You could perform surgery on it if you really wanted to. But because I have nothing else to do.

I glance at the clock. 3:42 PM.

It has been eight hours and forty-two minutes since I officially opened The Kaiser's Mug, and so far, my grand entrance into the Shoreditch coffee scene has been... underwhelming.

Jasper, my younger brother and part-time professional wind-up merchant, is perched on a bar stool at the end of the counter, sipping his second free coffee of the day and scrolling through his phone like he hasn't got a care in the world. He has been here since opening, doing absolutely nothing except watching me have a slow-burn existential crisis.

"Would you stop glaring at the door like it owes you money?" he says, not even looking up.

"I'm not glaring."

"You are. You look like a Victorian widow staring out to sea, waiting for her husband's ship to come home."

I let out a heavy sigh and toss the cloth into the sink. I could wipe down the counter a fifth time, but even I have my limits. Instead, I lean against it and stare at the beautifully arranged pastries in the glass display. *Linzer Torte. Apfelstrudel. Sachertorte.* Each one made fresh at five o'clock this morning by my Austrian pastry chef Klaus, each one tragically uneaten.

Jasper finally puts his phone down. "Theo. It's day one."

"Day one should have been busier."

He shrugs. "Maybe. Or maybe you should give it more than eight hours before spiralling into a meltdown."

I groan, running a hand through my hair. He's got a point, but still—I spent months planning this place. I wanted it to be perfect. And it is perfect, objectively speaking. The café is exactly how I imagined it, all dark wood panelling, velvet seating, and shelves lined with antique coffee tins. The espresso machine is a thing of beauty, the pastries are flawless, and the coffee? Easily the best in Shoreditch.

And yet.

The door remains firmly shut, the world outside indifferent to my carefully crafted vision. Me and my two waiters got all dressed up in shirt, waistcoat and tie for nothing.

"Maybe the concept is too niche," I say finally.

Jasper raises an eyebrow. "Theo, you're acting like you opened a café that only serves soup in wine glasses. It's a Viennese coffeehouse. It's not that weird."

"No, but maybe people don't want old-school charm. Maybe they want oat milk matcha lattes and rainbow bagels."

Jasper sighs, setting down his cup. "Listen. People in London will queue for two hours to eat a pancake the size of a two-pi coin if the place looks good on Instagram. You just need time. And marketing. Have you actually done any?"

I shift slightly. "I made an Instagram account."

He waits.

"I posted a photo of a coffee cup this morning."

His eyes narrow. "And?"

"...That's it."

He groans. "Theo."

"What? It was a very nice coffee cup."

Jasper pinches the bridge of his nose. "This is why Geoff and I are silent partners."

I sigh, drumming my fingers on the counter. Geoff, our eldest brother, is only involved in this café in the sense that he transferred me money, told me to "go live my dream," and then promptly disappeared to whichever glamorous location he's currently photographing impossibly beautiful people. Last I heard, he was in the Maldives, shooting a Vogue spread with a supermodel. He doesn't exactly relate to my struggle.

Jasper, on the other hand, made a fortune developing some computer component that now exists in nearly every machine on the planet. He could be running a tech empire, but instead, he's semi-retired and spends his time floating between expensive hobbies and annoying me.

"If it makes you feel better," Jasper says, "Mum just texted me to say she's proud of you."

I snort. "Did she say proud, or did she say, 'worried but supportive'?"

"...Both."

Sounds about right.

Before I can respond, the door swings open. My heart leaps at the sight of the elderly couple peering inside. They exchange a glance, nod approvingly, and step in.

I straighten immediately. "Welcome!"

The woman smiles. "Oh, what a lovely space."

I beam, ready to launch into my rehearsed speech about authentic Viennese coffeehouse culture, but she continues before I can start.

"Do you do English Breakfast tea?"

I hesitate. "...Yes?"

"Oh, wonderful," she says. "Two teas, please."

I shoot Jasper a look as I prepare the order. He bites his lip, visibly trying not to laugh.

Tea. My first real customers, and they've come to The Kaiser's Mug, an Austrian coffeehouse, for a bog-standard cuppa.

But hey, at least it's a start. I try to make it the best tea on the planet before sliding it across the counter for Pavel, one of my waiters, to carry it with all the right drama to the customers.

The bell above the door jingles again, and I brace myself, hoping for a customer who actually cares about coffee rather than just asking for tea like it's a roadside café off the M25.

Instead, two women stroll in, completely oblivious to their surroundings, deep in conversation. Well—one is talking at high speed while the other nods along, making noises of agreement.

"...And I'm just saying, it was a bad idea from the start," the blonde one insists, flicking her hair over her shoulder as she walks right past the pastry display without even glancing at it. "Honestly, Christa, I should've seen it coming."

The other woman—shorter, darker, wearing enough eyeliner to qualify for a punk rock band—snorts. "I did see it coming. I literally told you it was a bad idea, and you waved me off."

"Yes, well." The blonde sighs dramatically. "I was being optimistic."

Christa—at least I assume that's her name—gives her a look. "You were being delusional."

"I was being hopeful."

"Oh, hopeful. Is that what we're calling it now?" Christa smirks. "Because I'd call it throwing yourself into a foursome like a human buffet for some knobheads and then acting surprised when half the party left for football."

I blink.

Foursome?

My head snaps up properly now, eyes narrowing slightly as I take a look at them.

The blonde is curvy, with wild waves of hair that have a mind of their own, bright eyes, and a naturally expressive face that seems to shift emotions at an alarming rate. She's wearing a navy-blue dress and boots, and her body language suggests she's telling the greatest tragedy of all time, despite the fact that her friend looks like she's enjoying her pain a little too much.

The other one, Christa, is the complete opposite. Shorter, leaner, dressed in ripped jeans and an oversized leather jacket, with a collection of rings that look like they could double as weapons. She has that effortless cool-girl look—like she either plays in a band or at least used to date the lead singer of one.

Neither of them is paying attention to where they are.

Neither of them has even looked at me.

And yet, I am completely hooked on this conversation.

I grab the cloth and wipe down the counter again, pretending I'm not blatantly eavesdropping.

The blonde—still completely unaware of my existence—lets out a long sigh. "Anyway, it doesn't matter anymore, because as of today, I am on a dating ban."

Her friend snorts. "A what?"

"A dating ban," she repeats, more firmly this time. "Three months. No dates, no flings, no relationships, nothing."

Christa cackles. "You? Not dating for three months? That's like me giving up sarcasm—it's physically impossible."

"I can do it," the blonde insists, sounding both defensive and deeply unconvinced.

"Sure," her friend says. "And I can win *The Great British Bake Off*."

The blonde rolls her eyes. "Look, Pee-Pee says it's a good idea—" *Who or what is that Pee-Pee?*

"Oh, well, if Pee-Pee says so, then obviously it's the law."

The blonde groans. "It's not about the rule, it's about... I don't know. Me." She gestures vaguely, as if that explains anything at all. "Figuring out what I actually like, who I am when I'm not trying to impress someone, you know?"

I am so focused on listening—so invested in whatever this dating ban nonsense is—that I absentmindedly shift a mug a little too hard, sending it skidding across the counter.

It clatters loudly, nearly tipping over.

Both women finally look up at me.

I freeze, cloth still in hand, caught like a deer in headlights.

The blonde's eyes narrow slightly. "Were you listening to us?"

I clear my throat, wiping the counter one last time for dramatic effect. "No," I lie. "Not at all."

I regain my composure and straighten up, offering them my best customer service smile.

"Welcome to The Kaiser's Mug," I say, as if I haven't just been caught listening in on their conversation. "If you take a seat, I'll bring you the menu and—"

The blonde leans against the counter. "I'll have a *venti*, soy, hazelnut latte with extra foam and half cold milk."

I freeze unsure how to manage this situation diplomatically.

Jasper snorts quietly from his stool, no doubt waiting for my reaction.

I turn back to her, making sure I heard correctly. "You want a... *venti*, soy, hazelnut latte, extra foam, half cold milk?"

She nods, completely unbothered by the monstrosity she has just ordered.

I exhale slowly, running a hand over my jaw. "Right. So... we don't do that."

The blonde frowns. "What do you mean?"

I gesture vaguely to the café around us. "This is a Viennese coffeehouse. We don't have syrups. Or *venti* sizes. Or whatever that... situation was."

Christa smirks. "Oh, this is gonna be fun."

The blonde folds her arms. "So, what do you have?"

I sigh, rubbing the back of my neck before slipping back into my well-rehearsed, authentic Austrian experience mode. "I can make you a *Wiener Melange*. It's like a cappuccino but with a bit more milk and a fluffy, foamy top."

She blinks. "That sounds... nice?"

"It is nice."

She hesitates, clearly uncertain about trusting me with her caffeine needs, but then gives a slow nod. "Alright. Fine. I'll have one of those."

Her friend grins. "Make it two."

I nod, relieved that we've managed to land on something that doesn't involve cold milk and unnecessary sugar. "Take a seat, we'll bring it over," I smile. That also seems to be a new concept to them because the coffee chains they clearly frequent normally don't offer that service. The blond gives me a side eye before heading to a table in the corner.

As I start preparing their drinks, I steal another glance at her. She is now tapping on her phone. I'm still not over the dating ban thing. I mean, who bans themselves from dating? And why do I care? But then, who am I to talk? I'm kind of on a self-imposed dating ban, I guess. Being a single dad and business owner doesn't really leave a lot of time.

I shake off the thought and focus on making the coffee. Once both cups are ready, I carry them to their table and, without really thinking it through, decide to take my marketing strategy for a test run.

"These are on the house," I say, maybe a bit too quickly.

Both of them look up in surprise.

"Wait, really?" the blonde asks, narrowing her eyes slightly like she's waiting for the catch.

I clear my throat. "Yes. Uh, you know. First-time customers. And, um…" I shift awkwardly, trying to sound casual and failing miserably. "If you happened to post about it on Instagram, that wouldn't be the worst thing."

Silence.

The blonde stares at me, then slowly blinks. Her friend looks like she's physically restraining herself from laughing.

I hear a soft, muffled choking noise. I glance to the side. Jasper has his head in his hands.

…Was it that bad?

I clear my throat again, suddenly feeling hot under my collar. "Uh, yeah. You know. If you want. Just, uh… take a picture. Or—" I make an awkward, vague hand gesture, like I'm holding an invisible phone. "Or whatever people do. Hashtag it?"

Oh God, why did I say hashtag it?

The blonde bites her lip, eyes sparkling with what I desperately hope is amusement and not second-hand embarrassment. "Right. Hashtag it. Sure."

Her friend smirks. "Do you… want us to tag you?"

"Yes! Yes." I agree way too enthusiastic. "That. Tagging is… good."

There is a long pause before the blonde nods, still watching me like she's trying to figure out if I'm serious or not.

Then, in a moment of pure panic, I blurt out, "And you can have free *Apfelstrudel* too."

Jasper actually groans.

Both women glance at the pastry display like they hadn't even considered food before, but now they're intrigued.

"Alright," the blonde says slowly, exchanging a look with her friend. "Coffee and free strudel-thingy in exchange for an Instagram post?"

I nod, resisting the urge to look too pleased with myself as I turn back toward the counter. "Great. I'll get that strudel plated up."

As I busy myself arranging two slices of *Apfelstrudel* onto small plates—presentation is key, after all—I glance over at Jasper, who is watching me with the exhausted patience of a man who has just witnessed something truly painful.

I add a dollop of whipped cream before Pavel takes the plates to the two women. I give Jasper a look. A victorious, *I just nailed that business transaction* kind of look.

"Well?" I ask smugly. "That went well."

Jasper stares at me. "That was excruciating."

I scoff. "It was effective."

"You just bribed two strangers with free food because you don't understand how Instagram works."

I fold my arms. "And yet, did they agree to post about it?"

Jasper rubs his temples. "This is painful to watch."

I smirk, dusting my hands off like I've just successfully negotiated a high-stakes business deal. "Marketing, my friend. You wouldn't understand."

Jasper sighs, looking up at the ceiling like he's praying for patience.

I turn back to the blonde and her friend, still feeling rather pleased with myself.

This is definitely going to work.

4
Sun Salutation

Ivy

THE WAITER PLACES TWO plates in front of us.

"Enjoy," the peculiar barista shouts from behind the counter, like a man who is completely unaware of how much second-hand embarrassment he just inflicted on himself.

I nod politely. "Thanks."

Christa, however, has her eyes on him, not the strudel.

The second he turns back to the customer sitting at the end of the counter, she leans in, dropping her voice just enough that only I can hear. "It is an absolute tragedy that you're on a dating ban."

I roll my eyes, slicing into the pastry. "Here we go."

"I mean, honestly," she continues, completely ignoring me. "What are the odds that an incredibly fit guy opens a coffee shop literally underneath your flat, and you've just vowed to spend three months in romantic exile?"

I shake my head. "He's not my type."

She stares at me. "He is exactly your type. Tall, dark-haired, adorably dorky—"

"He wiped down the counter five times before we even ordered," I cut in. "That's unhinged."

She smirks. "Maybe he's just meticulous."

I shrug, stuffing a bite of *strudel* into my mouth. The warm apple and cinnamon practically melt on my tongue, and for a brief moment, I forget all about Christa's smug expression.

But only for a moment.

She watches me chew, unimpressed. "You're pretending you're not interested."

"I'm not interested."

"Uh-huh."

I sigh, deciding to change the subject before she gets any more ideas. "Anyway, I have a plan for the next three months. A dating-free plan."

Christa raises an eyebrow. "Tell me!"

I pull out my phone and open my notes app, showing her the list. "I've decided to try new hobbies."

She squints at the screen, reading aloud. "Yoga. Working with clay, maybe take up knitting, spa-ing... maybe camping."

She looks back up at me. "I have so many questions."

I take another bite of *strudel*. "Go on."

"Well, first of all, *spa-ing* isn't a hobby."

"It absolutely is," I argue. "Self-care is an art form."

She snorts. "Fine, I'll allow it. But camping?"

I grimace. "Yeah, I'm regretting that one already. I was trying to push myself out of my comfort zone."

"You hate the outdoors."

"I strongly dislike the outdoors," I correct. "Which is exactly why it's on the list. Growth, Christa. It's all about growth."

She shakes her head, but she's smiling now. "Alright, I'll give you points for effort."

I lean back in my chair, feeling smug. "See? I can survive without dating."

Christa takes a slow sip of her coffee, watching me over the rim of her cup. "Sure. Let's see how long that lasts with Hot Barista literally on your doorstep."

I huff. "His name is Theo." Yes, I may have checked out the name badge pinned to his waist coat. But I certainly didn't fantasise over the fact on how fan-yourself-hot he looks in his crisp-white shirt with the sleeves rolled up.

She grins. "Ohhh, so you were paying attention."

I groan, covering my face with my hands.

"Don't worry," she says breezily. "If I weren't happily engaged, I'd be all over him myself."

I peek at her through my fingers. "But you are happily engaged. To a very large man who could break Theo in half."

She sighs dreamily. "I am, aren't I?"

I shake my head, laughing despite myself. "You're the worst."

She winks. "Nope. Just happily unavailable, which means he's your problem now."

I steal another glance at Theo. *This is going to be the longest three months of my life.*

Three days into my dating ban, I am lying flat on my living room floor, having a full-blown existential crisis.

It started off well enough. I was feeling motivated, determined. Like a woman on a mission to discover herself.

Which is why I find myself, on a Tuesday evening, in my best pair of supportive leggings, a comfy T-shirt and a sports bra that could double as industrial scaffolding, pressing play on a video titled *Yoga for Dummies*.

I should have known. I should have known that even that is beyond my capabilities.

The instructor, a woman with a voice so serene it's borderline hypnotic, begins by saying, "Welcome. We'll start with some simple breathing exercises to centre ourselves."

Alright. I can breathe. I can centre.

I sit cross-legged on my yoga mat, inhaling deeply through my nose like I'm an expert.

"This is called Ujjayi breathing," she says, voice calm and steady. "Engage your diaphragm, feel your breath moving through you."

Okay. Engage my diaphragm. Move my breath. Feel at one with—

I yawn.

Like, a big, dramatic, jaw-cracking yawn.

The video is already losing me.

I shake myself, trying to focus. Right. Breathing is important. Got it. Let's move on.

But the instructor just keeps going. She's talking about "finding my inner stillness" and "connecting with the earth," and honestly, I'm already bored.

After what feels like an eternity of sitting and inhaling, I decide to skip ahead.

I grab the remote and fast-forward to something that actually looks like movement.

Sun Salutation. That sounds promising. Warm. Glowy. Like something that will make me feel like one of those effortlessly bendy women who drink green smoothies and have matching workout sets.

I get into position.

Feet together. Arms raised.

This is fine.

I bend forward to touch my toes.

Okay. Not fine.

I have never touched my toes, not even as a child, and I'm not about to start now. My hamstrings are actively rebelling against me.

I make an undignified sound and attempt to bend my knees slightly, hoping that will help. It does not.

The instructor, still frustratingly calm, instructs me to step one foot back into a lunge.

I try. I really try.

Except my foot doesn't glide back gracefully like hers does. It sort of... flops.

I wobble. My arms flail.

I tip over entirely.

With a very loud "Oof", I land on my side, sprawled out on my yoga mat like a starfish that has just washed up on shore.

I stare at the ceiling. The instructor, unfazed by my suffering, moves on to the next position as if I am not currently dying.

I let out a long, defeated sigh.

This is only month one.

I'm doomed.

...Or, at the very least, I need a yoga routine that includes built-in snack breaks.

I lie there for a good minute, staring at the ceiling, before accepting that yoga has defeated me. At least for today.

With a groan, I roll onto my side and push myself up from the mat, every muscle in my body voicing its displeasure. Clearly, inner peace is not my destiny. At least not in the form of a Sun Salutation.

Right. Time for snacks.

I head into the kitchen, already fantasising about something delicious. Maybe a chocolate bar. A bag of crisps. A biscuit. Anything to reward myself for my—admittedly tragic—effort at exercise.

I open the fridge with high hopes.

...And immediately regret every single healthy-living resolution I made this month.

Because staring back at me is a collection of green, leafy sadness.

Spinach. Broccoli. A sad, lonely cucumber.

Where is the joy? Where is the comfort? Where is the bloody chocolate?

I close the fridge with a sigh and yank open the cupboard instead.

Oats. Herbal tea. A jar of almond butter.

Fucking hell, what was I thinking? I took this New Me thing way too far!

My stomach growls in protest, as if personally offended by my choices.

And that's it. I officially give in.

Fine. If my own kitchen is a health-conscious prison, then I'll just have to take my business elsewhere.

Which means... the coffee shop downstairs.

Which means... cake.

Which means... Theo.

For a moment, I hesitate. Because if I'm going downstairs, I should probably get properly dressed. Maybe brush my hair. Put on a little makeup. Nothing dramatic, just a quick *I woke up looking flawless* sort of situation.

I catch sight of myself in the hallway mirror and sigh. My hair is a mess, my skin is slightly red from the mini exercise, and I am currently wearing an oversized t-shirt that says *Namast'ay in Bed*.

Not exactly temptress material.

I pad into my bedroom, rummaging through my wardrobe for something a little more presentable. Maybe jeans? A nice top? Something that says, "effortless but put together"?

And then, just as I'm about to reach for my makeup bag, I freeze.

Because suddenly, I remember.

This whole experiment is supposed to be about not caring what other people think.

And that includes not caring what the dashing coffee shop hottie thinks.

I groan at myself, dropping the mascara wand like it's personally betrayed me.

No. No, I am not getting all dressed up for a man.

I yank off the presentable outfit and pull my yoga leggings back on—even if they show off my big arse and thunder thighs—and shove my hair into a messy bun. I march into the bathroom and wash my face, wiping away any trace of foundation.

And then, just to prove a point to myself, I grab my giant, fluffy hoodie—the one with a questionable stain on the sleeve that I think is from curry but can't say with full confidence.

There.

I am officially embracing my dating ban.

I glance at myself in the mirror again. I look... comfortable. Casual. Unbothered.

I nod at my reflection, satisfied. Time for some cake and cake only.

5
Attack of the Ladybug

Theo

I AM NEVER DOING table service again.

It seemed like a great idea at first—authentic Viennese coffeehouse experience, all that nonsense—but now, as I sprint between the counter and the floor, I can confidently say it was the worst business decision I have ever made.

Even with two waiters handling most of the tables and Klaus, my Austrian pastry chef, making sure the vitrine is constantly stocked with fresh *Apfelstrudel* and *Sachertorte*, I am completely rushed off my feet.

And to make matters worse, I have a tiny wildcard running loose.

"Daddy!"

I barely have time to register the small blur of movement before my daughter, Lucy, flings herself behind the counter again.

I let out a groan. "Ladybug, we talked about this."

She grins up at me, completely unbothered. "I'm bored."

Of course, she is. I had tried so hard to keep her entertained—set her up at a table near the counter with colouring books, snacks, even my phone—but five-year-olds don't do patience. Especially my five-year-old.

"Lu, I need you to sit at your table like a big girl," I say, gently guiding her back toward her designated spot.

"But I wanna help!" she insists, puffing out her tiny chest like she's about to start taking *Melange* orders.

I take a deep breath, keeping my voice calm despite the ever-growing pile of tickets on the counter. "Lucy, it's too busy, and I need you to stay at your table."

"But I can help!" she argues, hands on her hips now. "I can carry things. I can bring people spoons!"

I glance over at Klaus, who is very pointedly pretending not to hear any of this as he arranges the pastry display with military precision. The two waiters are whizzing between tables, and meanwhile, I'm stuck in a stand-off with a 3 ft 4 in homunculus who thinks she's ready to run front-of-house.

Before I can come up with a response, someone clears their throat at the counter.

"Hi, excuse me?"

I turn—and of course, it's her.

Ivy.

The woman who's name I learned from her Instagram account when she tagged my café. The woman who then mocked my social media skills on Instagram while still managing to make my coffee sound like a religious experience. The woman who, apparently, has now decided to show up looking like she rolled straight out of a nap but still somehow makes it work.

And Lucy, of course, immediately takes an interest.

She looks from Ivy to me, then back again. "You have a stain on your sleeve."

Ivy chokes on absolutely nothing, her cheeks turning pink. "Oh."

I pinch the bridge of my nose. "Lucy!"

"What?" she says innocently. "You were very angry when I didn't tell you that you had ice cream on your shirt at nanna's birthday party."

I glance at Ivy, expecting her to look horrified or awkward, but instead, she presses her lips together, actively trying not to laugh.

"But we don't tell strangers that," I exhale sharply. "Ignore her," I suggest to Ivy.

"No, no, she is right," she says, giving Lucy a wink. "Thank you for pointing it out. I'll pop it in the wash when I get home."

Lucy beams.

I glare. "You're not helping."

Ivy just grins.

And just like that, my day somehow gets even more chaotic.

"Ladybug, I need to take care of this *customer*."

Lucy lets out a dramatic huff. "Fine. I'll go sit."

She stomps back to her table, flinging herself into the chair like I've just ruined her life plans. She starts stabbing her colouring book with a crayon, making it very clear to everyone that she is deeply unimpressed.

I rub my temples, already exhausted, and turn back to Ivy, who is watching the entire interaction like it's the most entertaining thing she's seen all day.

"Sorry about her," I say, trying to regain some level of professionalism. "What can I get you?"

She taps her chin thoughtfully, eyes twinkling. "Well, what would you recommend for someone who is clearly a mess," she holds up the arm covered in the stained sleeve, "... and who doesn't fancy coffee today?"

I consider for a moment before offering, "A *Wiener Heiße Schokolade*—that's a Viennese hot chocolate—and maybe a *Zauner Kipferl*?"

She raises an eyebrow. "Okay, the hot chocolate sounds delicious, but the other thing?"

"It's like an almond croissant but better."

She hums, clearly weighing her options. "You had me at 'better'. I'll take both."

"Good choice," I say. She doesn't reply but instead moves to the table right next to Lucy's and sits down.

Lucy, still sulking, peeks up from her furious colouring, eyeing Ivy with open curiosity.

Ivy just leans back in her chair, completely at ease. "Nice table you've got here," she says to Lucy.

My ladybug shrugs dramatically, the way only a five-year-old can.

Ivy smirks. "Not much of a talker, huh?"

Another shrug.

I roll my eyes as I return my attention to preparing her order. A few minutes later, I set the hot chocolate and the *Zauner Kipferl* in front of her.

She eyes them approvingly. "This looks amazing." Then, without missing a beat, she grins up at me. "I'm surprised your boss lets you bring your kid to work."

Lucy's head snaps up. "Daddy is the boss," she corrects, as if Ivy has just insulted our entire family line.

Ivy's eyebrows shoot up. "Wait—you own this place?"

I nod, slightly amused at how surprised she looks. "Yeah. It's my café."

Her lips curve in amusement. "And here I thought you were just a very committed barista."

"I am a very committed barista," I say dryly. "But also the owner."

Ivy gives a slow, thoughtful nod. "Well, that explains why you're running around like a lunatic."

I sigh, looking at the counter where Pavel is preparing an order. "It's been one of those days."

Lucy, having apparently forgiven me for whatever great crime I committed earlier, grins at me. "Agatha is sick."

I rub my face. "Agatha has the chickenpox, Lucy. Not just sick."

She waves a hand, unconcerned by the details.

"Agatha is the childminder," I add for Ivy's benefit.

She glances between me and Lu, then tilts her head. "Do you want me to sit with her for a bit?"

"What?"

She shrugs. "You look like you're drowning, and she seems like she's about two minutes away from staging a coup."

I exhale a small laugh, glancing at Lucy, who—judging by the way she's tapping her crayon like a gavel—definitely looks like she's planning something.

"You really don't have to do that," I say, though I would be lying if I said the idea wasn't tempting.

Ivy just leans back, sipping her hot chocolate. "I know I don't have to. I'm offering."

I frown slightly. "Don't you have somewhere else to be?"

She shakes her head, setting her cup down. "Nope. Just a lonely Saturday."

Something in the way she says it makes me pause.

But before I can think too much about it, Lucy has already made the decision for both of us.

"Okay!" she chirps, scooting her chair closer to Ivy's, completely abandoning her grudge from earlier. "You can colour with me."

Ivy smirks, grabbing a crayon. "I would be honoured."

"What's your name? I'm Lucy and this is Daddy," Lu introduces us.

"Theo," I correct her and hold out my hand to Ivy.

"It's nice to meet you both. I'm Ivy," she grins and shakes my hand before shaking Lucy's who is mirroring me.

"I like the name Ivy," Lu giggles.

I shake my head, a reluctant smile tugging at my lips.

Well. That was unexpected.

By the time the café closes at five, I am exhausted.

It's been a full-on day—constant orders, endless running around, and trying to keep my little whirlwind entertained while simultaneously making sure she doesn't overthrow my entire business.

But somehow, Ivy is still here.

Not in an *overstayed her welcome* way, but in a *comfortably settled in* way. She's been sitting with Lucy for the past hour, helping her colour, listening intently to whatever my daughter has decided to ramble about, and generally making my life a lot easier.

After I lock the front door and flip the *Closed* sign, I grab three plates from the counter and bring them over to their table.

"Alright," I say, setting them down. "German sausages and chips, fresh from the kitchen."

Ivy eyes the food approvingly. "Is this part of the authentic Viennese experience?"

I smirk. "Not exactly. But Klaus had extra, and I figured you earned it after your babysitting shift."

Lucy, completely ignoring any adult conversation, is already reaching for a chip.

Ivy picks up a fork and gestures toward me. "So, since I'm being paid in food, I think I deserve to know—why a Viennese coffeehouse?"

I exhale, leaning back in my chair. "My grandfather, Franz, was Austrian. He moved to England in the '60s, married my grandmother, and never looked back. He loved it here, but the one thing he always missed was the coffee culture from back home."

Ivy studies me. "What's so different about it?"

"It's slower," I explain. "Less about grabbing a quick caffeine fix, more about sitting down, enjoying the moment, actually taking a break. You can sit in a Viennese café for hours and no one rushes you out. My grandfather loved that."

She hums thoughtfully, chewing on a chip. "And you decided to bring that to Shoreditch?"

I give a small shrug. "I wanted to do something different. Something that mattered to me."

She studies me for a second, then asks, "What were you doing before this?"

I hesitate for a beat before answering. "I was a lawyer."

Her eyebrows shoot up. "You were a lawyer?"

"Yep." I stab a piece of sausage with my fork. "Corporate law. Contracts, negotiations, all that exciting stuff."

Ivy gives me a long, sceptical look. "No offence, but you don't look like a lawyer."

I smirk. "What does a lawyer look like?"

She waves a hand at me. "I don't know. Smoother. More sleeze, less... scruffy, rugged coffeehouse owner energy."

I chuckle. "Yeah, well, I gave it up."

Her expression shifts slightly—less teasing, more curious. "Why?"

I glance at Lucy, who is now happily dipping a chip into her ketchup, completely oblivious to the conversation.

I sigh. "Four years ago, her mum walked out on us. Just... left. No warning, no big dramatic fight, just—gone."

Ivy stills, her smile fading. "Oh."

"I tried to do both for a couple of years—be a single dad and keep up with my job. But I burned out. Badly." I let out a short breath, shaking my head at the memory. "So I quit. Took a year off to just be with Lucy. I needed to figure out what I actually wanted."

She's quiet for a moment, watching me carefully. "And that's when you started planning this place?"

"Yeah." I glance around the café, feeling the familiar mix of pride and exhaustion that comes with it. "It wasn't easy, but I wanted to build something that made sense for our life. Something stable. Something that is ours."

Ivy smiles softly, her eyes warm. "That's... really lovely, actually."

I shrug, trying to downplay it. "It's something."

She looks like she wants to say more, but before she can, Lucy suddenly pipes up.

"Daddy, can I have more ketchup, please?"

The moment breaks.

I chuckle, grabbing the bottle from the table. "Yeah, Ladybug, you can have more ketchup."

As I squirt some on her plate, I catch Ivy watching me again, but this time with something different in her expression—something I can't quite place.

I suddenly realise how easy it's been, sitting here, talking to her despite me barely knowing her.

And I don't know why that unnerves me so much.

6
Bendy Yoga Friends

Ivy

I POP A CHIP in my mouth, chewing thoughtfully as Theo wipes Lucy's ketchup-covered hands with the efficiency of a man who has done this a thousand times before.

"You are disturbingly good at that," I say, nodding at Lucy, who is currently squirming but ultimately letting him clean her up.

He raises an eyebrow. "At what? Parenting?"

"At controlling the mess," I clarify. "If that had been me, the ketchup would have somehow ended up in my hair, on my shirt, and possibly in my shoe."

Theo smirks. "I've had five years of training."

Lucy beams proudly. "Daddy says I'm very messy."

I nod solemnly. "You should be. It's a child's job to be messy. You're doing important work."

She grins before turning back to her plate, clearly satisfied with my answer.

Theo shakes his head, picking up his own fork. "So," he says, giving me a look, "I've spent the last half hour spilling my entire backstory to you. Tell me something about you."

I freeze mid-bite. "Oh, you don't want to know about me. Very boring. Nothing to report."

He gives me a pointed look. "You talk about…" He mouths the word foursomes, "…in public, willingly signed up for three months of not dating, and somehow ended up having dinner with a five-year-old you just met and her rather clueless dad. I highly doubt you're boring."

I gasp, placing a hand over my chest in mock surprise. "So you did listen."

Theo smirks. "Hard not to when someone casually drops… certain topics into conversation while standing three feet away."

Across the table, Lucy pauses mid-chip, looking between us with open curiosity. "What topics?"

I bite back a laugh. Theo, however, doesn't look quite as amused.

"Oh, nothing," I say breezily, stirring my hot chocolate. "Just… very boring adult things."

Lucy's nose scrunches up. "Taxes?"

Theo clears his throat, hiding a smirk. "Exactly. Boring adult things. Definitely not worth repeating."

Lucy hums, narrowing her eyes suspiciously before returning to her food.

I smirk at Theo. "Smooth save."

He sighs. "I'm starting to think I need to keep a 'things Ivy should not discuss in my café' list."

"Oh, you're such a delicate flower," I tease, resting my chin in my hand.

He gives me a dry look. "I'd prefer 'a man just trying to run a respectable business without innuendo disasters in front of his staff and child.'"

I chuckle, but decide to spare him—for now.

"So," he says, changing the subject. "Now that I know way too much about you, tell me something normal. Something... child friendly."

I sigh dramatically. "Fine. Since you're so desperate for a wholesome fact, I'll give you the mildest one I have."

"I'm on the edge of my seat."

I smirk. "I'm a forty-one-year-old divorcee who can't cook. Oh, and I'm an urban planner."

Theo blinks. "Wait—really?"

Which bit is he questioning?

"Yes, definitely can't cook. I burn water."

"Water doesn't burn," Lucy pipes up through a mouth full of food.

"I meant... you are really an urban planner?" Theo asks.

I nod.

He frowns slightly, like he's trying to fit this into his mental image of me. "So you... plan London?"

"Well, more like I help design urban spaces, make sure buildings and transport systems work together, and try to stop people from ruining everything with bad infrastructure decisions."

Theo looks at me like I've just told him I secretly run MI5. "That is so much more serious than I expected."

"Wow," I say, narrowing my eyes. "What did you expect?"

He hesitates, glancing at Lucy, then lowers his voice slightly. "Honestly? Something a bit... flashier."

I smirk. "Like what? A job in entertainment?"

He presses his lips together, clearly suppressing a laugh. "Something... customer-service-adjacent."

I gasp dramatically. "How dare you."

He chuckles, shaking his head. "I just can't picture you in a suit, standing over a giant map, making life-altering decisions about where to put a new bus lane."

"Oh, I have that power," I say, tilting my head. "I could personally make your morning commute hell if I wanted to."

Theo raises an eyebrow. "You'd... adjust transport logistics out of spite?"

"Absolutely."

"Unfortunately for you, we live just around the corner. No commuting involved. Regardless, remind me never to get on your bad side."

"Smart man." I grin, taking a sip of my third hot chocolate this afternoon.

Theo watches me, like he's still trying to figure me out.

Good luck, mate! I'm still trying to figure me out, too.

Before I can take another sip, Lucy suddenly perks up, eyes wide with excitement.

"Can you build me a playground?" she asks, her little hands gripping the edge of the table.

I blink. "Uh... what?"

Theo sighs, shaking his head. "Ladybug, that's not how it works."

"But she plans cities," Lucy insists, as if I have the power to summon swing sets out of thin air. "She can put a playground here!"

I bite my lip, trying not to laugh at how serious she looks. "It's a nice idea, Lucy, but I don't actually get to choose where things go. I mostly work on roads and boring stuff."

Lucy deflates a little, frowning. "But there's no playground around here. And the one at Uncle Jasper's is so good."

Theo nods. "She's not wrong. There's hardly anything for kids within walking distance. My brother lives in a small village in Kent and it has this massive playground. Every time we visit, Lucy acts like it's Disneyland."

"It has a zip line," Lucy adds dramatically.

I chuckle. "Well, I get it. Playgrounds are very important business."

Lucy nods seriously, like I've just validated her entire worldview.

"Sadly," I continue, "Shoreditch isn't one of the areas I'm working in, so I can't sneak in a last-minute swing set."

Lucy sighs heavily, slumping back in her chair. "That's so unfair." She huffs and stabs at a chip, her playground dreams dashed.

"The only thing around here for Lucy is the library—we go there sometimes," Theo says, running a hand through his hair. "And there's a yoga class for parents and kids on Mondays in the studio just down the road."

I blink. "You do yoga?"

He shrugs. "It's a good way to stretch out. And, you know, not collapse from the stress of running a café."

I shake my head, processing this new piece of unexpected information. "So let me get this straight. You're a former lawyer, Viennese coffee house owner, and a yoga dad?"

Theo smirks. "Multifaceted."

Lucy, still sulking about her lack of a playground, mutters, "He's very bendy."

I burst out laughing.

Theo groans, running a hand down his face. "Thank you for that, Lucy."

She shrugs, completely unbothered. "It's true."

I shake my head, still grinning, but as I reach for my hot chocolate, I remember the actual reason I ended up here in the first place.

"You know," I say, stirring my drink absentmindedly, "I actually tried yoga today."

Theo raises an eyebrow. "Tried?"

I sigh dramatically. "I started with Yoga for Dummies, which was already pushing my attention span to its limits, and then I attempted something called a Sun Salutation and ended up in what I can only describe as a human car crash."

He laughs. "Sounds dramatic."

"Oh, it was spectacular. There was flailing. There was swearing. At one point, I crashed to the floor."

Theo looks far too amused. "Crashed?"

"Listen, things happened, Theo. It was traumatic."

He chuckles, shaking his head. "Sounds like you need proper instruction."

I roll my eyes. "And where, pray tell, do you suggest I find this proper instruction?"

He smirks. "Well, funny you should ask. Some of us are very bendy and happen to attend a class on Mondays."

I blink. "Wait. Are you inviting me to kids' yoga?"

"Parents and kids practice separately," he points out. "No kids required."

I hesitate. "I don't know…"

"Why not?"

"Well, for one, I don't have a child."

He shrugs. "Not an issue if you come with me."

That... that feels like a loaded statement.

I glance at my nearly empty cup, choosing my words carefully. "I do work on Mondays."

Theo nods, as if that settles it. "Fair enough."

I wait for him to push back, to find another argument, but he just takes a sip of his drink like the conversation is already over.

And for some annoying reason, that makes me want to clarify.

"I mean," I continue, shifting slightly, "I do work, but... I work from home, so technically, I can be flexible with my schedule."

Theo tilts his head, amusement flickering across his face. "Ah."

I narrow my eyes. "What?"

"Nothing," he says, though he's clearly holding back a smirk. "Just enjoying you arguing with yourself."

I huff, stabbing a piece of sausage with my fork. "I'm not arguing with myself."

"You literally just proved your own excuse wrong."

I open my mouth, then snap it shut because, fuck, he's right.

To avoid looking at him, I focus on Lucy, who is carefully lining up her chips in a neat row, completely oblivious to my minor crisis.

After a moment, I clear my throat. "When is this yoga class, anyway?"

"Eleven-thirty."

I do a quick mental calculation. Eleven-thirty isn't too bad. I could start early, shift a few tasks around, and technically still get a full workday in...

I lean back in my chair, staring at the ceiling. "I might be able to make that work."

Theo raises an eyebrow. "That sounded dangerously close to a yes."

I exhale sharply, shaking my head at myself.

Because I do want to go.

I know it. He knows it. Even Lucy—who is now humming to herself while dipping a chip in ketchup—probably knows it.

But there's still something holding me back.

I fiddle with my fork, staring at the last few chips on my plate, trying to ignore the way my stomach is doing something at the idea of saying yes.

"I shouldn't really be... going out with a man," I say finally, though even I can hear how unconvincing I sound. "Because, you know, the ban."

Theo chuckles. "One day, you're gonna have to tell me that story."

I scoff. "Oh, it's a thrilling one, let me tell you. Full of self-reflection and—"

"Questionable decision-making?" he supplies.

"Exactly," I say, pointing my fork at him.

He smirks, then he leans forward. "But it's not a date. Just yoga."

I exhale, still hesitating.

He leans forward slightly. "Surely you're allowed to have male friends, Ivy."

I purse my lips, tapping my fingers against the table. What would Pee-Pee say?

She'd probably ask me why I was so reluctant to do something I clearly wanted to do. She'd probably tell me that just because I'm taking a break from dating, it doesn't mean I have to shut down every interaction with a man.

And, let's be honest, she'd definitely tell me that my excuses were getting flimsier by the second.

I sigh, running a hand through my hair. "Fine. But only because I don't want to die doing a Sun Salutation in my living room."

Theo laughs out loud. "Whatever helps you sleep at night."

Lucy claps her hands together. "Yay! Daddy's gonna do the cool poses again!"

I raise an eyebrow. "Oh? No Shaking Warrior pose?"

Lucy shakes her head fervently. "Nope! Daddy's really good."

Theo shrugs, looking far too pleased with himself. "I am very bendy." His voice goes all deep and sultry when he says that and I want to fan myself.

I open my mouth, then shut it, because there is no good way to respond to that.

Instead, I just hide my smirk. "Alright, fine. Monday. Yoga. As friends."

Theo nods, "Looking forward to it."

And just like that, I have plans for Monday.

7
Dazzled by the Warrior

Theo

I check my watch. 11:27 AM.

Lucy shifts excitedly beside me, swinging her arms as we wait outside the coffee shop. "Do you think she's coming?" she asks, bouncing on her toes.

"She said she was, didn't she?" I say.

"Yeah, but sometimes grown-ups say things and then change their minds."

I smirk. "Is that so?"

She nods seriously, as if she has years of wisdom on the subject.

I chuckle, but before I can respond, the narrow unassuming blue door next to the Kaiser's Mug opens and a familiar blonde figure rushes out, dressed in yoga trousers and an oversized hoodie, looking slightly flustered but very much here.

Lucy lets out a small squeak of excitement. "She came!"

I glance down at her. "Told you."

Ivy comes to an abrupt halt when she sees us, tucking a loose strand of hair behind her ear. "I almost talked myself out of this, just so you know."

I smirk. "And yet, here you are."

She exhales. "Here I am."

Lucy grins up at her. "You're gonna love it."

Ivy gives her a sceptical look. "You sound very sure about that."

"I am," Lucy insists. "Daddy's class is way harder than mine, but he's so good."

Ivy lifts an eyebrow at me. "Oh? So I'm about to be shown up?"

I shrug, feigning modesty. "I do have excellent balance."

She narrows her eyes. "I feel like you're setting me up for something."

I grin. "Come on, let's get going before you change your mind."

"Does Lucy not go to school yet?" Ivy asks whilst we walk the short distance.

"No, her birthday is in May so she starts in September. Until then, the café is closed on Mondays so I can spend some time with her," I sigh. It is sometimes scary to see how quickly Lu is growing up.

"She adores you," Ivy says.

"Well, she has only me... and my family."

Ivy lowers her voice when she asks, "Do you think her mum will ever come back?"

"Nope," I shake my head, "Katherine never bonded with Lu and it was clear she didn't want to be a mother very early on. We weren't in love either. We tried to make it work but, in the end, we had to call it a day. It just was better for everyone around. She has never been in touch or sent a birthday card or anything. Last I heard, she moved to Australia with her girlfriend."

"Oh," is all Ivy says. Yeah, people generally don't know what to say to our situation.

"Does Lucy ask after her?" Ivy asks carefully. "You don't have to tell me if you don't—"

"Nah, it's fine. She rarely asks after her. She's never really known any different. She was too little when Katherine left. My brothers are always there to help and my mum would be here in a jiffy if we needed a female perspective. So, she has all the family she needs," I shrug.

"Yes, she does." Ivy gives my arm a gentle squeeze.

The studio is just down the road, tucked away in a quiet little side street. It's one of those places that looks small from the outside but opens up into a surprisingly large space inside.

As soon as we step through the doors, Lucy beams and immediately bolts toward the kids' section, where a group of tiny humans is already gathered on their mats in the far corner of the room.

"See you later, Daddy and Ivy!" she calls over her shoulder, barely looking back before diving straight into conversation with a little girl who has a stuffed rabbit perched next to her mat.

Ivy watches her go with mild amusement. "Well, she settles in fast."

"She's a social butterfly," I say, scanning the room.

The adults' class is at the other end of the studio, a calm, soft-lit space where people are already rolling out their mats, stretching, and getting ready for the class.

I gesture toward a shelf stacked with yoga mats. "Grab one from here."

Ivy hesitates before pulling a mat out, holding it in front of her like it might attack her. "So, what's the protocol? Do I just... put this down and hope for the best?"

"Pretty much," I say, setting mine down in my usual spot.

She glances around at the other people warming up. "They all look very capable."

I smirk. "You nervous?"

She scoffs. "No. Of course not. I love humiliating myself in front of strangers."

I chuckle. "Don't worry. If you fall over, I'll pretend not to see."

She shoots me a look. "You will not."

I place a hand over my heart. "I absolutely will."

She sighs, shaking her head. "Why did I agree to this?"

"Because you secretly wanted to," I say, stretching my arms overhead. "And because you want to learn from a master."

Ivy presses her lips together, trying not to laugh. "I mean, that was a strong selling point."

I smirk. "Come on, Ivy. Time to get bendy."

She groans. "I already regret this."

Before Ivy can complain further about her impending humiliation, Safiya approaches us with a warm smile.

"Good morning, Theo," she says, her voice smooth and confident. She wears a cropped top and tight leggings as always and is the epiphany of a yoga instructor.

I smile. "Morning, Safiya."

She turns to Ivy, giving her the same friendly smile. "You must be new."

Ivy hesitates, then nods. "Yeah, first class. Go easy on me."

Safiya chuckles. "Beginners are always welcome." Then she glances at me and gives my arm a gentle squeeze. "You bringing in recruits now?"

"Just doing my part to spread the joy of yoga."

She hums, "I always appreciate all *your* support."

Ivy watches this exchange with an expression I can't quite place.

Safiya's eyes flick between the two of us before she smiles again. "Well, welcome, Ivy. I'll keep an eye on you today—make sure Theo doesn't intimidate you too much."

Ivy forces a chuckle, but it's slightly delayed.

"I appreciate that," she says, shifting her grip on her mat.

Safiya gives a small nod before moving off to the front of the room, leaving us alone again.

I stretch my arms over my head, not thinking much of it, but when I glance at Ivy, she's frowning slightly.

"You alright?" I ask.

She blinks, shaking her head a little, as if snapping herself out of something. "Yeah! Yep. Totally fine."

I tilt my head. "You sure? You looked—"

"Fine," she cuts in quickly, forcing a too-bright smile. "Just... mentally preparing for my inevitable public disgrace."

I chuckle. "You'll be okay."

She exhales and unrolls her mat, but there's something slightly off about her expression. Her lips are pressed together like she's holding something back, and her eyes keep flicking toward where Safiya is now setting up at the front of the room.

Then, very casually, she says, "So... Safiya seems nice."

I nod. "Yeah, she's great. Really good instructor."

Ivy hums. "Hmm. And she clearly enjoys your company."

I glance at her, frowning slightly. "What's that supposed to mean?"

She gives me an innocent look. "Oh, nothing. Just that she was very happy to see you."

I shrug. "She's friendly." The thought of Safiya being interested in me is laughable. I think she is even dating the guy who owns the yoga studio.

Ivy raises an eyebrow. "Theo, she was flirting with you."

I snort. "What? No, she wasn't."

She lets out a laugh, shaking her head. "Oh my God, you're one of those."

I cross my arms. "One of what?"

"The oblivious ones! The ones who have beautiful women flirting with them and just do not see it."

I scoff. "I think I'd know if someone was flirting with me." Of course I would. It's just been a while since... come to think of it, I'm not quite sure when a woman last flirted with me. *I need to get out more.*

She snorts. "Would you, though?"

"Yes!" I insist.

"Okay, let's examine the evidence. The way she smiled at you? That was flirting." She holds up one finger. "The way she praised you? Flirting." A second finger joins the first one. "And the way she kept glancing between the two of us, as if checking if I was a threat? Definitely flirting," she grins triumphantly holding up three fingers as prove of her absurd theory.

I shake my head, utterly unconvinced. "You're reading into things."

Ivy sighs dramatically, looking to the ceiling pleading for patience. "Wow. Men really do live in a different reality."

I smirk. "Or maybe you see things that aren't there."

She rolls her eyes. "Sure, Theo. Keep telling yourself that."

I chuckle, "Well, even if she was flirting—which she wasn't—I wouldn't have noticed because I was too busy making sure you didn't back out."

Ivy scoffs. "Oh, please. I was totally committed."

Just as Safiya is about to start the class, a little voice rings out from across the studio.

"Daddy! Ivy!"

I turn toward the kids' section, where Lucy is standing on her mat, arms flailing enthusiastically. When she sees she has our attention, she gives us a giant, proud wave.

Ivy waves back. "Looking good, Lu!"

Lucy beams, then immediately flops into what I assume is her version of a stretch.

I shake my head, chuckling, as Safiya claps her hands to gather our attention.

"Alright, let's start in Tadasana—Mountain Pose."

Ivy follows my lead, straightening up, feet firmly grounded, arms relaxed at her sides. She exhales slowly, looking surprisingly serious about this whole thing.

"Nice," I say quietly.

She flicks me a glance. "Don't patronise me, Theo. I can stand just fine on two feet."

I chuckle. "Impressive stuff."

She gives me a withering look before Safiya moves on.

"Now let's shift into Vrksasana—Tree Pose. Find your balance, press one foot to your calf or thigh, and focus on a fixed point."

I smoothly lift my foot and press it against my thigh, hands in prayer position. Ivy, to her credit, does the same—wobbling slightly but keeping herself upright.

She grits her teeth. "I swear if you say anything—"

"Nothing at all," I say innocently, though I can't hide my grin.

She narrows her eyes at me but stays focused, determined to not fall on her face.

"Now," Safiya says, moving to the next exercise, "I want everyone to line up along the wall. Place one foot against it, so we can work on our Virabhadrasana II—Warrior Pose."

We all move into place, and I find myself directly opposite Ivy as we stretch into position.

And that's when it happens.

Her eyes meet mine.

I don't know how long we stand there like that, close to the wall, staring at each other. Her lips part slightly, her breath steady but just a little shallow, and something shifts in the air between us.

The studio fades away. The sounds of breathing, shifting mats, and even Safiya's instructions blur into the background.

I don't know what it is—maybe it's the focus, the way her eyes soften as she holds my gaze, or the ridiculous fact that we're locked in some kind of accidental yoga standoff.

But I don't look away.

And neither does she.

Somewhere in the distance, I hear a voice.

"Hello, you."

It's faint. Barely noticeable.

"Hello?"

Ivy doesn't react. Neither do I.

"Hello?"

Still nothing.

Then, on the fourth repeat, someone behind me clears their throat.

"I think she means you," a man laughs.

Ivy blinks rapidly and whips her head around, realising that she is the only one facing away from the instructor.

The entire class is turned the opposite direction, all watching Safiya.

And Ivy?

Ivy has been staring directly at me.

Her face goes bright red. "Oh. Right. That makes sense."

"Lost in the moment?" I whisper. I can't help myself. My heart is still racing and somehow, I am willing her to just give me a sign that this was also... something to her just like it was to me.

She glares at me, mortified. "Psst."

I grin, shifting effortlessly into the next pose.

Best. Yoga class. Ever.

8

I like Brunch

Ivy

I AM NEVER SHOWING my face in this yoga studio again.

The moment I realise I've been standing the wrong way, locked in some ridiculous, romance-novel-level eye contact with Theo while an entire class watches us, my soul leaves my body.

The guy behind Theo, the one who called me out, gives me a knowing smirk as I finally turn the right way.

And Theo? Theo looks far too pleased with himself.

I will be getting my revenge.

I shake it off, force myself to focus, and try to actually listen as Safiya moves us through the rest of the class.

It's... not as bad as I expected.

Don't get me wrong—I am wobbling, and my muscles are already protesting, but at least I haven't fallen flat on my face yet. Small wins.

By the time we're in the final resting pose, I'm almost feeling serene. Who knew that lying flat on the floor with your eyes closed counts as yoga. This is my kind of yoga.

And then, of course, Theo has to ruin it.

"Comfortable?" he murmurs.

I crack one eye open, peering at him out of the corner of my vision. "You're not supposed to talk in this part."

He chuckles, eyes still closed, completely relaxed. "You looked like you were actually enjoying yourself."

I shut my eye again. "Don't make it weird."

"Too late."

I huff but don't respond. I refuse to give him the satisfaction.

A few minutes later, the class ends, and everyone starts rolling up their mats. I sit up, stretching out my arms, and spot Lucy running toward us from the kids' area.

"That was so fun!" she beams, plopping down into Theo's lap. "Did you do good?"

Theo grins. "I did great." He places a gentle kiss on her head and I swoon a tiny little bit. Never knew that single dads do it for me.

Lucy turns to me. "What about you, Ivy?"

I sigh dramatically. "Well, I only embarrassed myself once, so I'd say that's a win."

Theo finds my eyes again and I cut him off before he can say anything. "We are not talking about it," I warn him.

Lucy looks between us, confused. "Talking about what?"

"Taxes, Ladybug," he chuckles.

I shoot him a warning look, which he completely ignores, and pick up my mat, desperate to move on. "Right, well. That was fun. Thanks for the invite, but I should get going."

Lucy gasps. "Wait! We always get smoothies after yoga!"

I hesitate. "You do?"

She nods enthusiastically. "You have to come! It's tradition!"

I glance at Theo, who just shrugs like he had nothing to do with this obvious setup. "She's right. It's tradition."

I chew my lip. I could just go home. That was the plan. But I could also be half an hour late for work. I'll just work a little longer in the evening. It's not like I have anywhere to go.

Theo is watching me expectantly. And Lucy is looking at me with ridiculously big, hopeful eyes. And... well.

Maybe one smoothie wouldn't hurt.

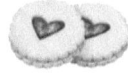

It's just past five o'clock, and through my open window, I hear Theo's voice from the street below.

"Alright, see you tomorrow," he calls out to someone. There's a muffled response—probably one of his staff—and then the unmistakable sound of keys turning in a lock.

He's closing up.

Going home.

I haven't seen him or Lucy since yoga on Monday. Five days.

I tell myself it's because I've been busy with work, which is technically true—deadlines have been piling up, emails have been relentless, and I've had a shocking amount of meetings for someone who works from home.

But if I'm really honest with myself? I've been avoiding him.

Because I'm pretty sure there was flirting happening at yoga and when we had our smoothies.

And I cannot risk it.

I cannot fail in the first month of my dating ban. That would be tragic.

Theo is... nice. And funny. And dangerously easy to be around. Which is exactly why I need to keep my distance.

Which brings me to tonight's plan:

Yoga.

Specifically, Yoga for Dummies, take two.

I roll out my mat in the middle of my living room, take a deep breath, and, after pressing play, make one very important adjustment from last time: I take the remote control and hide it under my sofa cushion. No skipping ahead. No fast-forwarding. No quitting halfway through. This time, I am doing the whole thing.

I straighten up, take a deep breath, and try to relax. The instructor's serene voice fills the room.

"Welcome. We'll begin with some gentle breathing exercises to centre ourselves."

I exhale slowly, determined.

I am taking this seriously.

Inhale through my nose.

I am not getting distracted.

Exhale through my mouth.

I am definitely not thinking about Theo. This time, I am committed.

I sit cross-legged on my mat, hands resting on my knees, and take a deep breath.

I can do this. I will do this. I will not get bored, skip ahead, or dramatically collapse halfway through.

"We'll start with Cat Pose. Come onto your hands and knees, press through your palms, and round your back gently as you exhale," the instructor says.

Alright. Hands, knees, spine up like a stretching cat—easy enough.

I move into the pose, feeling a slight stretch in my back.

Okay. This is fine. This is actually... quite nice?

We repeat the pose five times before the instructor moves on.

"Now rise to Mountain Pose, standing tall, feet firmly rooted to the ground."

I push myself up, straightening my spine, feet planted.

I take a deep breath.

Standing here, with nothing to do but breathe, my mind starts wandering.

Who am I?

I mean, really.

What do I truly like?

The instructor continues, leading me through the next steps. Each one gets repeated five times whilst inhaling through my nose and exhaling through my mouth.

"From here, move into Standing Forward Bend."

I fold forward, reaching for my toes. My hamstrings protest, but I breathe through it.

The thing is... I don't know what I like.

Not really.

I've always just kind of adapted. I went from being married to being single to serial dating without ever really pausing to figure out what I wanted.

"Step one foot back into a Lunge."

I carefully shift, wobbling slightly, but managing to stay upright.

I'm forty-one years old, and I don't even know what my own hobbies are. That's insane, right?

I know I like brunch. And cake. And... what else?

"Move into Tree Pose."

I press one foot against my thigh, finding my balance, arms raised.

I glance at the sofa cushion where I've hidden the remote, momentarily tempted.

No. Focus.

I take a deep breath, grounding myself.

"Next, we'll stretch into Standing Side Stretch Pose."

I extend my arms overhead and lean to one side, feeling the pull along my ribs.

Ivy, you are supposed to be using these three months to figure this out.

But what if I come out of this and realise I don't actually like anything?

What if I'm just... nothing outside of dating and work and brunch? When I was younger, I thought in my forties I'd be happily married with two kids, living somewhere in the countryside. The perfect family. Being on my own with no plan for my future wasn't quite what I had imagined.

The instructor carries on.

"Shift into Downward Facing Dog."

I press my hands and feet into the mat, hips raised. My arms shake a little, but I hold steady.

I mean, I'm good in my job. I was one of the youngest members of the Royal Town Planning Institute. When it comes to my career, I know what I'm doing. But I want to be more than just my job; I need to start actually paying attention to myself.

Not in a self-improvement, drink-green-smoothies way, but in a *who the hell am I* kind of way.

"Lower into Cobra Pose."

I stretch forward, pressing up with my arms, feeling the arch in my back.

Pee-Pee was right. It's time to start figuring out what makes me happy.

The instructor's voice is soothing.

"Shift into Child's Pose, letting your body rest."

I fold myself down, arms extended, forehead touching the mat.

I close my eyes.

But the truth is, I have no idea where to start. Yet, for the first time, I actually want to.

"We'll move into Seated Spinal Twist."

I sit up, crossing one leg over the other and twisting gently.

It's time to stop coasting.

"Extend into Seated Forward Bend."

I lean forward, reaching for my toes even if I don't quite get there yet.

Time to stop avoiding myself.

Finally, the instructor's voice softens. "Now, rest in Final Relaxation Pose."

I lie there, stretched out in my all-time favourite pose, staring at the ceiling, letting my breath settle

And then it hits me: I did it. I made it through the whole thing. No skipping. No quitting halfway through. No dramatically collapsing onto my mat in frustration. I did the whole yoga routine. Okay, someone's mind is supposed to be blank and calm when doing yoga, not full of life's questions, but I somehow made it through.

And the weirdest part? I actually liked it.

I exhale slowly, feeling a tiny swell of something that I think might be... pride? It's such a rare emotion for me when it comes to anything vaguely athletic, I barely recognise it.

But there it is. I enjoyed this.

Sure, I wobbled, and my hamstrings definitely hate me, but I feel... good. I let out a small laugh, the sound bouncing off the quiet walls of my flat.

Maybe this is what I've been missing. Not necessarily yoga itself—although apparently, I don't hate it—but the feeling of doing something just for me. No expectations. No impressing anyone. No outside validation. Just... me, a yoga mat, and an hour spent figuring out what my body can do.

9
Just Friends

Ivy

EVERY SINGLE MUSCLE IN my body is screaming.

I was sore after the yoga class with Theo and Lucy, but after my deeply unwise decision to do another full session at home, I've officially ascended to a new level of physical misery.

Walking to Pee-Pee's office feels like some kind of cruel endurance test. Every step sends a fresh wave of pain through my legs. My arms ache every time I lift them. Even my ribs hurt.

What kind of exercise makes your ribs hurt?

I reach the steps of her office and grip the railing like it's the only thing keeping me upright. One step. Two. Three—ow.

If Pee-Pee asks how I'm feeling today, I might just collapse, stare at the ceiling, and inform her that self-improvement is a scam.

I lower myself onto Pee-Pee's therapy sofa with the grace of a one-legged giraffe, groaning as my legs protest the movement.

Pee-Pee watches me over the rim of her glasses. Her trusted cardigan is a pastel shade of peach today. "Rough morning?"

I let out a dramatic sigh. "Phyllis, I have made a terrible mistake."

She clasps her hands together, looking far too intrigued. "Do tell."

I wave a limp hand. "Yoga."

She smiles knowingly. "Ah. First step of finding yourself."

"The only thing I found was pain," I correct. "No one warns you about that part. They all make it sound so calm. So zen." I gesture vaguely in the air. "'Oh, just breathe through it, Ivy. Just find your inner stillness, Ivy. Just contort yourself into unnatural shapes while pretending this is completely fine, Ivy.'"

She chuckles. "Walk me through it."

I sigh. "Well, I failed on my first try and then Theo dragged me to the parent and kids' yoga session. And after that I thought I can do the stupid Yoga for Dummies thing. So I promised myself, this time will be different. I'll be serious about it. No skipping ahead. No quitting halfway through. No dramatic flopping onto the floor and declaring myself unfit for human movement."

Pee-Pee nods, looking amused. "Go on."

"So, there I am, stretching, bending, definitely not shaking," I lie. "But don't even get me started on Downward Facing Dog—because apparently, I have zero upper body strength."

Pee-Pee bites back a smile. "And yet, you did the whole session."

I pause, slightly begrudging. "I did."

She raises an eyebrow. "And?"

I sigh again, slumping dramatically. "And it wasn't horrible until I woke up this morning."

She looks far too satisfied with that answer. "So, you might actually enjoy it?"

I scoff. "Let's not get carried away."

She leans back in her chair. "You said before that you've always fallen into things... relationships, activities, decisions, without really choosing them for yourself. Would you say yoga was something you chose?"

I frown slightly. "I mean... technically, yes."

She nods. "And how did it feel to commit to something just for you?"

I hesitate.

Because, if I'm really honest... it felt good. Not in a *Wow, I've found my life's calling* way, but in a *Huh, maybe I don't completely suck at following through* way.

I huff. "I hate how well you know me."

She chuckles but then tilts her head slightly. "And this whole experience... you did it entirely on your own?"

"Yep," I say quickly.

Pee-Pee just looks at me. I shift under her gaze, suddenly feeling like a teenager caught sneaking in past curfew.

One eyebrow lifts. "Who is that Theo you mentioned?"

I wave a dismissive hand. "I may have attended one class with him and his Lucy... I mean, his daughter, first, just to get a feel for it." There is no reply from Pee-Pee. Clearly, she wants more. I clear my throat. "He owns the café underneath my flat and we got talking and he told me about this yoga class. On Mondays. But that's not relevant."

"Of course not," she says smoothly. "Completely irrelevant."

I narrow my eyes. "I don't like your tone."

She just smiles. "So, tell me more about this entirely irrelevant Theo."

"You're making this a thing, and it's really not a thing."

"I'm simply asking about the entirely unremarkable Theo."

I groan, letting my head fall back against the sofa. "He's just this guy. A single dad. He had the weird idea to open a Viennese coffee shop. We met by coincidence, and now, somehow, I've been recruited into his daughter's yoga routine."

Pee-Pee nods, her expression unreadable. "And you're just... friends?"

"Yes," I say, sitting up a little straighter. "We are just friends."

"And why would that be a problem?"

"It's not a problem."

Pee-Pee just waits. I fidget.

"I just... I don't know. I don't want to fall into old patterns."

She nods. "And what would that look like?"

"You know, getting too comfortable, prioritising someone else's presence over figuring out what I actually want.

This whole thing is about focusing on myself, and if I let someone in too much, I might not do that."

Pee-Pee considers my reply. "That's fair. But does being his friend mean you're abandoning yourself?"

I hesitate. "Not... necessarily."

She leans forward slightly. "So then, what would it take for you to feel secure in the friendship? What boundaries would you need?"

I chew on my lip. "I guess... I'd need to make sure I'm still making decisions for me. Not changing my plans just to fit around his. And I'd need to be honest with myself if I ever started feeling like I was slipping into something more."

Pee-Pee nods. "That sounds reasonable."

I exhale, some of the tension easing out of my shoulders. "Okay. But how do I know the difference? Like, if I help out with Lucy sometimes, am I just being a good friend, or am I subconsciously moulding myself into whatever he needs?"

Phyllis nods slowly, pausing as if contemplating what best to say. Although I'm pretty sure she knows exactly what to say. That woman has an answer to everything.

"That's a really good question. What do you think the difference is?" *I thought I pay her to give me the answers?*

I frown. "I guess... if I actually want to do it, that's one thing. But if I feel like I have to, or like saying no would disappoint him, then maybe that's a red flag?"

Pee-Pee nods. "Exactly. Friendship isn't about obligation. If you're doing something because you genuinely want to—not because you're afraid of letting him down—then you're still making choices for yourself."

I let out a slow breath. "Okay. That makes sense."

Pee-Pee smiles but then studies me for a moment before asking, "Can I ask you something?"

I lift a brow. "Have you ever stopped yourself before?"

She smirks. "Fair point. But seriously—why do you even think you might be interested in him?"

I blink. "What?"

She shrugs. "You're acting like you need to keep your distance to avoid something. But if he's really just a friend, why does that even cross your mind?"

I hesitate.

Because, well... huh.

"I don't know," I admit slowly. "I guess... maybe because it would be easy? He's nice. I like spending time with him. He makes me laugh. I can be myself with him." I wave a hand. "But none of that means I actually like him like that."

Pee-Pee nods. "Then maybe the real question is: Are you afraid of falling into something you don't want, or are you afraid of wanting it?"

I scowl. "I'm starting to regret ever talking to you."

She grins. "I know. But you keep doing it anyway."

I groan, flopping back against the sofa again. "Ugh. Why do you always make so much sense?"

Pee-Pee smirks. "It's a gift."

To be honest, Pee-Pee has been a life saver after the divorce from Barry... Baz, as he likes to be called. Knobhead.

My brother put me onto Phylis. She helped his husband Henry come out when he was at SOAS, back when he was still trying to date women and convince everyone he was just really into existentialism. Thomas and I aren't close, not really, but when he found out Barry had been cheating—after everything, after the appointments and the tests and me still trying to hope for some sort of miracle—he went all big brother and was ready to drive down from Birmingham and knock some sense into him. Said it didn't matter if we hadn't spoken properly in ages, Barry needed a reality check. He is in the gym five days a week and looks like he could bench press a hatchback. Barry wouldn't have stood a chance. It took me and Henry to convince him that the knobhead wasn't worth it.

I roll my eyes at Phylis but smile at the thought of my brother going after Baz. "Alright, fine. Maybe I'll stop actively dodging him."

Pee-Pee's eyes twinkle. "How generous of you."

I snort. "Yeah, yeah. Just don't say 'I told you so' if it backfires."

She grins. "I would never."

I squint at her. "Lies."

Pee-Pee just chuckles, and for the first time in days, I feel like I might have a handle on this.

As I push open the door to the coffee shop, the bell overhead gives a half-hearted jingle, like it's too tired to fully commit this late in the day. The place is mostly dark, save for the warm glow of the counter lights, and behind them, Theo is wiping down the espresso machine with the kind of focus usually reserved for brain surgery.

"We are closing," he says without looking up.

"I think I'll survive."

He glances at me then, his mouth curving into an easy grin. "I don't know. I've seen you uncaffeinated. It's not pretty."

I gasp in mock offense. "I'll have you know, I am a delight at all hours."

Theo hums like he's considering it. "Hmm. Jury's still out."

I make a face at him, sticking out my tongue like a mature adult.

His grin widens. "Ah, yes. The universal sign of emotional intelligence."

I huff but can't quite fight back a smile as I slide onto my stool at the counter. Not my stool, obviously, because I don't have a usual stool. That would imply I spend too much time here. Which I don't. Obviously.

He finishes wiping down the machine, then leans against the counter, arms crossed, looking at me expectantly. "So... to what do I owe the pleasure?"

"Just passing through," I say breezily. "Thought I'd make sure you haven't set up some kind of underground yoga cult in my absence."

He smirks. "Not yet. But Lucy's been asking about you. She seems to think your presence improves the class."

I scoff. "Doubtful."

"Well, she disagrees." He stacks some coffee cups, glancing at me. "You made an impression."

I shrug. "She's five. I could have done a star jump, and she'd think I was an Olympic gymnast."

Theo chuckles. "True, but she was pretty sure you'd be back. She told me you like yoga."

I hold a laugh. "Lies. Slander. Defamation." I shift in my seat and grimace. "Although… I did do yoga yesterday. And now I regret everything."

His eyebrows lift. "You did yoga? On your own?"

"Don't sound so shocked," I say, crossing my arms. "I'm very disciplined."

He leans on the counter, smirking. "Mmhmm. So, how'd it go?"

I groan. "Terrible. Everything hurts. I think my hamstrings are staging a coup." I roll my shoulders and wince. "If I have to do one more downward dog, I might just stay down."

Theo grins. "See, that's why you've got to stick with the class. At least then you'll suffer with moral support."

"More like communal humiliation."

"Depends on how you look at it," he says, boxing up some cake from the vitrine. "You could always come back Monday. We'll be there."

I hesitate, stretching my sore arm like that'll somehow loosen the internal tension, too. "I don't know…"

Theo shrugs, like he genuinely doesn't care either way. "Up to you. Just saying, suffering's more fun when it's a group activity."

"That sounds like something a cult leader would say."

"If I start handing out matching robes, you'll know to run."

I laugh, but even as the sound fades, something tugs at the back of my mind.

Pee-Pee's words. *Do it for you.*

I hadn't really considered that before. That I might actually want to go.

Because, pain aside, yoga has been... weirdly nice. Not just the movement itself, though that part surprises me.

Exercise and I have never exactly been on friendly terms. At my size, it's not always easy. There's that unspoken expectation that working out should be about shrinking myself, about changing, about fixing. But yoga hasn't felt like that.

I mean, sure, I wobble in certain poses, and some stretches feel like they were designed by an actual sadist, but none of that has made me feel like I don't belong. My body still works in yoga—it moves, it adjusts, it holds its own. And even when it doesn't, there's no judgment.

And, okay, maybe I enjoyed hanging out with Theo and Lucy. It's hard not to enjoy Lucy's unfiltered enthusiasm, the way she throws herself into everything like she's the main character in a high-stakes action movie. And Theo... well.

And maybe—maybe—I liked the feeling of being part of something.

I glance at him. "How did you even get into yoga, anyway?"

He wipes his hands on a tea towel, thinking for a second before answering. "Cornwall."

I blink. "Cornwall?"

He smirks. "Yeah. Not exactly where you'd expect, right?"

"I thought you are going to tell me about some exotic *ashram* in India or so." I shift on my stool. "Why Cornwall?"

He leans against the counter. "Two years ago, I had my burnout, and my family basically staged an intervention. Told me I had to take two weeks off, no arguments. They all pooled together to take care of Lucy, and I—reluctantly—agreed."

I rest my face on my hand. "They sent you away?"

"They strongly encouraged me," he corrects with a dry smile. "I was barely functioning at that point, so I didn't have much of a fight left in me. And I figured if I was going anywhere, it might as well be somewhere I had good memories of. When I was a teenager, I went to Cornwall to surf, and it was great. Thought I'd relive my glory days."

I raise an eyebrow. "And?"

He exhales a laugh. "Waves were shit."

I snort. "Brutal."

"Yeah. So I was stuck in this tiny beach town, no surf, no real plan, and kind of miserable. And then the lady who ran my B&B, Margaret, decided I was a 'troubled soul' and dragged me to her senior citizen yoga class."

My lips twitch. "You did yoga with retirees?"

"Every morning for two weeks. I was the youngest person there by about thirty years. And also the least flexible."

I let out a short laugh. "That's amazing."

"Honestly? It kind of was," he admits. "It forced me to slow down, to actually be in my body instead of just running on autopilot. When I got back, I kept it up. Now I do yoga three or four times a week... mostly at home when Lu is in bed."

I pout, pensively. "And the Monday class?"

"That one's for Lucy." His smirk softens slightly. "She likes it. Monday's our thing. Family yoga."

Something about that sticks with me, settling somewhere deep in my chest.

Family yoga.

I swallow, looking down at where my fingers are idly tapping on the counter. I don't know why that hits me, but it does.

"You're a good dad," I say, almost without thinking.

Theo's brows lift slightly, like I've surprised him. He lets out a small breath, shaking his head. "I try. Why did you give yoga a try?"

"My therapist put me on the dating ban to find myself. After my divorce, which wasn't really amiable although by now I am glad I'm no longer with the knobhead. We weren't right, I just couldn't see it. So, after my divorce, I went a bit rogue and became a serial dater." I'm not sure why I tell him all of this. I didn't need to.

I carefully glance at him. There is no judgment, no pity in his face, just curiosity. He wants to know things about me; he wants to get to know me. A tiny alarm bell goes off, but I silence it with the thought that friends do that as well. Doesn't have to be a romantic thing.

"Barry... my ex, cheated on me. We had a rough few years in our marriage after we found out I can't have children, but I didn't want to believe the doctors."

"I'm sorry to hear that, Ivy." He leans forward and gently squeezes my arm. I know he means the children thing but I don't elaborate. I don't like talking about it.

"To be honest, I think I only married Barry because I wanted a family. I'm definitely better off without him, only I was focused on one goal so long, I kind of don't know myself. So here I am, trying to find myself... by not dying doing yoga."

"You should be proud of that." I can see in his eyes that he means it. Even more, he is proud of me.

For some reason, that makes me want to say something else, to fill the space with a joke or a quip, but nothing comes to mind. Before I can figure out what to say, my stomach betrays me with a loud, undeniable grumble.

"Hungry?" Theo breaks the tension with a smirk.

I sigh, pressing a hand to my stomach as if I could physically silence it. "Apparently."

He chuckles. "I was just about to make dinner. You're welcome to join."

It's a nice offer. And after my conversation with Pee-Pee, I know there's no actual reason to say no. Spending time with Theo isn't dangerous, it isn't breaking any rules. It's just dinner.

But something in me hesitates.

Maybe it's because I've spent all day talking about my feelings, and I need to just exist in my own space for a while. Or maybe I just want to sink into a hot bath and not think about anything for a bit.

I shake my head, offering him a small smile. "Tempting, but I think I need a long, scalding-hot bath to recover from yesterday's yoga session."

Theo's frown makes him look concerned for a moment. "That bad?"

I groan dramatically. "My hamstrings are crying out for some relief."

"Well, in that case, I won't stand between you and your recovery." He grabs a tea towel and tosses it over his shoulder. "But you're still coming Monday, right?"

I hesitate, but only for a second this time.

"Yeah," I say. "I'll be there."

Again, he doesn't gloat, doesn't push—just gives a small, satisfied nod. "Good."

I shift on my feet. "Alright. I'll let you get to your dinner before your child stages a real revolt."

Theo chuckles. "Appreciate it. But take this." He pushes the box he filled with cake earlier my way. "Dessert is on me," he winks. *Winking needs to be outlawed.*

I am about to politely reject but I am supposed to do what I *really* want, and I really want that cake.

"Thanks, Theo!" I turn toward the door, but just before stepping outside, I glance back over my shoulder. "Enjoy your evening."

His gaze flicks up from the counter, his mouth twitching slightly. "You too."

And then I'm stepping into the cool evening air, carefully balancing my precious cake.

Monday.

I'm going to yoga on Monday.

Not because I have to. Not because I'm worried about expectations. Not even because of Lucy.

Just because I want to.

10

The Frozen Hulk

Theo

BY THE TIME I unlock my front door, I'm running on fumes.

Closing shifts at the café aren't usually that bad, but tonight had been one of those long, slow slogs where I spent more time wiping down already clean surfaces than actually serving customers. And then there was Ivy, dropping by, keeping me on my toes with her usual sharp wit and warm smile. I'm not going to lie, it caught me off guard when she opened up. So far, she has kept details about her life to a minimum. But I like to get to know her... all of her, even her heartache. Even if I can't fix it, as much as I would like to.

I shake my head as I step inside. *She's coming on Monday. That's all that matters.*

What I'm not prepared for, though, is the absolute carnage that awaits me.

It looks like a unicorn exploded in my living room.

The coffee table is buried under an avalanche of tiaras, plastic teacups, and a mountain of stuffed animals, some of which have been dramatically wrapped in toilet paper like they're starring in a low-budget mummy movie. A pink feather boa dangles from the TV, a wand is precariously wedged into the potted plant, and there's a disturbing amount of glitter coating the floor.

And in the middle of it all, like this is the most normal thing in the world, are my five-year-old daughter and my fully grown forty-five-year-old brother.

Both dressed as princesses.

Lucy spots me first, beaming. "Daddy!" She scrambles to her feet, her pink satin skirt tangling around her hips as she runs toward me. "Uncle Geoff said we could have pizza for dinner!"

I slowly turn my head towards him. "Did he now?"

Geoff—who is six foot two, built like a retired rugby player, and currently squeezed into one of Lucy's Frozen dresses—gives me a lazy wave from his throne of stuffed animals.

And when I say squeezed, I mean it looks like Bruce Banner caught mid-Hulk transformation. The seams of the baby blue fabric are holding on for dear life, and the tiny, capped sleeves have given up entirely, having rolled up to his shoulders in surrender.

He adjusts the tiara perched precariously on his head and gestures at himself. "Before you say anything, I was left unsupervised with a five-year-old and a bag of dress-up clothes. This was inevitable."

I exhale. "Geoff, you're supposed to be the responsible adult."

Geoff gestures down at himself, then at the general disaster around him. "And I was responsible. I committed to the bit."

Lucy tugs at my hand, eyes wide with hope. "Daddy, pleeease can we have pizza? Uncle Geoff promised."

I sigh, rubbing a hand over my face. I should say no. I should tell Geoff off for spoiling her, for letting the house turn into some kind of glitter coated royal court while I was gone. But honestly? I don't have the energy.

And the idea of cooking something? Not happening.

I glance between my daughter, practically vibrating with excitement, and my idiot brother, who looks dangerously close to ripping that dress apart at the seams if he so much as breathes too hard.

"Fine," I say, already regretting it. "But I get to pick the toppings."

Lucy squeals in triumph and immediately starts listing her own demands. "Pepperoni! And cheese! And pineapple!"

Geoff grimaces. "We were doing so well until the pineapple."

I shoot him a look. "You have no right to judge anyone when you look like that."

Geoff looks down at himself, then shrugs. "Fashion is pain."

I shake my head, stepping over a pile of fairy wings to grab my phone. "Fine. But if I see glitter in my food, both of you are banned from dinner decisions indefinitely."

Lucy and Geoff exchange a look. Then, at the exact same time, they cross their hearts.

I don't trust them for a second.

By the time dinner is over, my stomach is full, my kitchen is a mess, and Lucy is in her room, supposedly tidying up. In reality, she's probably getting distracted by her toys and making an even bigger mess, but as long as I don't have to see it, I'm calling it a win.

Geoff, now free of his princess attire, stretches with an exaggerated groan, rubbing his shoulder. "Right. That's enough quality uncle time for one evening. I'm off."

I lift a hand. "Not so fast."

He turns, eyes narrowing. "What now?"

I shove a pile of stuffed animals into his arms. "You helped make the mess. You help clean the mess."

He scowls at me like I've personally betrayed him. "I did my part. I provided entertainment and pizza."

"You also turned my living room into a crime scene." I gesture at the piles of toys, glitter, and dress-up clothes still scattered across the floor. "So, unless you want to explain to Lucy why the princess kingdom has been shut down for good, you're staying."

Geoff mutters something under his breath but doesn't argue, bending down to scoop up a pile of sparkly fabric. We work in comfortable silence for a few minutes, gathering tiaras and tossing stuffed animals into the basket by the sofa.

Then, too casually, he says, "So, Jasper mentioned something about a woman."

I pause mid-reach for a plastic teacup, then straighten. "And?"

"And he says you've been spending time with her."

I roll my eyes and keep stacking Lucy's books. "You both need new hobbies."

Geoff smirks. "Well, Lucy did mention something about yoga."

I pause just for a second before grabbing another book. "So what?"

"You've been doing yoga with Lucy for ages, but now suddenly someone else is coming along too?"

I shake my head, sighing. "It's not sudden. Ivy joined one class, and now she's coming again. That's it."

Geoff lifts an eyebrow. "So this Ivy just happened to join, and now she's sticking around?"

"As I said, she's coming again on Monday," I admit. "But it's not like that."

Geoff hums like he doesn't believe me.

I groan, tossing a throw blanket onto the sofa. "She's... nice. Smart. Funny. A bit chaotic in a way that keeps things interesting. But we're just friends. She's on this whole self-discovery, no-dating ban thing, and I respect that."

Geoff watches me for a beat, then nods. "And that works for you?"

"Yes."

His expression doesn't change.

I know that look. It's the same one he used to give me when I was fifteen and trying to convince him I hadn't stolen his jacket, even though I was standing there wearing it.

I shake my head. "You can drop the sceptical older brother routine. There's nothing to dissect here."

Geoff makes a vague, unconvinced noise, folding his arms.

I exhale, dragging a hand through my hair. "Ivy and I are friends. That's it. She's not dating, I respect that, and honestly, I like having a friend, someone in my life aside from you and Jasper."

After I left my job, I realised that most of my friends were my work colleagues. We tried to stay in touch, but our lives were so different. They would work hard and play even harder. I had Lucy to look after. So, overtime my brothers became my best friends, but to be honest, I wouldn't mind a friend outside the family. A friend who doesn't rat me out to my mum if I do something silly, like grow a moustache. I looked like Borat.

"But you do like her," Geoff insists.

I pause—not because I don't have an answer, but because I know exactly how Geoff is going to interpret anything I say next.

I keep my voice even. "Of course I like her. She's a good person, and she makes Lucy laugh. But that doesn't mean I like her in the way you're trying to suggest."

He lets that sit for a moment, like he's waiting for me to take it back.

I don't. Because it's the truth. And yet, there's an odd flicker of something I can't quite place in my chest.

Geoff sighs, running a hand over his jaw. "Alright. If you say so."

"I do say so."

He studies me for another long moment, then shrugs. "Fair enough."

I grab the last of Lucy's fairy wings off the floor and toss them into the dress-up bin, signalling that this conversation is over.

Geoff smirks like he knows he's getting under my skin. "Jasper's going to ask about her next, you know."

I groan. "Brilliant. Can't wait for the full family interrogation."

"Just giving you a heads-up." He pats me on the shoulder, far too amused for my liking. "I'll leave you to sit with your totally non-existent feelings in peace."

I shake my head as he grabs his jacket and heads for the door.

Just before he steps out, he pauses. "For what it's worth, you do seem lighter these days."

I frown. "Lighter?"

He shrugs. "Less weighed down. Whatever it is, whoever it is—I'm glad you got some joy back in your life... aside form Lucy of course. You've been alone for too long."

Before I can figure out a response, he's gone, leaving me alone in my mostly clean living room.

I stare at the door for a moment, then exhale, shaking my head. Geoff and Jasper are reading too much into things. Ivy's a friend. That's it. And I'm fine with that.

Lucy and I are waiting outside the coffee shop, soaking in the late morning sun. Lu is practically buzzing with excitement, her little hands gripping the ends of her jumper sleeves as she rocks on her heels.

"She's coming, right?" she asks, tilting her head up at me. *Here we go again.*

"She said she would," I reply, though I barely get the words out before the upstairs flat door swings open.

Ivy steps out, shoving her hands into her jacket pockets, her hair slightly tousled like she's just woken up.

Lucy gasps, as if Ivy appearing is the most shocking and exciting thing to ever happen. "Ivy!"

Ivy grins. "Morning—no, wait. Almost afternoon. Time is fake."

Lucy giggles. "You're silly."

Ivy smirks. "Silly is good, right?"

Lucy waves a hand. "The best."

I nudge Lucy forward so we actually start walking. "Come on, we'll be late if you start getting sidetracked."

We set off at an easy pace, the early summer sun feeling nice on my skin.

For all of two seconds, there's peace. Then Lucy turns to Ivy, her eyes wide and sparkling with that particular kind of joy that tells me we're about to hear the full retelling of a major event.

"Guess what we did on Saturday?" she asks, not waiting for an answer. "We played dress-up with Uncle Geoff, and he wore my princess dress!"

Ivy's eyebrows lift. "Wait—your dress?"

Lucy nods, looking absolutely delighted. "It was so funny! It was way too small for him, and his arms were too big, and it almost broke!"

Ivy lets out a snort. "Oh, I would pay to have seen that."

Lucy sighs dramatically. "Next time."

Ivy grins. "Looking forward to it."

"Oh! And then we had pizza, and I picked the toppings, but Uncle Geoff said pineapple was wrong."

Ivy gasps in mock horror. "Did he now?"

Lucy nods gravely. "He doesn't understand the truth."

I glance at Ivy, who's barely holding in a laugh. "Sounds like I missed an eventful evening."

Lucy hums thoughtfully. "Maybe next time you can come too. But you have to be a princess."

Ivy grins. "Deal."

I don't know whether to be concerned or amused by the fact that Lucy is already recruiting more people for her chaos. Probably both.

We keep walking, Lucy still animatedly recounting every detail of Saturday's excitement.

I glance at Ivy more than I should, Geoff's words replaying in my mind. I really am starting to hate the dating ban.

11

Collapsed Star

Ivy

BY THE TIME YOGA is over, my legs feel like jelly, my arms are somehow sore even though I'm fairly sure we didn't do that much with them, and Lucy is still full of boundless energy as she skips beside us on the way to the smoothie bar.

Honestly, it's impressive. Concerning, but impressive.

Theo holds the door open as we step inside, the smell of fresh fruit and something vaguely tropical hitting me instantly. It's one of those small, overpriced places that makes you feel healthier just by existing in it.

Lucy runs straight to the counter, already deep in decision-making mode as she studies the brightly coloured chalkboard menu. I order a berry smoothie, Theo gets something green (Mr Healthy, of course), and Lucy predictably ends up with the most sugar-packed option available.

We find a table by the window, Lucy happily slurping away at her drink as she watches people walking past the shop. I take a sip of mine, enjoying the rush of cold sweetness, before stretching out my legs with a small sigh.

Theo watches me over the rim of his cup. "You alright there?"

"I'll live," I say, rubbing my calf. "Probably."

He smirks. "So, now that you're practically a pro, you planning to stick with this?"

I pause, swirling my straw in my cup. "Well, I'm coming to the end of my yoga month in a bit over a week."

"And then what? You give it up?"

"No," I say, shaking my head. "I actually... like it. Weirdly enough."

He raises an eyebrow. "Not weird. But surprising, considering how much you complained about it at the start."

"I stand by my complaints," I say, pointing my straw at him. "But I also have to admit it's... good. It does something for me."

Theo nods like he already knew that answer. "So, what's next?"

I blink. "Next?"

"For your self-discovery thing. You said you're coming to the end of yoga, right?"

"Oh. Yeah." I pause, thinking. "I was looking at trying something with clay."

His brows lift. "Like a pottery class?"

I shake my head. "No, not like the whole potter's wheel, *Ghost* reenactment thing. I've seen loads of people on Instagram using air-dry clay, just making stuff at home. It seems fun, and I like the idea of making something with my hands."

Theo takes a slow sip of his smoothie, considering this. "So you're saying next month's mess potential is high."

"Oh, extremely high."

"Well, at least you're keeping things interesting."

I smirk, taking another sip of my smoothie. "That's the goal."

Lucy looks up from her drink, blinking at us. "What's air-dry clay?"

"It's like normal clay, but you don't have to put it in a super-hot oven," I explain. "You just shape it, let it sit, and it hardens on its own."

Lucy's eyes widen with wonder. "Magic clay?"

Theo chuckles. "Not quite magic, Ladybug."

Lucy hums thoughtfully before going back to her drink, and I get the feeling she's already planning something. Probably involving a lot of clay.

He takes another sip of his smoothie, then shifts slightly in his chair. "So, since you're sticking with yoga, does that mean you'll keep coming to class with us?"

I pause, running my thumb over the condensation on my cup. "I mean, I was going to find a new class or just do it at home, but..." I trail off, considering.

Theo just watches me, like he already knows where I'm going with this.

Lucy, however, is far less patient. "You have to keep coming with us!" she says, nearly knocking her smoothie over in her enthusiasm. "Mondays are family yoga days!"

I bite my lower lip. Family yoga days.

There's something tight in my chest again. Theo's eyes are on me, but he doesn't say anything. I can't read his expression and it is unsettling. I don't want him to think I am pushing my way into his family.

I clear my throat, keeping my voice light. "Well, I don't want to intrude on your time with your dad."

"You won't!" Lucy insists. "Right, Daddy?"

Theo exhales a small laugh. "You're welcome anytime." Then, after a beat, he adds, "If work allows, of course."

I glance between them, and honestly? The idea of not going next Monday suddenly feels strange.

I exhale, then nod. "Alright. As long as my schedule doesn't get in the way, I'll keep coming."

Lucy beams, completely satisfied with this outcome. "Yay!"

Theo just nods, like this was inevitable. "Good."

I take another sip of my smoothie, then hesitate for a second before reaching into my pocket and pulling out my phone.

"Actually," I say, unlocking it, "I should probably give you my number. Just in case something comes up and I can't make it."

Theo pulls his own phone out as well. "Good idea."

I type my number into his phone and show it to him before pressing save. He taps something on his screen, and a second later, my phone vibrates in my hand.

I glance down at the incoming call, unknown number flashing on the screen.

"Efficient," I say, saving his number in my contacts "Now I've got yours too."

"Mutual accountability," he says with a smirk.

I grin. "Or mutual excuses, depending on how things go."

Theo chuckles. "Now I have to make sure we never miss a class out of pure spite."

"Perfect," I say, lifting my cup in a toast. "Mutually assured yoga."

He clinks his smoothie against mine, and Lucy eagerly does the same, even though she probably doesn't know what we're agreeing to.

Looks like Monday yoga isn't ending anytime soon. And that's all for me. Because I want it.

The intercom buzzes, crackling slightly.

I pause mid-sip of my tea, then set the mug down and shuffle over, pressing the button. "Hello?"

"Delivery for Ivy Gillman," a gruff voice replies.

Right. That must be the clay.

I press the button again. "Be down in a sec."

Slipping on my trainers, I grab my keys and make my way out, locking the door behind me. The entrance is next to the coffee shop, an unremarkable doorway opening up to a narrow staircase leading up to my place. As I step outside, the delivery guy is waiting on the pavement with a plain cardboard box balanced against his leg.

I sign the handheld scanner, barely paying attention, then reach to take the box... and immediately regret every decision that led me here. The moment the weight shifts into my arms, my back nearly gives out.

"Fuck!" I stumble slightly, shifting my grip, but it's like someone's filled the bloody thing with cement. It's not particularly big, but it's dense, like I'm holding a collapsed star.

The delivery guy watches, completely unfazed. "You alright, love?"

I grit my teeth, hoisting the package up with more effort than I'd like to admit. "Yep. All good."

He gives a half-hearted thumbs-up before heading off down the street, while I try not to drop the box—or myself—right there on the pavement.

By the time I make it upstairs, my arms are burning, and I've acquired a deep and personal hatred for whatever is inside this thing. I manage to wrestle it onto my dining table with a loud thud, then stand there, catching my breath.

Right. What the hell did I order?

Grabbing some scissors, I slice through the tape and pull open the flaps. Inside, neatly wrapped in plastic, is clay.

A lot of clay.

I stare at it, confused. This doesn't look like 2.5 kg.

Frowning, I push back the cardboard flaps and get a better look. There's no neat stack of smaller packages, no tidy little bundles. Instead, there's just one massive slab of dirt-brown clay, sealed inside a thick, see-through plastic bag. The label on the front reads:

12.5 kg.

I blink.

That can't be right. I ordered 2.5 kg, not... this.

I double-check the box, as if smaller packages might be hiding inside, but no. It's just one huge, solid block. I press a hand against it, feeling the cool, dense slab beneath the plastic.

What the hell am I supposed to do with 12.5 kilograms of clay?

This isn't some cute little craft kit; this is industrial levels of material. I'd planned to make a few trinkets, maybe a dish or a little sculpture, but this? This is commitment. This is pottery bootcamp.

I grab my phone and check my order confirmation. Yup, I'm the idiot who can't read and missed the one before the 2.5 kg.

I let out a slow breath, shaking my head. What the hell am I supposed to do with this much of it?

12
Massive G and Wonky J

Theo

LUCY SMACKS THE WATER with both hands, sending a wave over the side of the bath and straight into my lap. Warm, soapy water seeps through my jeans. Fantastic. Exactly what I wanted.

She grins at me, triumphant. "Again!"

I shake my head, flicking water from my sleeve. "If you flood this place, we're moving into a tent."

She giggles and kicks her feet, making the rubber duck do an unnecessary backflip. Then, just as quickly, she goes quiet.

Her fingers trail absently over the edge of a floating boat. "Where's Ivy?"

I shift, leaning my arm on the edge of the tub. "She's still busy with work."

Lucy frowns. "She was s'posed to come to yoga." Lu wasn't the only one who was disappointed when we received the text from Lucy that she had to skip class this week. But she made sure we knew she hadn't given up on yoga.

"She was," I say, pulling out my phone. "But she still did some at home." I open Ivy's message and show her the proof—a blurry photo of Ivy mid-tree pose, in her living room, looking half-asleep but determined.

Lucy studies it with all the seriousness of a judge on one of those dance shows. "She's still not very good."

I snort. "No, she's not. But she's trying and that is all that matters."

"She wobbles more than you."

"Well, yeah, because I've been doing it a lot longer than her," I say, nudging her gently. "She's still learning."

Lucy nods but doesn't drop it. She leans her damp head against my arm, voice small. "When's she coming back?"

I exhale slowly, reaching for the towel and wrapping it around her before scooping her up.

"Dunno," I say, keeping it light. "Soon, probably."

I carry Lucy out of the bathroom, her damp curls sticking to my shoulder as she cuddles up. I drop her down on her bed and she gently bounces on the mattress. Lu giggles rolling herself tighter into the towel.

"Can we call her?" she asks, tilting her head back to look at me, eyes hopeful.

I grab her pyjamas from the drawer and shake my head. "She's probably still working, Ladybug. Let's text her instead, yeah? Then she can reply when she's free."

She thinks it over, then nods. "Okay."

I sit beside her on the bed and open the chat. Lu is peering at the screen like she can actually read it all.

> **Me**
> Lucy's asking after you. Still surviving?

Lucy watches the screen with wide eyes, like she expects Ivy to burst out of it at any moment. A few seconds later, the little typing bubble appears.

> **Ivy**
> Barely. Work is hell. Also, I have a cold. Kill me now.

I wince. Yeah, definitely not reading that out loud.

Lucy tugs at my sleeve. "What did she say?"

I clear my throat, adjusting the message slightly as I read it aloud. "She says work is really busy and... she's got a cold."

Lucy gasps dramatically, clutching my arm. "She's sick?"

I bite back a grin. "It's just a cold, Lu. She'll be fine."

"But we have to help her!" she insists, wriggling into her pyjama bottoms with sudden urgency.

"Oh yeah?" I ask, helping her getting the pyjama top on. "And how exactly do we do that?"

She pauses, thinking hard, then brightens. "Soup! You always make me soup when I am ill."

I chuckle as she places her arms around my neck. "Right."

She nods seriously. "And a card."

I sigh, already knowing there's no way I'm getting out of this. I'm also considering it not one of Lucy's worst ideas. Ivy lives only around the corner and soup is the universal cure for the common cold.

"Fine," I say, shaking my head. "Maybe we can take her some of the chicken soup I made last week. I'll defrost it."

Lucy cheers like I've just told her we're off to save the world. "Really?"

"Really," I confirm, ruffling her damp curls. "But first, we need to get you dry unless you want to catch a cold too."

For once, she holds still while I blow dry her hair, sitting patiently on my bed. She must be really invested in this mission. Once her dark curls are mostly dry, she wriggles out from under my hands and scrambles to her little craft box.

"I'll make her a card!" she announces, dragging out paper, crayons, and a pile of stickers.

I leave her to it while I head to the kitchen, popping the frozen soup into the microwave to thaw. The apartment fills with the familiar scent of garlic and herbs as I watch the pot moving in circles, keeping half an ear on Lucy's occasional huffs and mutters from the living room.

When I check on her, she's sprawled across the floor, tongue poking out in concentration as she adds the finishing touches to her drawing. She finally sits back and holds it up proudly.

I study it, biting back a laugh. It's... definitely a drawing. Ivy is there, curvy with a wild bun and what appears to be a massive red nose. Next to her, there's a wobbly bowl of soup (at least, I think it's soup).

I press my lips together. "That's brilliant, Ladybug."

She beams. "She's sick, so I made her nose big."

"Yeah, I got that." I tap the paper. "What's this bit?"

"The soup."

I got that right then.

She stares at it, then frowns. "I need words."

"Go for it," I say, turning back to the stove.

She picks up a crayon, presses it to the paper—then stops. "I don't know how."

I smirk. "Want me to do it for you?"

Her eyes go wide with horror. "No! I have to do it."

"Right, of course." I grab a separate sheet of paper and a pen, crouching beside her. "I'll write it here, and you can copy it."

I print *Get well, Ivy* in clear, bold letters. Lucy leans in, nose practically touching the page, as she carefully copies each letter onto her card. The G is massive, the I is wonky, and the V looks like a seagull, but she gets there in the end.

She leans back, inspecting her work. "That's good."

I nod solemnly. "It's perfect."

Satisfied, she folds up the card while I finish packing the soup and some bread rolls into a tote bag. She can wear her pyjamas for the short distance but even if it is a mild June evening, I grab a light jacket for Lu before we head out.

We stroll the short distance to Ivy's building, Lucy practically bouncing with excitement. When we reach the coffee shop below her flat, I steer her inside for a quick detour.

She gives me a suspicious look as I grab a slice of lemon drizzle cake from the counter. "We're just bringing soup," she reminds me.

"And cake," I correct. "Because even sick people need dessert."

She considers this, then nods. "True."

Armed with our care package, we step outside and turn to the entrance to the flats above the café. I press the intercom, and after a second, her tired voice crackles through the speaker.

"Hello?"

Before I can say a word, Lucy stretches up on her toes and shouts, "IVY! WE BROUGHT YOU SOUP!"

There's a pause over the intercom, and for a second, I think Ivy might refuse. Then, with a crackly sigh, she says, "Come up."

I exchange a look with Lucy, who grins in victory, before we push through the door and head up the stairs. When Ivy opens her flat door, she looks—well, pretty much like Lucy's drawing.

Dark rings under her eyes. A flushed, pinkish nose that rivals the one on the card. Her hair is tied in what I assume was a bun at some point but is now just a lopsided mess. She's wrapped in a huge hoodie, which seems out of place on this warm evening.

She catches me looking and straightens up. "I'm fine," she says before I can get a word in. "No fever, no cough, just a bit of a stuffy nose. I barely even feel ill anymore."

"Uh-huh," I say, unimpressed.

"Promise," she insists, sniffling slightly before giving Lucy a tired smile. "Thanks for the soup, Lu. That was very sweet of you."

Lucy holds up the card proudly. "I made this too!"

Ivy takes it, eyes widening slightly as she takes in the artistic rendering of herself. She chuckles, voice still a little hoarse. "Wow, this is very... accurate."

Lucy nods eagerly. "Your nose is really red."

Ivy snorts, then winces like she regrets it. "Yeah, well. It's been through a lot." She folds the card carefully, but something about the way she shifts in the doorway feels... off.

She hasn't moved to let us in.

I glance past her shoulder. The flat isn't a mess or anything that I can see. Maybe I made a mistake bringing Lucy.

I open my mouth to suggest we leave when Lucy suddenly gasps and points past Ivy.

"Look at all the Santas!"

13

Chicken Soup for the Army of Gnomes

Ivy

I GROAN, RUBBING MY temple.

Lucy is practically vibrating with excitement; her eyes locked on my coffee table as if it holds the greatest treasure she's ever seen. Theo, meanwhile, looks utterly lost.

"Santas?" he repeats, eyebrows raised.

I sigh, stepping aside. "They're not Santas."

That's all the invitation Lucy needs. She dashes past me, straight to the coffee table, and crouches down, her hands hovering just above the collection of carefully arranged figures.

"They look like Santas," she announces, inspecting them closely.

"They're not," I correct, tucking a strand of hair behind my ear before shutting the door behind them. "They're gnomes."

Theo takes in the scene—the coffee table covered in fully painted figures, each one detailed with pointed hats in either deep red or dark blue, all decorated with intricate Nordic white patterns. Their round noses are pink, peeking out from beneath their hats, and their faces are nothing but fluffy white beards dusted with a subtle shimmer. No eyes. No cheeks. Just an army of faceless, festive little creatures.

Then he notices the breakfast bar.

"Oh, wow," he mutters.

That's where the unfinished ones sit—dozens of them, still grey, waiting to dry. Some are completely shaped, others still need details carved into their beards, but they're all lined up like tiny recruits awaiting inspection.

Theo gives me a look. "I feel like I should be more surprised by this, but somehow, I'm not."

I scowl at him. "I needed something to do while I was stuck inside."

He smirks. "So, naturally, you made a small army of gnomes."

"It's not an army," I cross my arms, fully prepared to defend my choices. "I ordered too much clay."

Theo raises an eyebrow. "And you had to use all of it?"

"Well, obviously," I say, as if that should be clear. "At first, I thought I'd try making a bowl." I grab the thing from the shelf behind me and hold it up. It's supposed to be round, but it's—well... not. More like a lumpy oval with uneven edges, a slight dip in one side like it gave up halfway through drying.

Theo stares at it, then blinks. "Right. That's... a bowl."

I huff. "It was my first attempt."

Lucy peeks up from the coffee table, looking intrigued. "It looks wobbly."

"Thanks, Lu," I mutter, setting it back down. "Then I thought, okay, jewellery. So, I made some little pendants and beads. But it turns out, the clay was too brittle when it dried, and most of them cracked. Some just snapped when I tried to thread them onto anything."

I grab a small dish where I've stashed a few. Some of the pendants are still intact, but a couple have jagged edges where they broke. Theo picks one up, turning it over in his fingers.

"Yeah," I say, sighing. "Not exactly a success."

"So, after all that... gnomes?" he asks, eyeing my coffee table.

I shrug. "I saw some online, thought they looked fun. And they are fun. Plus, they're easy to make. You don't have to worry about symmetry or anything. Just a hat, a nose, and a beard." I gesture to the coffee table, where my little flock (no, it is definitely *not* an army) stands proudly. "See? No faces, no stress."

Lucy has been staring at them this whole time, completely entranced. Her little hands hover just above the table, like she's dying to pick one up but doesn't quite dare.

I smirk, then crouch down beside her. "You know," I say casually, "I could let you have one."

Her eyes snap to mine, wide and sparkling. "Really?"

I nod. "If you want one, you can pick from the painted ones."

She gasps, looking back at the table like I've just asked her to choose a favourite star in the sky. "But which one?"

she whispers, overwhelmed by the sheer responsibility of the task.

Theo chuckles. "Take your time, Lu. It's a big decision."

Lucy nods seriously, then begins her inspection, picking up each gnome gently, turning them over in her tiny hands, and murmuring things like, "This one's got a nice hat," and "Ooooh, look at this beard."

Meanwhile, Theo nudges one of the little figures with his finger. "You know, you could sell these."

I snort. "Yeah, right."

"I'm serious," he says, folding his arms. "People would buy them."

I roll my eyes. "They're not that good."

"They don't have to be perfect. They just have to be cute. And these?" He gestures at the coffee table. "They're cute."

I shake my head, unconvinced. "No one's gonna buy my weird little gnomes."

"They would," he insists. "In the right setting."

"Oh yeah?" I cross my arms. "And where exactly do you plan on selling them?"

Theo shrugs. "I'll put them up in the café."

I blink. "What?"

"In November," he clarifies. "Not now, obviously. No one's thinking about Christmas in June."

I scoff. "So what, you're just going to display them next to the strudel and hope someone impulse-buys a gnome with their Melange?" *I am getting better at that Austrian coffee stuff.*

He grins. "Stranger things have happened."

Before I can argue, Lucy finally gasps dramatically and holds up her chosen gnome. A red-hatted one with a particularly fluffy-looking beard.

"This one!" she announces proudly.

I nod. "Good choice."

She beams and cradles it carefully, like she's just won a grand prize.

Theo just shakes his head, smirking. "Well, congrats, Ivy. You're officially in the gnome business."

I snort, shaking my head. "Yeah, yeah. I'll send you an invoice for my first million."

Theo just smirks, but before he can reply, he pulls the soup container from the bag and holds it out to me. "Here," he says, his voice softer now. "Eat something proper."

I take it from him, fingers brushing his for the briefest second.

"Thanks," I say, and for some reason, this thanks feels so much more meaningful than the thousands of thanks we throw around each day.

For a moment, neither of us moves. It's quiet, apart from Lucy singing to herself as she inspects her gnome. Theo watches me, something unreadable in his expression, and for the first time in weeks, I realise how nice it is to have a man... someone looking out for me. Not because they expect anything back, not because they're waiting for me to do something in return—just because we're friends. Because they care.

And apparently, I don't know what to do with that.

"Can I help you make them?" Lucy pipes up suddenly, shattering the moment.

"What?"

"The gnomes!" She holds up her chosen one proudly. "I wanna help!"

I chuckle, shaking off the weird feeling still lingering in my chest. "Tell you what—I'll keep some clay aside. When I'm better, you can come over and make some with me."

Lucy gasps, delighted. "Really?"

"Really," I promise.

She clutches her gnome to her chest like she's just been given the greatest honour in the world. "Okay! But I want to make lots!"

"We'll see how you do with one first, yeah?" I tease.

Lucy nods, satisfied, and Theo lifts her in his arms. "Alright, gnome queen, I think we should let you get some rest," he says, looking at me again. "You are going to rest, right?"

I roll my eyes. "Yes, Sir."

He smirks, but there's something softer behind it. He doesn't push, doesn't make a big deal out of it, just checks. And weirdly, I don't hate it.

I walk them to the door, Lucy leaning against Theo's shoulder, already chatting to her gnome like it's a new best friend.

"Thanks again," I say, lifting the soup slightly.

He nods. "Feel better, Ivy."

Then they're gone, and I'm left standing in my doorway, staring at the space where they just were.

The office of Woods & Dubois is exactly as I remember—too bright, too loud, and already filled with the unmistakable scent of someone's overly ambitious meal prep, despite it barely being nine in the morning.

I step inside, adjusting the strap of my bag, and spot Christa at the front desk, typing aggressively, her brows furrowed in frustration.

"Either you're hard at work or drafting a furious resignation email," I say, leaning against the counter.

She startles slightly, then looks up, eyes lighting up with a grin. "Oh my God, look who it is! Back from the dead."

"It was a cold, Christa, not the plague."

She leans back in her chair, arms crossed. "Yeah, well, judging by the way Theo the Hot Barista was talking about you last week, I was expecting a tragic farewell announcement."

I groan. "Do not call him that."

She shrugs. "I can't help it. It's accurate. And it annoys you."

I shake my head. "He's not even a barista. He owns the place."

"Right, but Theo the Hot Coffee Shop Owner doesn't have the same ring to it."

I sigh. "Why were you even talking to him?"

Christa gives me an exaggerated look. "I was getting coffee. Like a normal person. And he was asking how you were." She tilts her head, eyes sharp with amusement. "Very concerned, by the way."

My face warms slightly, which is ridiculous. "He was just being polite."

She smirks. "Sure."

I ignore her. "Anyway, he did look after me. Brought soup. Lucy made me a get-well card."

Christa clutches her chest. "That child is too precious."

"She's a cheeky monkey... but adorable, I give you that."

"All Theo's doing, I guess," she muses. "He's got the doting single dad thing down. He'll be fighting off school mums left and right."

I huff a laugh. "His yoga instructor definitely fancies him." *Ah, there is the bitter taste again.* The same one I have every time Safiya talks to Theo.

Christa grins. "Can you blame her? A man who owns a coffee shop and knows how to braid hair? He's basically a rom-com lead waiting to happen."

Before I can reply, a too-polished voice cuts through the air behind me.

"Oh, Ivy! Lovely to see you in the office."

I don't even have to turn around to know who will ruin my day in like five seconds. Caroline.

I school my expression before facing her. She stands there, immaculate as always—perfectly pressed blouse, sharp bob, a polite smile that doesn't quite reach her eyes.

"It's been so long since we've had the pleasure," she continues, tone light but pointed.

I return her smile, just as polished. "Nice to see you too, Caroline."

She looks at me with content. "I imagine it must feel good to be back. There's just something about working in the office, don't you think?"

And there it is.

Caroline is one of *those* people—the ones who believe that if you're not physically at your desk, you're not really working. She's never outright said that remote workers do the bare minimum, but the undertones are always there. The subtle remarks about team culture. The casual digs about dedication. The pointed way she phrases things, like she's not quite accusing you of slacking, but you know that's exactly what she's implying.

I could let it slide. I *should* let it slide. But Caroline is the same level as me and I don't let her boss me around.

So, I flash my best, most professional smile. "Oh, absolutely. Where else would I get to enjoy Colin narrating his emails out loud like he's recording an audiobook?"

Beside me, Christa lets out an undignified snort, covering it quickly with a cough.

Caroline's smile twitches, but she recovers fast, smoothing a hand over her blouse. "Well," she says, tone clipped, "I suppose some people just work differently."

"Suppose they do," I reply brightly.

She gives me one last glance before turning and heading back to her lair, the click-click of her heels sharp against the floor as she walks away.

Christa is still shaking her head, trying to stifle her laughter. "One day, Caroline is going to snap, and I will be there with popcorn."

I smirk. "Make sure it's salted." I give her a wink before heading towards the meeting room.

The meeting is exactly what I expected—far too long, filled with slides that could have been emails, and sprinkled with the usual buzzwords that make my soul shrink. By the time

I step back out into the corridor, I feel like I've aged a decade.

I make a beeline for reception, where Christa is scrolling through her phone.

She looks up the moment she sees me. "Survived?"

"Barely," I say, dropping my bag onto the counter. "I swear, if I hear the phrase 'synergy in urban planning' one more time, I might start throwing things."

Christa grins. "Sounds like you need a reset."

I raise a brow. "You *think*? And what do you suggest, oh wise one?"

She leans forward, eyes sparkling with mischief. "Spa day. This Saturday. You, me, facials, massages, and absolutely no talk of work."

I hesitate, but she sees the crack in my resolve before I can even think of an excuse.

"Spa-ing was on your list, Ivy. And you owe me. I've been carrying this office's entertainment needs while you've been holed up at home. Plus, you clearly could do with some treatments." She gestures vaguely at my face. "No offence, but you still look like you've been through it."

I sigh dramatically. "Wow. Love the support."

She grins. "I'm just looking out for you. And before you come up with any pathetic excuses, I already have a voucher, and Alex doesn't need the car this weekend. So, we're going to our favourite spa in Kent, and you are not getting out of it."

Alex, her fiancé, is probably staying home watching rugby, just like he does most weekends. I'm not going to say something though, Christa already thinks that I don't like him. It's not that per se, it's just that I feel she deserves better. But what do I know? I'm on a dating ban because I have no clue about men or relationships. Maybe what Christa and Alex have is the best there is.

I narrow my eyes at her. "You really planned this whole thing, didn't you?"

"Obviously." She smirks. "I know you. If I didn't box you in with logistics, you'd wiggle out of it."

I shake my head, but a smile is already creeping onto my face. "Fine. But no massage! I hate that. I feel like they are torturing me to extract some state secrets, and I don't know what they are."

"Deal." Christa claps her hands together, victorious. "Saturday, it's happening. No backing out."

I roll my eyes but feel a little lighter already. "Wouldn't dream of it."

Just as I push myself off the reception counter, ready to escape back to my home office sanctuary, a voice calls out behind me.

"Ivy! Before you go…"

I swear I clench my jaw on instinct before I even turn around.

Caroline approaches with the usual polished smile—practised, professional, and just a little too smug for my liking. "Just a quick reminder about the big Macmillan Cake Extravaganza in four weeks," she says, her voice dripping with enthusiasm.

I blink at her. "The what now?"

Christa mutters under her breath, "Oh, here we go," before making herself look very busy with something on her screen.

Caroline's smile tightens just a fraction, as if I've personally insulted her by not immediately knowing what she's talking about. "The charity event? You do read the company newsletter, don't you?"

"Oh, the newsletters." I nod, playing innocent. "The one probably buried under a mountain of meeting invites? Must've slipped through."

Caroline exhales, though she keeps her expression pleasant. "Well, it's a big deal. We're raising money for Macmillan, and everyone is encouraged to bring in a homemade cake." She tilts her head, eyes twinkling with something far too knowing. "Of course, we all know baking isn't exactly your strong suit, so no one will hold it against you if you just attend. We mums have it covered."

Ah. There it is. I feel Christa freeze beside me, probably holding her breath to see if I take the bait.

I do.

"Actually," I say, pasting on my brightest smile, "I will be attending. And I'll be bringing a cake."

Caroline's brows lift ever so slightly, just enough to suggest she's highly doubtful. "Really?"

"Really," I say, crossing my arms. "A proper, homemade cake. By me."

Christa chokes on nothing.

Caroline gives me one last unreadable look before nodding. "Well then, I look forward to it."

She waves awkwardly before disappearing down the corridor with the same purposeful click-click of her heels that follows her wherever she goes.

The second she's out of sight, Christa bursts out laughing. "Oh my God. You so took the bait."

I groan, rubbing my temples. "I know."

"Do you even own cake tins?"

"I will by the end of the month."

She cackles. "This is gonna be amazing."

I glare at her. "You're supposed to be supportive."

"Oh, I am!" She grins. "I fully support this disaster you've just signed yourself up for."

I sigh, already regretting every life decision that has led me to this moment.

14
SOS from Kent

Ivy

I ZIP UP MY bag and set it by the door after glancing inside one last time to make sure I've got everything. Bathrobe, towel, swimsuit, shower gel, shampoo... check. Book for lounging, snacks for the car ride... also check.

Christa will be here any minute to pick me up for our spa day, and I'm actually looking forward to it. A whole afternoon of facials and soaking in a heated pool without a single email notification in sight. Heaven.

I grab my phone to see if she's texted, but the screen lights up with a message from Theo instead.

Theo
> SOS.

I frown. That's it? No explanation? No follow-up? I fire off a reply.

Me
> What's wrong?

No response.

I wait for the little typing bubble to appear. Nothing. Great.

I sigh, grabbing my bag and slinging it over my shoulder before heading downstairs. Whatever's happening, it must be urgent—Theo never texts like that. Since we exchanged phone numbers we have been messaging on and off a bit. About the weather, his brothers bugging him, my growing army, and my personal favourite: videos of Lucy telling me goodnight. Friends stuff. But he doesn't do dramas... usually.

I push open the door to The Kaiser's Mug, and the scent of rich coffee and freshly baked pastries wraps around me instantly. The place is already heaving for it being barely eleven in the morning—every table occupied, the gentle clatter of waiters stacking crockery mixing with the low hum of conversation.

Despite the morning rush, everything still runs with the precision Theo demands. His staff, dressed in crisp white shirts and neatly pressed waistcoats, move effortlessly between tables, balancing trays of coffee and delicate slices of *Sachertorte*. The polished wooden counter gleams under the soft lighting, and the glass cake display is fully stocked—*Apfelstrudel*, *Gugelhupf*, and perfectly layered cakes waiting to be served.

Theo is behind the counter. His jaw is tight, his movements just a little too sharp, and there's a tension in his body that immediately sets off alarm bells in my head.

He glances up as I step forward, and the second he sees the bag slung over my shoulder, his expression falls.

"Oh," he says, voice tight. "You have plans."

I shake my head. "Ignore that. What's up?"

He hesitates, his fingers gripping the edge of the counter like he's weighing his options. I know that look—he's trying to figure out how to handle this alone, even though it's already clear he can't.

I arch a brow. "Theo."

That does it. He exhales sharply, sliding the finished coffee onto a tray before leaning in slightly, voice low over the noise of the café.

"Jasper took Lucy for the day," he says. "They went back to his place. But he just called me—he's fallen, and he thinks he's broken his arm."

My stomach clenches. "Is he okay?" *Stupid question, Ivy, the man broke his arm!*

"He says he will be," Theo replies, but his expression is strained. "The problem is, he needs to get himself to hospital, but he can't exactly take Lucy with him. Geoff's not available, and I don't know what to do."

I don't even think about it.

"Give me the address," I say immediately.

Theo's jaw tightens. "Ivy...no. I can't ask you to cancel your plans."

I roll my eyes. "You're not asking. I'm offering."

He hesitates, his shoulders tense with that familiar internal struggle—grateful but reluctant, torn between accepting help and insisting he'll figure it out himself.

"Theo," I say firmly. "Just give me the address."

He exhales, defeated, and pulls his phone from his pocket. "I can tell you how to get there by train—"

"Don't bother," I cut in, already unlocking my own phone. "I'm getting Christa to drive me."

That makes him pause. "Wait. You're really—?"

"Yes," I grin, already texting. "Now stop wasting time and send me the address."

The Kent countryside stretches out around us, all rolling fields and winding country lanes, the occasional hamlet breaking up the endless green. Christa drives with one hand casually on the wheel, the other fiddling with the volume of the radio as we make our way deeper into what feels like the middle of nowhere.

I glance at my phone. The blue dot on the map confirms that we're about fifteen minutes away from Little Hadlow, the tiny village where Jasper lives.

I exhale. "I still feel bad for dragging you into this."

Christa scoffs. "Ivy, if you say sorry one more time, I'm kicking you out of this car."

I smirk. "While it's moving?"

"I'll slow down."

I chuckle, shifting in my seat. "It's just... I know you were looking forward to today. And now instead of relaxing at the pool, you're driving me around the country so I can look after someone else's child."

Christa waves a hand dismissively. "And yet, weirdly, I don't mind? Lucy needs looking after. That takes priority over a steam room. Plus," she throws me a sly look, "I'm kinda curious to see where Theo's brother lives. From what you've said, I am picturing some countryside bachelor pad with questionable furniture choices."

"Same," I admit. "I've only seen him once, when you and I went to the café for the first time."

"Well, we're about to get a front-row seat to his life," she says as we turn onto a narrower road, lined with stone walls and wildflowers.

A few minutes later, we drive past the sign for Little Hadlow, a picture-perfect village if I've ever seen one. It's all thatched roofs, ivy-covered brickwork, and a high street that consists of a pub, a post office, and a tea shop. The kind of place where everyone probably knows everyone, and news spreads faster than broadband.

Christa whistles. "Cute."

I nod. "Very."

We follow the sat nav through the village and onto a quieter road, passing some charity shops and an old church before turning into a long gravel driveway.

Our jaws drop.

The house is massive. More villa than cottage, with sprawling gardens, elegant stonework, and large sash windows gleaming in the late morning sun. There is an extension to the left that looks like a weird add on—might be a granny flat—but the rest belongs in a magazine spread rather than a sleepy village.

Christa parks in front of the extension. "When exactly were you planning on telling me that Theo's brother is secretly aristocracy?"

I shake my head, still staring. "I didn't know."

Before I can process the sheer size of the place, the front door swings open.

Jasper stands in the doorway, tall and broad like Theo, but with a scruffier edge. He is clean shaven whilst Theo always has a bit of a stubble. Jasper's hair is also a bit lighter and has some streaks in it that look like his genes couldn't decide if they wanted him to be dark haired or blond. His eyes are currently clouded with pain. His arm is cradled against his chest in a stiff, awkward position, but he still manages a grin.

"Welcome to the countryside," he says as if we've just popped by for afternoon tea.

I hop out of the car, closing the door behind me. "Jasper, are you—"

"Fine," he interrupts smoothly, waving me off with his good hand. "A bit of a tumble, nothing dramatic."

Christa side-eyes me. I side-eye her back.

Lucy suddenly appears at Jasper's side, beaming. "Ivy! You came!"

"Of course I did," I say, crouching down to hug her. "You okay?"

She nods eagerly. "Uncle Jasper fell, but he said he's super strong, so it's probably okay."

Jasper grins, but his fingers twitch slightly against his injured arm. *Yeah. He's in pain.*

He gestures for us to come inside. "Come in, come in. I'll give you the quick tour before I head off."

We step inside, and my jaw drops again.

The interior is just as stunning as the exterior—high ceilings, exposed beams, and a blend of classic architecture with modern furnishings. The place somehow manages to feel both luxurious and lived in. I love this place.

Jasper leads us through a massive open-plan living room and into an even more impressive kitchen. It's sleek but warm, with a ridiculous farmhouse-style table, hanging copper pots, and one of those professional-grade ovens that look like they belong in a Michelin-starred restaurant.

"Help yourselves to anything," he says, motioning to the kitchen. "Food, drinks, whatever you need."

Before I can argue, Lucy tugs at my sleeve. "Ivy! Guess what?"

"What?"

She bounces on her feet. "You can swim in the pool!"

I blink. "The—wait, what?"

Jasper chuckles. "Hot tub, technically. It's next to the patio." His grin turns sheepish as he points through the open French doors that lead from the kitchen to the garden. "That's actually how this whole thing happened. I was getting it ready, slipped on the decking, and—" he tries to lift his bad arm slightly, wincing. "Gravity won."

Christa and I exchange a look.

"I mean," she says, "if the hot tub is already set up..."

"Christa!" I laugh.

She shrugs. "What? We did pack towels."

And honestly... she has a point. The thought of sinking into warm bubbling water, letting all the stress of the week melt away, is extremely tempting. I glance at Lucy, who is practically vibrating with excitement, and start to think that maybe this isn't such a terrible idea.

But before I can voice it, Christa claps her hands together. "Right. Jasper, hop along. I'm taking you to the hospital."

Jasper blinks. "Wait, what?"

"You heard me," she says, already grabbing her car keys. "No offence, but you look like you're dying inside, and I am not about to let you sit here trying to pretend you're fine."

He lets out a dry chuckle. "I appreciate the concern, but I can call a taxi."

Christa narrows her eyes. "And wait for one to actually show up out here in Little Piddleborrow or whatever this place is called? No. We're going now."

Jasper looks between us, clearly trying to find an escape route. "I really don't—"

"Jasper," she interrupts, her voice taking on that firm, no-nonsense tone she usually reserves for unhelpful contractors. "Out. Now."

He stares at her for a moment, then sighs heavily. "You're terrifying."

She smirks. "I know."

With one last look at me, Jasper shakes his head in defeat and heads toward the door. Christa follows, all but herding him outside like a stubborn sheepdog.

"Be good, you two!" she calls over her shoulder.

The front door swings shut, leaving just me and Lucy standing in the obnoxiously nice kitchen.

We look at each other and giggle.

Lucy dashes toward the stairs. "Pool! Pool! Pool!" she chants as she scurries up, her little feet thudding against the polished wood.

I follow behind, a little slower but definitely not *not* looking forward to sinking into warm water and pretending for at least an hour that my life is not mild chaos.

I reach the top of the landing and find Lucy in a room that looks like a guest bedroom. She is kneeling over a small backpack. Eventually she pulls a pink bathing suit from it and spins on the spot, throwing her arms in the air. "I'm so ready for the pool!"

I rub a hand over my face, suppressing a laugh. "Lu, it's not a pool, it's a hot tub."

She frowns. "But it's full of water."

"Yes."

"And it has bubbles."

"Also, yes."

She narrows her eyes like she's about to dismantle my argument with five-year-old logic. "And you sit in it."

I nod. "That is correct."

She crosses her arms. "Then it's a pool."

I sigh. "Fine. It's a very tiny, very warm pool."

Satisfied, she holds out her bright pink swimsuit covered in little starfish, holding it up triumphantly. "I love my pool swimsuit!"

I grin. "Good, because you're going to need it."

Lucy flings off her T-shirt without a second thought and wrestles her way into the swimsuit, arms getting momentarily tangled before she pops her head out through the right hole. She wiggles her toes against the floor and bounces slightly.

"I'm ready."

"Almost," I say, grabbing an equally pink dressing gown I can see peaking out of her backpack.

Lucy's nose wrinkles. "I don't need that."

"You absolutely need this," I declare solemnly.

She scowls. "Why?"

"Because," I say, crouching down to her level, "it's spa day rules."

"I don't know the rules," she says with a sad voice.

"Well, let me tell you." I hold up a finger like I'm revealing ancient wisdom. "Rule number one: Bathrobes are very important. All spa guests must wear them on their way to the pool."

Lucy narrows her eyes. "Why?"

"Because it makes you fancy."

She tilts her head, clearly considering this. "Fancy like the ladies in the movies?"

"Exactly."

She gasps, grabs the robe, and practically throws it around her shoulders like she's stepping onto the red carpet. "Ooooh, I am fancy."

I grin. "Rule number two: You have to walk like you're a VIP... a very important person."

She immediately stands taller, lifting her chin like she's royalty. "Like this?"

"Perfect," I confirm, tying her gown properly before grabbing my own. "I'll just get quickly changed. Wait here for me, Lu," I say, slipping into the bathroom across the hall that I had seen on the way in. I pull on my black one piece and my white dressing gown and return to Lucy.

With towels in hand, we make our way downstairs, Lucy practically floating like the Queen.

The back garden is just as ridiculous as the rest of the house—sprawling lawns, flower beds that look like something out of a National Trust estate, and next to the stone patio, a very inviting-looking hot tub, the water already bubbling in the afternoon air.

Lucy throws off her dressing gown dramatically onto a chair. "I'm going in first!"

I shake my head. "Carefully!"

Lucy stops just before the hot tub, her face lighting up with excitement. "Wait!" She spins on her heel and dashes to the little shed at the corner of the house, leaving me standing there, confused.

A few seconds later, she bursts back out onto the patio, waving a pair of neon orange swimming armbands in the air like she's just won a prize.

"I need these!" she announces proudly.

I blink. "Lucy, it's a hot tub, not a swimming pool."

"But I want to float," she insists, already jamming one of the inflatable armbands onto her tiny arm with sheer determination.

"You do know you can just sit in the water, right?"

She puffs out her chest. "But this way, I can be like a jellyfish."

I pinch the bridge of my nose, but honestly, how do you argue with that?

"Fine," I sigh, kneeling down to help her wrestle the second armband onto her other arm. "But no wild splashing, okay?"

She nods seriously, though I can already tell she has zero intention of keeping that promise.

Once she's fully seaworthy, she struts to the small wooden steps and climbs carefully over the edge of the hot tub into the water. The second she leans back, her little arms pop up to the surface, and she giggles as the bubbles swirl around her.

"I'm floating!" she squeals.

I shake my head, laughing as I step in after her, letting the hot water instantly relax my muscles.

Lucy closes her eyes, drifting lazily. "This is so nice."

I let my head tip back against the edge, feeling the warmth sink into my skin.

Yeah. This was a very good idea.

Just as I'm about to fully relax, the sound of the door from inside the house draws our attention.

Christa strides onto the patio, handbag on one shoulder, two bulky shopping bags on the other— every bit a woman on a mission.

"You started without me?!" she gasps, looking genuinely offended.

Lucy giggles, kicking her legs. "You were taking Uncle Jasper to the doctor!"

"I was!" she huffs, setting the shopping bags down with a dramatic flourish. "And then I very kindly stopped to pick up some essentials."

I eye the bags warily. "What kind of essentials?"

Christa smirks, grabbing her things. "I brought the spa here."

Before I can question her further, she spins on her heel and marches inside, disappearing into the house like she's about to execute some grand plan.

I blink after her, then glance at Lucy, who is watching with wide eyes.

"What's in the bags?" she whispers.

"No idea," I whisper back.

Lucy giggles, then tilts her head. "Do you think she got snacks?"

I laugh. "If she knows what's good for her."

Christa's head pops back out of the doorway. "Oh, by the way, Jasper gave me his keys in case we need to pop out for something." She waves them in the air. "Now please tell me there's still room in that hot tub."

I shake my head. "That depends. What's actually in those bags?"

She grins. "You'll see," she whispers mysteriously before sliding into the water and taking a seat next to me.

Whatever she's got planned, I have a feeling this day is about to get even more ridiculous.

15

Quack and Other Treatments

Theo

It's just after four when I finally pull up outside Jasper's place. The café had quietened down enough that I could leave my head waiter in charge, and I'd made good time getting to Little Hadlow. Still, the whole drive, I couldn't shake the feeling that I owed Ivy and Christa big time for stepping in.

I kill the engine and step out, stretching my legs as I take in the absurdity of my brother's house. It doesn't matter how many times I see it—this place still looks like the kind where they interview some rich artist who moved to the country to 'find inspiration' and now exclusively drinks herbal tea from handmade pottery.

I unlock the front door with my key—my brothers and I have always had keys to each other's places, it just makes life easier with everyone chipping in looking after Lu.

Stepping inside, I immediately hear laughter coming from the garden. I follow the sound, stepping onto the patio—only to stop dead in my tracks.

I blink.

I actually blink, just to make sure I'm seeing this right.

Ivy, Christa, and Lucy are sprawled out on a massive outdoor sofa, all three in bathrobes, all three with towels wrapped around their heads, and all three with what looks like a thick layer of moisturiser smeared across their faces.

Oh, and cucumber slices. On their eyes.

My lips twitch. "Do I even want to ask what's happening here?"

Ivy lifts a cucumber slice and peeks at me. "Spa day."

Before I can respond, Lucy casually grabs one of her cucumber slices, pops it into her mouth, and starts chewing.

Christa loses it. She howls with laughter, clutching her stomach. "She keeps eating them!" she wheezes. "We put them on her eyes, and two seconds later—gone!"

Lucy, completely unbothered, licks a bit of the mask off her fingers. "It's yummy!"

I cross my arms, fighting back a grin. "Wait—what is on your faces?" I ask concerned.

Lucy sits up, her other cucumber slice sliding off. "It's quack!"

Ivy snorts. "It's quark, Lu."

"That's what I said," she replies, looking up at her. "Quack."

Something warm spreads through me, the way it always does when Lucy is unintentionally hilarious.

I glance at Ivy, who's watching Lucy with that soft, affectionate look she gets when she thinks no one is noticing. And damn, if that doesn't make something else tug at my chest.

I clear my throat. "So you're telling me you're all sitting here, covered in cheese?"

"It's not cheese," Ivy says, wiping a little off her cheek. "It's quark with honey and lemon juice. It's actually good for your skin."

Christa nods sagely. "It's very European."

I shake my head, exhaling through a laugh. "Of course it is."

I glance at the side table where three glasses of what looks like sparkling wine are sitting. My brows lift. "And you're drinking—"

"Fizzy apple juice," Ivy cuts in before I can even finish the question. "We're not that irresponsible."

I chuckle, shoving my hands in my pockets. "So... you are introducing my daughter to the finer sides of life?"

"She loves it," Christa defends, still giggling.

Lucy nods seriously, wiping her hands on her bathrobe. "It's a real spa day."

I shake my head, sighing. "And where exactly did all of this come from?"

Ivy tilts her head toward Christa. "She brought the spa here."

Christa waggles her brows. "If the mountain will not come to Muhammad, then Muhammad will go to the mountain."

I watch them for a beat—the way Christa is still chuckling to herself, the way Lucy is wriggling to get comfy in her pink robe, and the way Ivy is reclining with zero shame, looking like this is exactly where she's meant to be.

And honestly? I don't know if I should be impressed or completely charmed.

Definitely both.

Before I can dwell on that thought, Lucy tugs at her dressing gown with little fists as she turns to me with wide, serious eyes.

"Daddy, you have to come in the pool," she demands.

I raise a brow. "I really don't."

"Yes, you do!" She gestures dramatically at the hot tub. "It's so warm, and it makes bubbles, and it's like a bath but better!"

"I think I'll survive without it, Ladybug."

She huffs, then points at the fancy watch on Christa's wrist. "When the beep happens, we wash off the quack—"

"Quark," Ivy corrects with a giggle, not even bothering to open her eyes.

"That's what I said," Lucy insists. "The quack comes off and then we go back in the pool. That's the spa rules."

I shake my head. "Still gonna pass, Lu."

Before she can argue, the sound of a closing door draws our attention to the house.

Jasper and Geoff are crossing through the kitchen and step outside; Jasper looking pale, with his arm in a cast but otherwise in relatively good spirit. Geoff, as always, looks effortlessly put together—sleeves rolled up neatly, hair barely out of place, exuding that calm, slightly smug older-brother energy that he's way too good at.

I frown and cross my arms. "What are you doing here?"

Geoff raises a brow. "Nice to see you too, Theo."

"I thought you had a photoshoot today."

"I did," he says easily, rolling his shoulders. "Finished as soon as I could. And since you made it very clear in the family chat that Lucy was looked after, I figured I'd head straight to the hospital to make sure Jasper had someone to bring him back."

I bite my tongue. "Oh."

Jasper sighs. "It's very touching having two grown men fuss over me, really."

Geoff smirks. "You did break your arm falling out of your own hot tub."

"I slipped."

"Right," Geoff says. "*Slipped*."

Jasper mutters something under his breath before waving his good hand toward the hot tub. "Anyway, since I can't enjoy it, the rest of you might as well."

Geoff eyes the bubbling water with interest. "Now that is a good idea. Three hours at a hospital is the opposite of relaxing. I think I've earned a hot tub soak."

Christa claps her hands. "Excellent. Everyone in."

I shake my head. "No, thanks."

Geoff gives me a pointed look. "Theo. Don't be boring."

"I'm not boring."

"You kind of are," Ivy chimes in.

Lucy bounces up onto her knees, grabbing my hand with her little fingers as their spa alarm goes off. "Daddy, pleeease?"

And just like that, my last shred of resolve crumbles.

Before I can even attempt to refuse again, Geoff claps me on the back. "I'm sure Jasper's got spare swim shorts for us."

Jasper waves his good hand. "The black ones should fit you."

"Hold on—" I try, but Christa is already shooing me toward the house.

"Go, go, before we drag you in."

I sigh heavily, but Lucy's hopeful little face is beaming up at me, and I know I've already lost.

I shake my head, muttering under my breath as I head inside. "Completely outnumbered in my own family."

As I turn toward the house, my gaze flickers back to Ivy, almost unconsciously. She's watching me, a pink hue spreading from her neck upwards, disappearing under the thick layer of quark, her fingers fiddling with the edge of her bathrobe.

She blushes.

And for some reason, that tiny reaction hits me more than it should.

My stomach tightens, and my brain—useless, traitorous thing that it is—decides to remind me that beneath that dressing gown is definitely a swimsuit.

And Ivy in a swimsuit?

I swallow hard and force myself to look away before my thoughts go somewhere they really shouldn't, especially not when I am surrounded by my brothers and my five-year-old daughter.

I am so in trouble.

By the time I've changed into Jasper's black swim shorts and made my way back downstairs, the girls have already washed off the quark and are back in the hot tub.

Christa and Geoff are sitting on one side, chatting easily, while Lucy bobs happily in the centre, her swimming armbands keeping her upright as she sings her favourite nursery rhyme. That leaves the only available spot right next to Ivy.

Of course.

I step into the water, letting the heat wrap around me as I sink down into the seat beside her. The jets hum quietly beneath the surface, sending a gentle current swirling around us, and I can feel the warmth seep into my muscles.

Ivy shifts slightly, and under the bubbling water, our legs brush.

It's nothing. Just an accident. But the contact is like a tiny shock to my system, and suddenly, my entire focus narrows to the fact that her bare skin is against mine.

Ivy doesn't move away.

I tell myself not to overthink it. But now, every time she so much as shifts, I notice it. The way her thigh just barely presses against mine. The way the water moves around her, sending little ripples against me. The way the fragrance of whatever coconut-scented thing she uses is way too distracting this close.

Across from me, Geoff is still watching with that insufferable grin.

And that's when it clicks. He's doing this on purpose. He left the seat next to Ivy free for me because apparently, he is now in the bloody matchmaking business.

I narrow my eyes at him in warning, but he just looks delighted with himself, like he knows exactly what he's doing.

I had been clear. We are just friends. But of course, Geoff had decided that my words meant absolutely nothing.

Before I can give him another warning look, Jasper, sitting miserably on a patio chair, lets out a loud, exaggerated sigh.

"Enjoying my hot tub without me," he says dramatically. "Truly, this is betrayal of the highest order."

"You invited us," I remind him, stretching my left arm along the edge of the tub.

He scowls. "I take it back. You should all be suffering in solidarity with me."

Geoff snorts. "I did my suffering at the hospital, thanks. You were very needy for a grown man."

Jasper levels a glare at him. "I was literally injured."

"You still made me get you a snack whilst waiting."

"I hadn't eaten in hours!" he grumbles. "I was in pain. In fact, I'm hungry again. Someone else should be feeding me."

I smirk. "What do you want? A bib and a spoon?"

Christa chuckles, while Lucy, still floating between us, giggles. "Uncle Jasper, you should have yogurt," she declares. "Daddy always says yogurt is good when you don't feel well."

"Want me to feed you some yoghurt?" I chuckle.

Jasper curses under his breath, rubbing his face with his good hand trying to hide that he is giving me a very clear one finger salute. "I can feel my dignity evaporating."

Geoff smirks. "You had dignity?"

Jasper glares. "You're so lucky my arm is broken."

"Ignore him," Geoff says to Christa, "Jasper's the baby in the family."

"Should have known he is the third child. They always are attention seekers," Christa winks. Jasper's protest is drowned out by mine and Geoff's laughs; he just sinks lower in his chair pretending to ignore us whilst scrolling on his phone.

"So, Christa, what does a man have to do to woo you?" Geoff wiggles his eyebrows.

"You have to be called Alex and be my fiancé," she flashes her engagement ring at him with a smug smile, dashing any hopes he may have had. Geoff is a constant flirt, so you never know if he is really interested in a woman or just toying with her.

"Ah, bad timing on my side," he winks at her.

"Definitely wrong time," she says dryly.

Geoff grins. "So you're saying that in another life—"

"Nope."

"Not even a little curious?"

"Not even a little."

Jasper and I share a look. Then, in perfect sync, we both turn to Geoff.

"Ouch," I laugh.

"Brutal," Jasper adds.

Geoff tilts his head back dramatically. "Fine. I can take rejection."

"You should be good at it by now," I say.

Jasper grins. "It's almost impressive, really."

Geoff narrows his eyes at us. "You both suck."

"Language!" I warn.

"Ivy is the single one," Christa says with a mischievous glint in her eyes.

I catch the look that passes between my brothers—one of those silent, devious exchanges that means nothing good is about to happen for me.

Geoff turns to Christa, looking far too pleased with himself. "Well, Christa, since you are clearly the expert on happy relationships, got any tips for Theo? He's been single so long, I'm starting to worry he's forgotten how it works."

I frown. "Excuse me?"

Jasper jumps in, grinning. "Yeah, maybe you two can give him some pointers. You know, help him out a bit."

I shoot them both a warning look whilst trying to ignore that my ears are burning. "I do not need help."

Christa leans back against the edge of the hot tub with a thoughtful expression. "Well, Theo does have some good qualities. He makes excellent coffee. He's not terrible to look at. He's occasionally charming."

"Wow," I deadpan. "So generous."

Geoff nods, playing along. "Yeah, but he works too much. He's always busy. That's probably his main issue."

Jasper strokes his imaginary beard like he's Sigmund Freud analysing my psyche. "Maybe he should practice flirting? You know, get back into the game."

I groan loudly. "Okay, we're not doing this."

But before I can fully shut it down, a little voice pipes up.

"My daddy doesn't need a girlfriend."

The entire hot tub falls silent.

Lucy, still floating between us, looks very serious. She lifts her chin with determination. "He has me and he has Ivy."

My mouth slams shut.

Ivy, beside me, stiffens slightly.

Jasper and Geoff share a look that screams victory whilst Christa is in a fit of giggles.

Geoff is the first to recover, pressing a hand over his mouth like he's trying so hard not to laugh. "Well. There you go, Theo. Sorted."

Jasper grins. "No need for a girlfriend when you've got Lucy and Ivy, huh?"

I feel Ivy shift beside me, but I don't dare look at her.

Lucy nods firmly. "Daddy and Ivy are best friends," she announces. "She's fun, and she makes nice Santas, and she brings me yummy snacks. That's way better than a girlfriend."

Jasper chokes on a laugh. Christa snorts into her drink.

I clear my throat. "That's... very sweet, Ladybug."

She beams at me. "See?" Then, like she's solved the most important problem in the world, she flops back into the water, kicking her feet with satisfaction.

I finally risk a glance at Ivy.

Her cheeks are pink... very pink.

She looks down, adjusting the strap of her swimsuit like it's suddenly the most interesting thing in the world. Then, as if feeling my gaze, she flicks her eyes up to meet mine for the briefest second before quickly looking away.

It's small.

Barely anything.

But it's there.

That moment of hesitation. The quiet awareness. The way her fingers fidget just a little before she forces herself to stay still.

Jasper notices, of course. "Ivy, that's quite an endorsement."

She recovers fast, flashing him a dry look. "What, that I bring snacks?"

Jasper grins. "Hey, food is important."

Geoff claps his hands together. "Alright, I think we've embarrassed Theo enough—for now."

"Lucky for you," Jasper adds.

I shake my head, but even as the conversation shifts, I feel Ivy next to me. So close yet so unattainable. This is not how I had seen my afternoon go.

16
The Wettest Dry Hump in History

Theo

THE NIGHT IS STILL. The stars stretch wide across the sky, their soft glow reflecting on the surface of the water. The air is cooler now, but the hot tub keeps me warm, the gentle hum of the jets filling the silence.

Everyone else has gone inside—Lucy, exhausted from all the excitement, had practically fallen asleep at the table. Jasper, still milking his injury for all it was worth, had disappeared to the sofa with a whisky in his good hand. Christa and Geoff had retreated to the kitchen, still locked in some ridiculous debate about burger toppings.

And Ivy...

I hear the faint creak of the door before I see her. Footsteps pad across the patio, slow and quiet. Then, her voice—soft, just above a whisper.

"Mind if I join you?"

I glance up.

She's standing just at the edge of the terrace, wrapped in her dressing gown again, her hair slightly damp from earlier. The glow from the outdoor lights catches on the soft curve of her face, her eyes warm but hesitant.

I should say no.

I should tell her I was just about to head inside. That I'd had enough of the water. That I wasn't sitting here thinking about things I shouldn't be thinking about.

But I don't say any of that.

Instead, I nod. "Yeah. Of course."

For a moment, she doesn't move. Then, slowly, her hands rise to the knot of her bathrobe, loosening it with a quiet pull.

As she shrugs it off, my brain short-circuits.

The soft fabric of her black swimsuit is clinging to the curves I have spent far too much time not thinking about. The light from the house casts a golden glow over her skin, and my mouth goes dry.

I look away fast, shifting in my seat like that'll somehow manage to keep myself in check but my cock is not playing along. He has been through hell this afternoon and now that Ivy and I are alone, he is taking control.

She takes a seat on the edge, dipping a toe in first before slowly sinking into the water opposite me. A small sigh escapes her lips as she relaxes against the edge, letting the warmth envelop her.

"This is nice," she murmurs.

I clear my throat, forcing my brain to function. "Yeah. Peaceful."

She tilts her head back, gazing up at the sky. "It's amazing how many stars you can see out here. It's nothing like London."

I follow her gaze. She's right. The sky out here is endless, speckled with stars so bright they almost don't look real.

For a moment, we just sit there, the quiet stretching between us.

And I should leave it like that.

I should let this be nothing more than a peaceful, quiet moment between friends.

But I'm still too aware of her. The way the steam rises between us. The way the water shifts slightly every time she moves. The fact that if I stretched my leg even slightly, my knee would brush against hers.

I risk another glance at her, and for the first time tonight, she's properly looking at me too.

And it's different.

It's not like before, not like the comfortable, easy looks we've shared a hundred times. There's something charged about it, something that makes the air between us feel heavier.

Her lips part slightly, like she's about to say something—

Then she blinks, looks away quickly, and rubs a hand over her arm, as if trying to shake whatever this is off.

I exhale slowly, running a hand through my damp hair, trying to ground myself. Trying to ignore the way my heart is pounding, the way my skin feels too warm, and not just from the water.

I should say something.

I should make a joke, cut through the tension, turn this back into what it should be—just a quiet moment between friends.

But before I can, something shifts.

I'm not sure who moves first.

Maybe she leans in. Maybe I do. Maybe it's both, pulled together by something inevitable, something neither of us fully understands but neither of us wants to fight.

All I know is one second, we're sitting there, barely breathing, too aware of the space between us.

And the next—

Her lips are on mine.

It's soft at first, hesitant, like we're both afraid to acknowledge what's happening, afraid that the second we do, it'll shatter.

But then she shifts closer, her hands finding my shoulders, her fingers pressing against my skin, and I lose every last thought in my head.

I kiss her back.

Properly.

There's heat and something achingly familiar about it, but also something completely new. Her lips are soft, her breath is warm against mine, and the world outside of this moment ceases to exist.

I don't think.

I just feel.

The way her fingertips dig into my skin, the way the water moves gently around us, the way she lets out the faintest, barely-there sigh against my mouth when I pull her just a little closer.

Ivy's body, wet and shining, moves smoothly as she straddles me. My cock is hard and throbbing by now and she just must feel it when she settles into my lap. Her hands grip my shoulders, nails digging slightly into my flesh, as she begins to ride me with a newfound ferocity. Dry humping in water, is that a thing?

The hot water makes everything feel more intense as our bodies move together. My hands explore her curves, squeezing her arse and pulling her closer as our moans fill the steamy air.

"Oh, Ivy, you feel so fucking good," I groan, my eyes closing in ecstasy. "I love the way you move on me. So fucking hot. I wanted this so much."

Her confidence soars as she takes control, her breath coming in short, excited gasps. She leans forward, her breasts pressing against my chest, and whispers seductively, "I want to feel you. Show me what you can do, baby."

"You're mine, Ivy," I growl, my voice low and commanding. "I'm going to fuck you so hard, make you mine in every way."

Her body trembles, a mixture of pleasure and submission washing over her. She meets my gaze, her eyes shining with desire and trust, and nods slightly, encouraging me to take what I desire. I get rougher, grabbing her arse and pinching her nipples, making her gasp.

She wraps her legs around my waist, her arms around my neck, as I push the gusset of her bathing suit aside and slide my hard cock into her whilst our lips meet in a deep, hungry kiss. Her breath hitches, her eyes fluttering shut, waves of pleasure washing over me. My thrusts become more urgent, my muscles straining, as I drive into her with relentless passion.

"I'm gonna come, Theo," she whispers, her voice breathy and desperate. "I can't hold back, baby."

I feel her body clench around me and I almost loose it. I grip her tightly, my fingers digging into her arse, and I thrust harder into her warm pussy, my own orgasm building. The hot tub's water laps at our bodies.

"Come for me, Ivy," I growl, my voice hoarse. "Let's finish this together."

Her body shakes, her orgasm rippling through her. She cries out, her voice mingling with my deep groans as we reach our climax together. Our bodies shudder, our lips still locked, as our pleasure peaks.

Then, suddenly, it's gone.

I open my eyes.

Steam curls around me, the heat pressing against my skin, but it's not from the hot tub.

It's from my shower. My dick is softening in my hand.

I inhale sharply, the sound of running water hitting the tiles snapping me back to reality.

My other hand is braced against the cool ceramic, droplets trailing down my arms, my forehead pressed against the wall as I let out a slow, shaky breath.

Fuck. Fuck. Fuck.

It wasn't real.

Just a fantasy. A moment my brain had conjured up so vividly that, for a second, I'd let myself believe it.

I squeeze my eyes shut, frustration curling deep in my chest.

Because as much as I want to pretend it was just some stupid thought, something that drifted in and out of my head, I know better.

It felt real.

Because I want it to be real.

And that? That's a problem.

I take another breath, willing myself to shake it off. To let it go. To not think about the way Ivy's lips had felt in my daydream, about the way she had leaned into me, like it was the most natural thing in the world.

It wasn't real.

And that is the part that stings the most.

I force myself to stand up straight, running a hand over my face as the water continues to pour down over me. I need to get a grip.

Ivy is my friend.

She is off-limits.

No matter how good that kiss had felt in my head. No matter how much my heart is still hammering in my chest, like it hasn't caught up to the fact that it was all a dream.

I reach for the shower tap, twisting it off with more force than necessary.

The water stops.

Reality settles in.

And I'm left standing here, completely alone.

17
Being Human

Ivy

Pee-Pee peers at me over the rim of her glasses, waiting.

"So, Ivy," she says, her voice as calm and measured as always. "How's it going?"

I lean back in the slightly-too-stiff armchair, letting my fingers play with a loose thread on my sleeve. "Good. Great. Life ticks along."

"That's not really an answer."

I sigh. "I'm still doing yoga three times a week."

She nods approvingly. "And how's that going?"

"Shockingly well," I admit. "I mean, I still struggle with some of the poses, but I actually feel better afterwards. I don't want to throw my laptop out the window every time I get a frustrating email, so I guess that's progress."

Her mouth twitches. "That is progress."

I nod. "And I've also taken up… a bit of a side project."

She waits, because she knows I'll keep talking if she just gives me enough silence.

I cross my legs. "I, uh, may have accidentally started an army."

Both her brows lift. "An army?"

I wave a hand. "Not a real one. A gnome army."

Pee-Pee laughs, which is shocking enough. Even she seems surprised and bites her lip to shut it down. "A... gnome army?"

"Yeah, I ordered way too much clay and needed something to do with it. Tried making a bowl first, but it turned out looking like a first try of a Grayson Perry. Then I attempted some jewellery... also a failure. But the gnomes? The gnomes worked."

Pee-Pee, to her credit, barely reacts to this information. "And how many gnomes are in your army?"

I bite my lip. "Um... a lot?"

She just nods, as if this is completely normal. "And what do you plan to do with them?"

I shrug. "Right now, they're just existing. Watching over my coffee table. And my breakfast bar. And my bookshelves. Theo—" I cut myself off, glancing away. "Anyway. They're multiplying."

There's a pause. Then she says, "Theo?"

Damn it.

I pick at the thread on my sleeve again. "He thinks I should sell them."

"And what do you think?"

I scoff. "I think they're not nearly good enough for that."

Another pause. "You know, Ivy, you have a tendency to talk yourself out of things before you even try them."

I give her a look. "Yes, I know. That's why I pay you."

That earns me a small smile. "Fair enough."

She watches me for a moment, and I know she's waiting for me to say more. To mention something else.

I don't.

I don't tell her about the hot tub.

About how warm the water was. About how close Theo was sitting next to me, the way our legs brushed underwater, the way my heart did something completely ridiculous in response.

And I definitely don't tell her about the way I almost said something before I panicked and looked away.

Nope.

Not bringing that up.

I clear my throat. "So, I'm mentally stable. Shall we call it a day?"

She leans back in her chair, completely unimpressed. "Nice try."

I sigh dramatically. "Worth a shot. I took care of Lucy when Theo was in a pickle. And we ended up with his family and my friend Christa in the hot tub. And it still felt a little bit more like friends... especially when his daughter declared that Theo doesn't need a girlfriend because he has her and me. She included me in their little family. And I like that, I'm not going to lie."

Pee-Pee watches me closely, her gaze calm but focused, like she's watching the exact moment something clicks in my brain.

I shift under her stare, crossing my arms. "This is bad, isn't it?" I blurt out.

Phyllis doesn't react, just picks some fluff off her lavender cardigan. "What makes you say that?"

I throw up my hands. "Because I shouldn't need to feel like I belong somewhere, right? I should be fine on my own. I should be content just being me. That was the whole point of this! I wasn't supposed to let anyone else fill a space in my life. I was supposed to be enough on my own."

Pee-Pee leans back slightly, watching me with that unreadable expression. "Ivy," she says carefully, "do you think that wanting connection with people means you're not enough?"

I shift uncomfortably. "That's not—"

She lifts a hand, cutting me off gently. "You didn't say that in so many words. But you seem to believe that needing people... that feeling like you belong somewhere is a weakness."

I frown. "Isn't it?"

Her brow furrows slightly. "No. It's being human."

I look down at my hands. "But what if I do need that? Doesn't that mean I've failed? That I haven't done what I was supposed to do?"

She tilts her head. "What exactly were you supposed to do?"

I shake my head, frustration bubbling in my chest. "I was supposed to... fix myself. Be happy being alone. Be strong enough to not feel like I need someone else."

Pee-Pee exhales softly. "Ivy, do you remember why we agreed on the dating ban?"

I hesitate, fingers curling against the hem of my sleeve.

She doesn't wait for me to answer. "It wasn't because you needed to learn how to be alone. You were already alone. You were keeping yourself alone." She pauses. "The problem wasn't that you were dating. It was how you were dating."

I swallow.

"You weren't looking for connection. You were looking for validation. You told me yourself—you would walk into a bar, pick out someone who seemed interested, and then..." She gestures vaguely.

I close my eyes briefly. "And then I'd pretend to be whoever they wanted."

She nods. "You made yourself easy to want. You made yourself into a fantasy, into something exciting. But the second they got too close, the second it was about you—not the version you were showing them, the real you—you pulled away."

My chest tightens.

I already know this. I've known it for ages. But hearing it again, laid out so plainly, still stings.

She keeps going, her voice steady. "The dating ban wasn't about isolation. It was about giving you time to figure out who you are—what you want in a relationship, and what the people you let into your life actually want from you."

I nod slowly, staring at my lap. "Right."

She waits a beat, then says, "A while ago you told me that with Theo you can be yourself. So let me ask you this—does Theo know you, the real you?"

I hesitate. "Yeah."

"And do you feel like you're pretending around him?"

I shake my head. "No."

She nods. "And do you think he only wants you because you're making yourself into something convenient for him?"

I blink. "No." The answer is immediate. And true.

Theo doesn't want something from me.

He just... wants me there.

The thought sends a strange, warm feeling curling in my stomach.

Pee-Pee nods. "Then maybe this isn't what you were avoiding."

I let out a slow breath, still staring at my lap.

She lets me sit with that thought for a moment before she speaks again, her voice gentler this time.

"You're not supposed to be an island, Ivy."

I swallow.

I know she's right.

But knowing it and accepting it? That's a whole different thing.

I stare down at my hands, my mind a mess of tangled thoughts. Pee-Pee has a way of making me see things—things I've been carefully ignoring or pushing aside. And now, I don't know what to do with all of it.

"I told him about me not being able to have a baby." Pee-Pee knows that is a big deal. I don't talk about it much and letting him into this knowledge, that says something. "He was so open, the way he talked about Lucy's mum, and I just wanted him to know something personal about me as well."

"You trust him." It's not a question. It's a statement and I know she is right.

"I do. That's crazy, right?"

"Why?"

"Because... we don't really know each other."

"I would argue you know a lot about each other." Pee-Pee is, as always, the voice of reason.

"But we haven't known each other for long," I argue back.

"What is the minimum time you need to know someone, before you trust them?" *Damn you, Pee-Pee!*

"I don't know."

Phylis gives me an encouraging smile, "Ivy, trust is earned and what you have told me so far, Theo has done everything right to earn your trust. So, it's only natural that you would open up to him."

"Hm." *Oh great, now I'm the one hm-ing.* I glance up hesitantly. "So... does that mean we shouldn't be just friends?"

Pee-Pee doesn't react, just watches me with that calm, infuriating patience.

I sigh, rubbing my hands over my face. "I don't even know if he wants more. He's never—" I pause, my heart picking up pace. "I mean, I don't think he's ever thought of me that way. Has he?"

Pee-Pee tilts her head slightly. "Has he ever treated you like just a friend?"

I open my mouth, ready to say yes, because that's what I've always told myself.

But then I think about it.

The way he always makes sure there's a cup of my favourite coffee waiting for me at the shop. The way he instinctively shifts closer when we walk side by side, like he needs to keep me near. The way he looks at me when he doesn't think I'll notice, like I'm something he can't quite figure out but isn't ready to stop trying.

My stomach tightens.

I close my mouth.

Pee-Pee nods slightly, as if she already knew I wouldn't have an answer to that. "Ivy, you're asking all the big questions when you don't even know what you want yet."

I let out a frustrated breath. "But that's the problem. I thought I knew what I wanted—I wanted to be independent, to feel whole on my own. And now..." I gesture vaguely. "Now I'm just confused."

Pee-Pee offers a small smile. "Then maybe that's your answer right now."

I frown. "What?"

"Slow down."

I scowl. "I hate slowing down."

"I know," she says, smirking slightly. "But you still have a little over a month left. So instead of trying to define something that hasn't even happened yet, maybe you focus on what's in front of you. Keep living your life. Keep being present. And when the time comes, you'll know what you want."

I slump back in my chair. "Great. Love that for me."

Pee-Pee just chuckles.

There's a long beat of silence before she asks, "So what are you planning to do?"

I sigh, shaking my head before finally sitting up, my expression set with determination.

"First," I say, "I need to learn how to bake a cake."

Pee-Pee's lips twitch in amusement. "And then?"

Something flickers across my mind, something certain and real, but I don't say it out loud. Instead, I just smile slightly and stand, grabbing my bag. "I guess we'll see."

Pee-Pee watches me, curious but letting it go.

I give her a small wave. "Same time next week?"

She nods. "Looking forward to hearing about the cake."

I smirk. "You and me both."

18

Lost, Soaked, Frozen, or Eaten by Foxes

Theo

THE ESPRESSO MACHINE HISSES as I rinse the steam wand, filling the café with the scent of dark roast and warm milk. It's the slow stretch before closing, that quiet pocket of time when the rush is over, and all that's left are the regulars lingering over their last sips.

Then the door swings open, and Ivy stumbles in, drowning in shopping bags.

She makes it to the counter whilst huffing and puffing, dumping herself onto a stool at the far end. One of the bags slips from her grip, toppling onto the floor, and out clatters a whisk. A big, professional-grade one, the kind you'd expect in a restaurant kitchen rather than a home. It rolls a little before coming to a stop against the leg of a near-by table.

I raise an eyebrow. "Expecting to whisk an entire vat of something?"

She exhales dramatically, pushing damp hair off her forehead. "If you value my life, Theo, you'll make me something caffeinated. Strong enough to bring me back from the abyss."

I glance at the whisk, then at her. "So... not a *Wiener Melange* then?"

Her eyes narrow slightly. "Will it fix my life?"

I smirk, reaching for a portafilter. "It's basically a Viennese take on a cappuccino, so it might help. But given your current state, I'm thinking something stronger. *Doppio mit Schlag*?"

She leans forward, suspicious. "And what exactly is that?"

"A double espresso with whipped cream."

She lets out a long breath. "Now that I can get behind."

Once done, I slide the coffee across the counter, watching as Ivy wraps her fingers around it like it's the only thing tethering her to the earth. She takes a sip, lets out a small, almost indecent sigh of satisfaction, then finally lifts her head enough to meet my gaze.

"So," I say, nodding at the mountain of shopping bags, "are you stocking up for the apocalypse, or is there another questionable hobby I should prepare myself for?"

She blows on her coffee. "Baking."

"Baking?" I can't help but snort.

"Baking," she confirms, taking another sip.

I glance at the whisk still lying on the floor like an abandoned weapon. "As in, making food people willingly eat?"

"Yes, Theo. That is the general concept."

I fold my arms, leaning on the counter. "And you've chosen to do this... voluntarily? The person who burns water, if I may quote?"

She huffs. "Look, I'm perfectly aware that I'm no Mary Berry, but I can follow a recipe."

"Can you, though?"

She gasps, mock-offended. "Excuse you! I am a highly intelligent woman."

"I don't doubt that." I say, amused. "But intelligence and baking are two very different skill sets. One requires precision, patience, and an ability to follow instructions."

She waves a hand. "Alright, calm down, Paul Hollywood."

I smirk. "Do you even own a measuring scale?"

Her lips press into a line.

"A set of mixing bowls?"

A beat.

I tap the counter. "Ivy."

She exhales through her nose. "I may have also panic-bought those today."

I fight back a laugh. "That inspires a lot of confidence."

She sits up straighter, lifting her chin. "I have to do this, okay? It's for a Macmillan coffee morning at work."

I prop myself against the counter, arms crossed. "You do know you can just buy a cake at the coffee morning, right? That's kind of the point. You show up, eat cake, donate some money, feel like a good person, and leave."

Ivy scoffs. "Yes, obviously. But that's not the issue."

I lift a brow. "Oh? And what is the issue?"

She exhales through her nose. "Caroline."

I frown. "Who's Caroline?"

Ivy rolls her eyes like I should already know. "A colleague. Smug. Bakes effortlessly. Probably has a tin with secret family recipes."

I smirk. "Sounds like a menace."

"She is a menace," Ivy says, pointing at me for emphasis. "She made jabs, Theo. Jabs about how I probably can't bake because I'm not a mum."

"Okay, she is a bit of bitch, I get it. That mum comment was entirely unnecessary." *Actually it was fucking ridiculous.* My mother can't bake even if you pay her, yet she is an amazing, if also crazy, mum. "But at the risk of drawing your wrath on me, you can't bake."

"That's not the point." She flaps a hand. "The point is, I refuse to give her the satisfaction of being right. I am a fully functional adult. I can make a sodding cake."

I nod solemnly. "I admire your determination. Misguided as it is."

Ivy ignores my comment entirely, her eyes suddenly lighting up with something suspiciously close to excitement. She leans forward, gripping the edge of the counter. "Do you want to know what else I bought?"

I sip my coffee, studying her. "Considering the sheer volume of those bags, I'm almost afraid to ask."

She grins, practically vibrating with energy now. "A tent."

"A tent?" I cough. *No, no, no, not a good idea.*

"And a backpack!" She gestures at the largest bag beside her, the one that looks like it could fit an entire kitchen inside. "That's why the bags are so huge. I'm going camping."

I stare at her. "You?"

"Yes, me," she says, lifting her chin like she's just announced she's scaling Everest.

I glance at the bags again. Then back at her. Then at the bags.

"You're going camping."

"Yes."

"At the risk of repeating myself... voluntarily?"

She scoffs. "Obviously."

I rub my jaw, trying to picture Ivy surviving in the wild.

I lean against the counter, smirking. "Are you sure you don't just want to go back to making more clay gnomes? That seemed less... life-threatening."

Ivy sticks her tongue out at me. "My gnome work is thriving, thank you for asking"

I raise an eyebrow. "Thriving?"

She nods solemnly. "I may or may not have steadily added to my army. They are currently gathering on my windowsill, awaiting further orders."

I shake my head, "Remind me to stay on their good side."

She grins, but then her expression hardens. "But no, Theo. This time, I am serious. I am going camping."

I watch as she folds her arms, her shoulders squaring like she's expecting me to challenge her.

I sigh. "Ivy, if I've learned one thing about you, it's that when you put your mind to something, you will do it. No matter how ridiculous or ill-advised it may be."

She props her chin up on her hands and looks at me from under her eyelashes. "But?"

I hesitate, rubbing the back of my neck. "But... unlike baking or yoga or—God help us all—the gnome factory, if something goes wrong with this, you could be in serious trouble."

Her eyes narrow. "You think I can't do it."

"That's not what I said."

"It's exactly what you meant."

I exhale. How do I tell her that I just want to keep her safe with every fibre of my being without sounding like a bloody creep or, even worse, anything more than a friend? "I mean that you're going into the middle of nowhere, in a tent, alone."

Her chin juts out defiantly. "Plenty of people do that."

"Yes, but plenty of people also end up lost, soaked, frozen, or eaten by foxes."

She snorts. "I think I can handle a fox, Theo. I live in London... plenty of foxes around here."

I drag a hand down my face. "That's not the point. Look, I get it—you want to prove something, and I know you can do this. But camping isn't just a hobby you can abandon if it goes wrong. If you mess up a cake, fine, you bin it. If you fall out of tree pose in yoga, no one dies. But if you get stranded in the middle of nowhere with no phone signal and a tent that won't go up..." I shudder thinking of everything that could happen to her. All the nutters that could hide behind the bushes and—*Theo now you are losing it!*

One look at her tells me I won't win this argument. I have to admire her determination even if it scares me more than I care to admit.

"I'll be fine," she grins and chugs back the rest of her espresso.

I nod slowly, biting back everything else I want to say. I cross my arms, watching as Ivy absentmindedly traces the rim of her coffee cup, her expression shifting between confidence and the realisation that she might not have thought this through.

"Alright," I say, nodding at the mountain of gear beside her. "When and where is this grand expedition happening?"

She hesitates. "Uh... sometime in the next few weeks?"

"That's vague."

She shrugs. "I need to do some research."

I smirk. "Right. And do you at least have a general idea of where you're planning to go, or are you just going to pitch a tent in Hyde Park and hope for the best?"

She swats my arm. "I was thinking Cornwall. Or maybe the Lake District. Or Kent?"

"So... you have absolutely no clue."

"Not no clue," she argues, licking a last drop of coffee from the rim of her cup. "Just... flexible options."

I glance at her bags again, the sheer volume of them taking up all the floor area around her stool. She's planning a full-scale outdoor adventure, and yet, she hasn't even settled on a location.

An idea takes shape. I tap my fingers on the counter. "What about Dorset?"

She tilts her head. "Dorset?"

I nod. "Yeah. Lucy and I are heading there in two weeks for a holiday. We're staying in a cottage, but there are plenty of campsites in the area. You could book one of those."

She considers this, her brows drawing together. "That... actually makes sense."

I almost punch the air with my fist when I detect victory. "I know."

She exhales, glancing at her bags. "It would make things easier."

"Much easier," I confirm. "I mean, unless you want to lug all of this—" I gesture at the camping haul, "—from a train station to a campsite, which, knowing your luck, will be at the top of a very steep hill."

She pulls a face. "That does sound miserable."

"Exactly. And setting up a tent after that?" I shake my head. "Not ideal." *Come on, Ivy, say yes, say yes to an option that gives me a vague feeling of safety.*

Her lips press together, and I can see the gears turning in her head, realising how impractical her original plan was.

"And," I add, keeping my tone casual, "if you camp somewhere near us, at least I'll be close enough to help if anything goes wrong."

She pauses at that, looking up at me properly now. "That's actually... not a bad idea."

I grin. "I'm known for them."

She huffs a laugh and leans back. "Alright, Dorset it is."

I glance at the bags again. "You are going to practice putting up that tent before you go, right?"

"Obviously," she says, waving a hand. Then, after a beat, she adds, "I'll do it in my flat."

I snort. "You're going to set up a full-size tent in your living room?"

"I need to know how it works!" she argues. "Better to struggle indoors than in a field with the wind trying to murder me."

I shake my head, smiling despite myself. "Please send me a picture when you inevitably get tangled in the tent poles."

She smirks. "You wish you had my level of preparedness."

I take a sip of my coffee, watching her, still not sure whether to be impressed or deeply concerned. But whatever adventures she gets up to, at least I'll be nearby to make sure nothing happens to her.

19
Indoor Survival Queen

Ivy

THE SUN IS BLAZING, my flat feels like a preheated oven, and the only thing standing between me and my impending camping triumph is a *Coleman Darwin 2* tent currently lying in an uncooperative heap on my living room floor.

The instructions claim it's "quick-pitch" and "intuitive to assemble"—phrases I now suspect were written by someone with a very dark sense of humour.

Dressed in my yoga pants and an old T-shirt that's clinging to me in ways no fabric should, I wipe sweat from my forehead and give it another go.

Step One: Lay out the tent

Easy enough. I shake out the fabric, spreading it over my floor. It immediately tries to refold itself into a wrinkled mess. I flatten it again, eyeing the pieces.

Step Two: Assemble the poles and insert into the pins

I frown at the two long, bendy, black fibreglass poles that seem to have a life of their own. After a brief wrestling match, I manage to slot them together, feeling vaguely accomplished.

Now, the pins.

I glance at the tent. There are no pins... although I am not sure what these pins are supposed to look like.

I consult the instructions again. *Insert the poles into the external pin and ring system.*

What the fuck?

I flip the paper upside down, as if that will suddenly make it clearer. It does not.

Right. Guessing it is.

I try threading a pole through the small fabric loops, but that doesn't seem right. The whole thing flops over, nearly dragging two gnomes off my coffee table.

"Oh, for fuck's sake!" I shout.

After some trial and error (and only one minor trip over a stray guy rope), I realise the poles need to arch. When I finally manage to slot them into the metal pins at the base, the tent suddenly springs up, its shape coming together in a way that feels a little bit like magic.

I gasp. "Oh my God, I did it."

Step Three: Attach the tent fly

Thank God for Google because without it, I wouldn't have a clue what a guy rope is or a tent fly. But now I do. The tent fly is the extra layer of fabric that I somehow forgot about and is currently discarded on my sofa. It's the waterproof bit.

I drape it over the top, securing it in place with a series of Velcro straps that seem to appear out of nowhere.

Step Four: Secure the guy lines

I find the thin white ropes hanging off the sides of the tent, "designed for stability in windy conditions," as

Google tried to explain to me. Not exactly necessary in my flat, but if I'm going to do this, I may as well go all in.

I try to knot one to a bookshelf. It immediately slaps me in the face.

"Brilliant."

By the time I finish tying them off—mostly to my furniture, since I don't fancy hammering tent pegs into my carpet—I step back and assess my work.

A fully upright, real-life tent, standing proudly in the middle of my living room.

I wipe my hands on my thighs, panting slightly. "Look at that. Queen of the great indoors."

Sure, it takes up most of my living room. Sure, I may have knocked over a lamp in the process. And yes, my pouffe is now trapped inside the tent, but I did it.

And if I can put up a tent in my flat, then surely I can do it in an actual field.

Right?

Feeling proud of myself—and needing to document this triumph before the tent inevitably collapses—I grab my phone and snap a selfie in front of it, slightly flushed, slightly sweaty, but successful.

I open the messaging app and fire off the evidence.

Me

> Behold! The Queen of Camping has arrived.

A reply comes almost immediately.

Theo

> You actually put the tent up in your flat?

> **Me**
> And I did a mighty fine job, I'd like to add.

> **Theo**
> I would've paid good money to watch this happen in real-time.

> **Me**
> Rude. This was a flawless operation.

> **Theo**
> There's a footstool trapped inside.

I glance at the pouffe, very visible through the opening of the tent. Fine. Maybe not entirely flawless.

> **Me**
> It's part of the aesthetic. Rustic. Homely. A modern take on outdoor living.

> **Theo**
> Right. And where exactly are your tent pegs secured?

I bite my lip, staring at the four guy ropes currently looped around my radiator, the leg of my sofa, and—regrettably—a dining chair that now looks like it might tip over at any second.

> **Me**

> **Don't worry about it.**

Theo

> **Oh, I'm definitely worried.**

I smirk, flopping onto the sofa, my phone resting on my stomach.

This... this is easy.

The way we talk, the way we are, it's natural. Friends. Always friends. And yet, my mind flickers back to the hot tub. That almost moment, the way the air felt different between us, the way his eyes had lingered just a little too long.

Then there was Pee-Pee, telling me maybe it wouldn't be the worst thing in the world if I did date... once the ban is over, of course. That I had learned things about myself now, that I wasn't just reacting to loneliness anymore.

But Theo hasn't indicated anything. No shift, no change—except, maybe, in the way he worries.

And that's what nags at me. Is it just concern? Or is there something else sitting beneath it?

My phone buzzes again.

Theo

> **Alright, I'll admit it. I'm actually impressed.**

I blink at the screen, rereading the message. Impressed?

I shouldn't care. It shouldn't matter what he thinks about my questionable indoor camping setup. And yet, a little spark of satisfaction flickers to life in my chest.

I tap out a response, keeping it breezy.

> **Me:** High praise! Bow before my superior survival skills.

> **Theo:** Let's not get ahead of ourselves. You haven't actually survived anything yet.

> **Me:** Details.

I toss my phone onto the sofa and stretch my arms above my head, groaning slightly. My entire body feels sticky, the heat clinging to my skin like an unwelcome second layer. The effort of wrestling with the tent has left me feeling both triumphant and gross, and there's only one solution for that.

Shower. Immediately.

I drag myself to the bathroom, peeling off my yoga pants and T-shirt, both damp with sweat, and step under the blissfully cool spray. The water runs down my body, washing away the stickiness, the tension, the lingering thoughts about Theo and his praise and why it made me happy.

When I'm done, I wrap myself in a towel, but the moment I step into my bedroom, the heat presses against my skin again, thick and suffocating.

Nope. Not happening.

The towel drops.

I collapse onto my bed, sprawling across the thin summer duvet, naked and completely done with the day. The fan hums softly in the corner, offering only the weakest of breezes, but I can't bring myself to care.

I stare at the ceiling, limbs spread like a starfish, the last messages from Theo replaying in my head.

I'm actually impressed.

It shouldn't make my stomach flutter. It's just Theo. We banter, we wind each other up—that's what we do. It's normal. But that stupid little compliment is now lodged in my brain, circling like a persistent mosquito.

I groan, rolling onto my side, but my thoughts refuse to settle. Instead, they wander back to that afternoon at Jasper's, when we were all in the hot tub.

Nothing had happened—of course nothing had happened—but now, lying here naked, my brain decides to dig up details I had absolutely not needed to store.

The way Theo looked in those black shorts, his chest bare, just some sprinkling of dark hair. I remember noticing the way his muscles tensed when he moved, the water clinging to him in a way that made my mouth feel dry.

And the trail of dark hair on his stomach, snaking down beneath the waistband of his shorts...

He has this lean, muscular physique that I put down to his determined efforts to feed Lucy healthy food and, by extension, himself — though the yoga is clearly doing things too. Unfair things.

At our last class, Lucy encouraged him to show me some of his advanced moves. The ones he does at home. Shirtless, I imagine. With serene breathing and zero shame.

He held himself up like gravity was a mere suggestion. He did crow pose and another one with a name that sounds like a mildly sensual pasta dish, and didn't even break a sweat. I, meanwhile, was trying very hard not to stare at his arms. Or his everything.

I swallow, shifting against the sheets. I press my palms over my eyes. "Nope. Not doing this."

I roll onto my back, trying to will away the memory, trying to remind myself that Theo is just Theo.

But then I remember the way Theo had leaned back in the hot tub, water droplets trailing down his chest, disappearing into the rippling surface. The way his voice had sounded, low and amused, when he'd caught me staring for half a second too long.

My thighs press together instinctively.

What if we had been alone?

The warm water wrapping around us like a soft caress, while his lips meet mine with a touch that is both gentle and insistent. His hands roam over my skin in slow, deliberate strokes, sparking a deep, burning desire that feels like it is setting me on fire from the inside out. He pulls me onto his lap, and I straddle him, the heat between us almost something you can physically feel.

His kisses trail up and down my neck, leaving a tingling wake, and he whispers in my ear, his voice husky with longing. His thumbs softly teasing my nipples through the fabric of my bathing suit before sliding the straps down to reveal me, and his eager mouth follows. I can't hold back a cry—a raw, honest sound of need and total surrender. When he asks me what I want, I barely manage to whisper that I need to come.

He slowly eases a finger inside, then another, each movement full of purpose and care. One hand begins to stroke me while his thumb traces rhythmic circles over my clit. The sensations build up like a tidal wave, drawing me ever closer to the edge until I finally explode in a shattering release that leaves me utterly breathless.

I open my eyes and I am back in my bedroom, the reality of the moment settling in. My fingers, still sticky with my own arousal, serve as a clear reminder of that intense, vivid fantasy.

Fantasy… yes.

It is all just fantasy.

20
Austrian Baking Logic

Theo

THE COFFEE HOUSE IS buzzing, the warm scent of freshly brewed espresso mingling with the sweetness of pastries. It's the kind of mid-morning rush that keeps my hands moving without thinking—pulling shots, steaming milk, placing orders on trays with automatic ease.

Then the door slams open.

Ivy storms in like a woman on a mission, her T-shirt slightly askew, flour smudged across her cheek, and something suspiciously brown smeared down the front of her top. It looks...questionable.

At the far end of the counter, Jasper—who's been lazily scrolling on his phone, sipping a melange like he owns the place (which, technically, he partly does)—snorts so loudly that a few customers glance over.

I look at Ivy, torn between amusement and something much more dangerous, much more instinctive.

She looks cute.

Flustered, messy, lickable.

I shove that last thought somewhere deep and unspeakable as she stomps up to the counter, planting both hands firmly on the surface.

"I have failed," she announces, chest rising and falling dramatically. "I am a failure."

I set down the portafilter. "Elaborate."

Her shoulders sag. "The cake. It's a disaster. I tried. I really tried. But it turns out baking is some kind of black magic and I was clearly not born with the gift."

Jasper snorts again, barely trying to hide his amusement. "Tell me you at least set something on fire?"

She scowls at him. "No, but I may have broken a whisk, curdled some butter, and created something that looks—and I cannot stress this enough—exactly like cat vomit."

I bite my lip to keep from laughing. "Ivy—"

She grips the counter tighter, leaning forward. "I need you."

I suck in sharply.

Her eyes go wide. "I mean—your skills. I need your skills, Theo. Your baking skills. Would you—" She takes a breath, exhales dramatically. "Would you please, please help me bake a cake?"

I let the moment stretch, just long enough for her to shift on her feet, before smirking. "Of course."

Her face lights up in pure, unfiltered relief. "Really?"

I wipe my hands on a towel and nod. "Yeah. I'll help. But I need to make sure Jasper can get Lucy later." Like I would have ever said no to her.

Jasper waves a lazy hand. "Yeah, yeah, I'll grab her. Just text me the details."

I glance back at Ivy, her hair slightly frizzy, the flour still streaked across her cheek. She's looking at me like I've just agreed to perform life-saving surgery.

I chuckle, grabbing a cloth to wipe down the counter. "I'll be up after the café closes."

"You're a lifesaver, Theo. Honestly, I could kiss you," Ivy exhales.

The words hang there for a beat.

Her eyes widen slightly as if she's only just registered what she's said. A flush creeps up her neck, and she immediately backpedals, waving a hand. "Not that I... I just mean... you know what I mean."

I do know what she means. But now the words "kiss you" are floating in my head like they belong there.

Before I can say anything, she spins on her heel. "Right! See you later!"

And then she's gone, practically jogging out the door, leaving a trail of flour-dusted chaos in her wake.

I stare after her, rubbing the back of my neck, still hearing those words. Kiss you.

A long, drawn-out laugh breaks my daze.

I glance to the side. Jasper is watching me over the rim of his cup.

"So," he smirks, setting the mug down. "When exactly were you planning on telling her that you can't bake either?"

I turn back to the espresso machine. "I can bake."

Jasper raises an eyebrow. "No, Klaus can bake. You can stand next to him and look like you know what you're doing."

I shoot him a look. "It's cake, Jasper. How hard can it be?"

Jasper lets out a laugh, shaking his head. "I think Ivy may have thought this too before she created cat vomit."

I ignore him and pull out my phone, scrolling for Klaus's number. Can't be that difficult with a few tips from the expert.

I lean against the wall outside Ivy's flat, a bag of hastily bought baking supplies hanging off my wrist. The scent of warm pavement and lingering espresso from the café below clings to my clothes, but my mind is on the cup cake.

Not cupcakes, mind you. Not the tiny, frosted things people stick candles into. No, this is some Austrian logic at work—a full-sized cake, measured out using a cup, which Klaus assured me was idiot-proof. His exact words.

Which is a little insulting, honestly. But also, reassuring.

I glance down at the bag: flour, sugar, eggs, yoghurt, nuts, cocoa powder, vanilla extract. A bottle of milk that I may or may not have panic bought because I wasn't sure if we'd need it. Everything was sourced from the corner shop down the street, where the owner gave me a bemused once-over when I dumped it all on the counter.

Now, I'm just waiting for Ivy to buzz me up.

I shift my weight, tapping my fingers against the plastic bag. The "kiss you" comment from earlier is still floating somewhere in the back of my mind, refusing to settle. It was nothing—just a throwaway phrase, a flustered slip of the tongue.

But she blushed.

And now I'm here, standing outside her flat, about to bake a cake I've never heard of, with a woman who keeps wedging herself deeper into my thoughts, whether I like it or not.

I take a breath just as the buzzer sounds.

Here we go.

The door swings open, and Ivy stands there, hands on her hips, hair slightly damp like she's just had a shower. She eyes the bag in my hand before her gaze flickers up to my face.

"Well, well, if it isn't my knight in shining apron," she says, stepping aside to let me in.

I smirk as I brush past her. "I left my apron downstairs. Thought I'd take my chances without it."

She gestures dramatically towards the kitchen. "Welcome to my domain. Try not to be intimidated by my gnome army."

I glance around. The counters are already dusted with flour, and there's an unmistakable burnt smell hanging in the air. Gnomes are no longer just on the coffee table, but the windowsill and on the floor in one corner of the room. I guess those are the ones banished from the breakfast bar which is currently covered in baking tins and flour dust.

I lift an eyebrow. "You already attempted round two without me?"

She crosses her arms. "No, that's round one. Or... what's left of it."

I lean over and peer at the cooling rack. What I assume was meant to be cake has collapsed into a dense, sunken mess. The top looks vaguely caramelised, but not in a good way.

I pick at the edge with my finger. "Did you try to cremate it for good measure?"

"Don't mock the fallen," she says solemnly. "It tried its best."

I shake my head, setting the bag of ingredients down. "Right. Let's do this properly."

She watches as I pull out the recipe Klaus sent, her lips twitching. "So, what are we making?"

"A cup cake."

Her brow furrows. "A cupcake?"

"No, a cup cake."

She stares. "Theo. That is the same word."

"Not in Austria, apparently. It's a full-sized cake, but you measure everything with a cup."

Her mouth opens, then closes. She points at me. "That is the dumbest baking logic I've ever heard."

I shrug. "I don't make the rules."

She sighs, rolling up her sleeves. "Fine. But if this goes wrong, I'm blaming Austria."

We start mixing, following the stupidly simple instructions Klaus gave me. Ivy takes over measuring the ingredients while I handle the actual mixing.

At first, it goes smoothly. Eggs, yoghurt, cocoa powder, oil and sugar—all mixed to a smooth, creamy liquid. Simple.

Then it doesn't.

The batter turns out weirdly lumpy when we add the nuts and flour mix, and when we try to smooth it out, it somehow curdles. I don't even know how that's possible, but Ivy stands back, hands on her hips, surveying the damage.

"Well," she says finally. "We made something."

I exhale, pinching the bridge of my nose. "I think we made a mistake."

She grins. "Oh? So, Chef Theo isn't actually an expert?"

I sigh, turning to her. "Fine. I admit it. I am not a baker."

She gasps, clutching her chest in mock shock. "Say it again, I think my ears deceive me."

I grab the ruined bowl of batter and dump it into the bin. "Let's just try again."

The second batch goes better—less lumpy, smooth, and looks more like something a human being might eat. We get it into the oven and set the timer, both leaning against the counter as the warmth of the oven fills the kitchen.

Ivy sighs, stretching her arms. "Well, we're practically professionals now."

I give her a wink. "Should we open a bakery?"

She waves a hand. "Too mainstream. We should do something niche. Only cakes that require cups as measurements."

I snort. "The Cup Cake Café."

She grins. "Exactly. Very exclusive."

I grab a dishcloth, wiping down the counter. "Right, let's clean this disaster zone."

Ivy nods, picking up the bag of flour—just as a small puff of white dust bursts out of the top and settles on her shirt.

She freezes. I freeze.

Then I smirk. "You know, white really suits you."

Her eyes narrow. "Don't."

I wipe my hands on the cloth. "Don't what?"

"Whatever you're thinking. Don't."

I grab the bag from her hands and tip it—just slightly. A tiny dusting of flour floats onto her arm.

Ivy giggles. "Two can play this game."

She lunges for the bag, but I twist away, laughing. "Oh no, you started this."

"I did not!" she shouts, but she's already grabbing a handful of flour from the counter and—before I can dodge—smacks it right onto my chest.

I stare down at the white imprint on my shirt. Then at her.

Her eyes widen slightly.

"Oh, you are in trouble," I warn with a chuckle.

She shrieks as I grab a handful and flick it at her, catching her hair. She retaliates immediately, and suddenly, there's flour in the air, on the counters, in my hair, on her face—

We're laughing too hard to care.

Somewhere between dodging a handful of flour and grabbing for the bag, my hand brushes against her waist, and for half a second, something shifts.

She freezes just slightly, her breath catching, her body warm beneath my touch.

And then she shoves an entire handful of flour straight into my face.

I cough, spluttering. "Right. That's it."

I grab her by the waist, lifting her clean off the floor as she howls with laughter, kicking her feet in protest.

"Theo, put me down! I'm too heavy!"

I tighten my hold, not letting her nonsense ruin the moment. "Absolute rubbish."

She squirms. "I mean it, I—"

"Ivy," I say firmly, adjusting my grip. "I could do this all day."

Her struggling slows, her hands resting against my shoulders, fingers curling slightly into my shirt. There's a moment—a beat—where her breathing evens out, and I realise just how close we are.

I lower her slowly, not because she's too heavy, but because something about this—her—makes me want to linger. Her body presses against mine for a second too long before her feet finally touch the floor.

She is not much shorter than my six-foot-three frame, but this close she still has to tilt her head back.

And then she looks at me.

Really looks at me.

The laughter fades, leaving something quieter, something heavier between us.

Her gaze drops to my mouth.

My fingers are still resting at her waist. I could move them. I should move them. But I don't.

She swallows, then—hesitantly, almost testing—lifts a hand and cups my cheek. Her thumb brushes against my skin, slow and warm, leaving behind a trail of something I can't quite name.

We lean in.

Just slightly.

Just enough for her breath to warm my lips.

Just enough for my heart to stutter in my chest.

And then—

DING.

The oven timer blares through the moment like a cold slap.

Ivy jumps, her hand dropping from my face as if she's been burnt. I force myself to take a step back, to put space where there should have been space all along.

She clears her throat, turning sharply towards the oven. "Right. Cake."

"Yeah," I say, raking a hand through my flour-dusted hair. "Cake."

Neither of us moves.

Neither of us looks at each other.

The timer beeps again.

And still, neither of us moves.

21

Victory to the Loser

Ivy

I STAND THERE FOR a moment, frozen, staring at the oven as the soft ping of the timer snaps me out of my thoughts. The cake.

I swallow, suddenly aware of how close Theo is, the air between us still thick with something unspoken. My hand trembles as I reach for the oven mitts, pulling them on, the fabric too tight around my fingers. I bend down, my heart hammering in my chest, and carefully open the oven door.

The warm air hits me first, followed by the familiar scent of baked goods—vanilla and nuts.

I grab the cake tin, my hands still shaky, and pull it out, setting it on the counter with a soft clink.

Theo stands next to me, watching. His gaze is intense, but he doesn't say anything. We both just stare at the cake, waiting for... something. A sign. Or maybe it's just that moment when things feel different, but neither of us wants to acknowledge it.

The cake looks good. Perfect, even. The golden top is slightly cracked, the edges crisp but not burnt. It doesn't look like a disaster. I've done it... we've done it.

But still, all I can focus on is the feeling of him standing there, too close, his presence wrapping around me like the flour dust still clinging to the air.

I take a step back, slowly, my hands pulling off the mitts. "Well," I say, my voice a little too high-pitched. "It's done."

Theo's gaze is still on the cake, but his jaw tightens just slightly. "It looks... great."

I try to clear my throat, awkwardly shifting from foot to foot. "I'll just—uh, let it cool."

Theo nods, then looks at me, his expression unreadable. "Yeah. Good idea."

I clear my throat again, trying to shake off the sudden tension hanging in the air. "Seriously, Theo, thanks. I couldn't have done it without you," I say, gesturing to the cake, but it feels a little too grand for what I'm really trying to express.

He gives a small, awkward shrug, a grin playing at the corners of his mouth. "You did most of it. I just added a little flour." He rubs the back of his neck, looking almost sheepish.

I laugh, the sound easier than I expected. "Well, I suppose that's the magic ingredient. Theo, if there's anything I can do to repay you," I say, my voice a little quieter now. "I owe you."

His eyes snap up to meet mine, and I catch the flash of surprise on his face. He stammers slightly. "Repay me?" He clears his throat, flushing just a touch. "Uh, well, actually..."

My curiosity piques, and I raise an eyebrow. "What's going on? You've got that *I-need-a-favour* look. Spill it, now is your chance!"

Theo shifts slightly, letting out a slow breath. "Well, it's kind of a big ask, actually," he says, running a hand through his hair. "Do you have any plans for Saturday?"

I pause for a moment, considering. "Nope. Nothing at all. Why?"

He hesitates before speaking again, clearly unsure how to phrase it. "Lucy's childminder's unavailable, and Jasper and Geoff are both tied up with work stuff. I can't really take time off either because of the trip to Dorset in a couple of weeks. I was wondering... would you be able to spend a few hours with Lucy on Saturday?"

I blink, surprised by the request but not put off. "Oh, you want me to babysit?"

Theo shifts uncomfortably, running a hand through his hair again. "Not exactly babysit. More like... hang out with her. She really likes you, and I know she'd have a good time. Plus, it'd take some of the pressure off me if I'm being honest."

Hanging out with Lucy sounds like a perfect way to spend Saturday. "I'd love to," I say, without a second thought. "I promised Lucy we'd make some of those clay gnomes together. Perfect opportunity."

Theo's face softens at the mention of the gnomes, a small smile tugging at the corners of his mouth. "She's been asking about that, actually. She says you're the best at making them."

I laugh lightly, the idea of making little clay creatures with Lucy sounds like a perfect Saturday afternoon. "Well, I've got a reputation to uphold now, haven't I?"

Theo grins, clearly relieved. "That would be amazing, Ivy. I'm sure she'll be over the moon."

"Yeah, no problem. Just text me what time, and I'll be there."

"Thanks. Seriously." Theo says, his voice softer now, his eyes holding something that feels like more than just genuine gratitude.

"No worries." I grin. "This is actually going to be fun."

I'm not sure if I'm doing him a favour or just giving myself an excuse to hang out with his lovely little human. Either way, it feels like the right thing to do.

It's Friday, and that means Macmillan time. I've made the rare pilgrimage into the office—lured in by the promise of cake and thinly veiled workplace competition. Christa spots me before I even make it to the lifts.

"Well, well," she calls out, "look what the hybrid policy dragged in."

I hold up my Tupperware. "I bring cake and mild social anxiety."

She grins. "Perfect. You'll fit right in."

By the time I get to the large meeting room, it's already packed with people pretending this is about charity and not passive-aggressively one-upping each other via sponge.

Caroline is in position, naturally. She's standing beside her Victoria sponge like it's about to be unveiled at the V&A, complete with handwritten labels and a cake stand that probably came with a certificate of authenticity.

She spots me and my slightly battered Tupperware.

"Oh!" she says, all faux surprise and weaponised kindness. "Looks like just one layer? That's so sweet. Minimalist."

I smile. "It's an Austrian cup cake."

She blinks. "Like... a cupcake?"

"No. A full-sized cake just made using a cup to measure everything. Very traditional. Very special. No showstopping layers, but it doesn't collapse under its own ego either."

Christa coughs behind me. Might be a laugh. Might be cake-induced choking. Hard to tell.

Caroline makes a little noise before smiling at me a bit too friendly. "Well, it's so lovely you brought something. That's the spirit."

Before I can reply she stalks off clapping to draw the attention of the room to where all the cakes are displayed.

The managing director drones on about team spirit and fundraising goals while everyone eyes the cake table like it's the buffet at a wedding they weren't technically invited to. Then the tasting begins. Forks clatter. Moans of appreciation fill the room.

I catch snippets of conversation and have to stifle a laugh because some people sound like they're auditioning to be the next judge on The Great British Bake Off.

Eventually, I try my own cake. It's not bad. Actually, it's good. Moist, subtly sweet, a bit nutty. Like something that wouldn't win a prize but would quietly sort out your whole day.

Christa nudges me. "Yours tastes like it's got a soul."

"Thanks. I was going for 'edible emotional support'."

Caroline wins, of course. She gasps like she's just been crowned Miss World and not given a paper certificate by Tony from HR. There's polite clapping, and someone says "Well deserved" in that vaguely threatening way people do when they want to be heard saying it.

I come second to last.

Just ahead of Colin, whose flapjacks were mostly hope and oats that never quite committed.

And somehow... I don't care.

Not even a little.

I look down at my slightly uneven Austrian cup cake, or what's left of it, and feel something I don't usually associate with public events involving judgement and Victoria sponge.

Pride.

Not smug, Instagrammable, influencer-style pride. Just... the quiet kind. The kind that settles in your chest and makes you smile when no one's looking.

It wasn't a showstopper. It didn't sparkle. But it tasted good. Actually good. Comforting and unfussy, with just the right amount of sweetness and a hint of chaos. Very me, really.

And we made it in my kitchen. Me and Theo. It had been a mess. A lovely one.

That cake wasn't just cake. It was laughter and a little flirtation and an unexpected moment where everything felt... right.

I box up the remaining slices carefully. One for me. A few for Lucy and Theo. And two slices of Caroline's, purely for scientific comparison.

I don't need a certificate. I've got something better: a cake I'd actually eat again and a day that didn't end in overthinking or embarrassment. Just crumbs and a pride in myself.

Progress, possibly. Or madness. Either way, I'll take it.

22
Peanut Butter Laundry Fraud

Ivy

THEO OPENS THE DOOR and greets me with a smile. "Hey, Ivy. Come in."

I step inside and follow him down the corridor. As we approach the living room, I notice Lucy sitting on a small chair in the hallway, facing the wall, her arms crossed tightly across her chest. She looks entirely unamused, her little body stiff with defiance.

I lean closer to Theo and whisper, "What's she doing?"

Before he can reply, Lucy's voice rings out, sharp and stubborn. "Daddy's unfair!"

Theo sighs, sounding a mix of exasperation and fondness. "Lucy," he gently warns her.

She doesn't respond, just continues to glare at the wall in protest.

Theo looks back at me. "She got a bit too excited about hanging out with you. When I asked her to tidy away her crayons, she told me to do it myself, so I gave her a five-minute timeout."

I glance back at Lucy, who's still frozen in her little timeout stance. "And how long has she been like this?"

Theo winces. "Two minutes left."

Lucy stays where she is, her back to us, and I hear a small sniffle escape her. It's barely audible, but it's enough to make my heart crack a little. I want to scoop her up and hug her but I don't think Theo will thank me if I'll do that.

He glances down at her, then sighs softly, leading me away from the hallway toward the living room. "Sometimes," he says quietly, "I feel like I'm not sure what I'm doing as a dad."

I look over at him as I place my tote bags with cake and clay for the gnomes on the counter. I'm surprised by the vulnerability in his voice. He's usually so confident when it comes to Lucy, but I can see that this moment has shaken him. I give him a reassuring smile. "Theo, you're doing fine. She's just testing boundaries, like all kids do. You're a great dad."

He gives a small, almost reluctant nod but doesn't quite meet my eyes. "I don't know. Sometimes I think I'm too forgiving with her because she doesn't have a mum. Maybe I'm not strict enough with her."

I give his upper arm a gentle, reassuring stroke. "Nonsense, she is a great kid. Every child plays up every so often. I was a wild child when I was little."

I wonder if he's questioning more than just his role as a dad, but I don't push. Not now.

The quiet stretches, until finally, the silence is broken by a soft, unmistakable sound—a very clear ping from the oven timer.

Theo clears his throat softly, calling out to Lucy, "Alright, time's up, Lucy. If you're ready to apologise, you can come in."

There's a pause, then a small shuffle from the hallway. Lucy slowly steps into the living room, her head down, looking slightly embarrassed. She's tugging at her sleeves, a sign of her discomfort.

She whispers, barely audible, "I'm sorry, Daddy."

Theo doesn't hesitate. He kneels down to her level, his expression softening. Lucy immediately launches herself into his arms, and he holds her tight. For a moment, they just stay there, wrapped up in each other, a quiet comfort between them.

Theo pulls back slightly and says gently, "Okay, Ladybug, now can you tidy your crayons away like I asked?"

Lucy sniffles, her face still flushed, and with a small, embarrassed sigh, she nods. "Okay, Daddy. Love you."

"Love you too, Lu."

I study Theo for a moment as he watches Lucy, and a quiet pride settles on his face. It's not a big showy thing, but it's there—the satisfaction of knowing he's doing something right.

I grin and nudge him gently, my voice playful. "See? First-class dad right here."

"Thanks," he murmurs, his gaze soft. He's grateful, though he doesn't say it directly. And somehow, that makes it mean more.

I wait until Lucy's crayons are safely back in their little plastic tub—with some creative interpretation of "tidy"—before clearing my throat with exaggerated ceremony.

"Right," I announce, picking up the cake tin I smuggled in like contraband, "I come bearing baked goods and a serious question."

Theo raises an eyebrow. Lucy perks up immediately, her time-out gloom already starting to lift.

I flip the lid off with a flourish.

"Behold! Exhibit A: the Austrian cup cake made by yours truly, with only minor flour-based disasters. Exhibit B..." I pull out a second container with theatrical reluctance "...is Caroline's Victoria sponge. Office legend. Looks like it was made by angels with access to precision tools."

Theo smirks. "You stole Caroline's cake?"

"I rescued it," I say. "For research purposes."

Lucy bounces over like a tiny judge at a dessert tribunal. "Are we allowed to eat both?"

"Absolutely. But you must be *brutally honest*. This is a highly scientific taste test."

She gives a solemn nod and clambers up onto the sofa like she's taking her place on the judging panel of *Junior Bake Off: Petty Edition*. I hand her small slices of each, then pass a plate to Theo, who takes it with a slightly amused shake of his head.

Lucy tries Caroline's first, giving her best Paul Hollywood impression. "It's nice," she says, "but it's kind of... fluffy. Not exciting."

"Noted," I say, scribbling nothing down on an imaginary clipboard.

She tastes mine next. Her eyes widen slightly. "Yours is... like pudding and cake had a baby."

"That's exactly the vibe I was going for."

Theo takes a bite of mine, then glances sideways at me. "Yours actually tastes like something. Caroline's is... polite."

I beam. "So, what I'm hearing is, I've won the informal, slightly biased home judging round."

Lucy frowns as she shovels another bite into her mouth, then points her fork at me. "It's not fair you didn't win. Yours is pure goodness."

"Pure goodness?" I giggle.

She nods with conviction. "It tastes like hugs and happy things and maybe a bit of magic." Then, without another word, she hops off the sofa and bolts out of the room at full speed, her socks skidding slightly on the floorboards.

Theo and I exchange a look.

"Should I be worried?" I ask.

He chuckles. "Always."

A few seconds later, she returns, triumphant, holding a slightly bent cardboard medal strung on what looks suspiciously like a shoelace. It's covered in flower stickers, glitter glue, and the vague whiff of Pritt Stick.

She hands it to me with both hands, like it's the crown jewels.

"You can have this one. I made it for Uncle Jasper but I can make him another one," she says, absolutely serious. "This is yours now. It's a special prize. For best cake that didn't win."

I stare at the little cardboard medal. My throat tightens in that stupid, unexpected way, like there's something stuck that's not cake.

"Oh, Lu," I say, my voice catching a bit too early. I blink quickly, looking up at the ceiling like it might help keep the tears from tipping over.

She watches me, slightly puzzled. "Don't you like it?"

"Are you joking?" I manage, voice wobbly. "I love it."

I reach out and pull her into a hug, holding her tightly, because she just made my day. This little munchkin has a way to get into your heart that just catches you off guard every time. She must have that talent from her dad.

Lucy hugs me back just as fiercely. "You're the best baker, Ivy."

"Well, I wouldn't go that far and your daddy helped me," I mumble into her hair, trying not to sniffle like I've just watched a puppy reunion video. "But I'll take it."

Theo says nothing, but when our eyes meet, my stomach does a flip.

He smiles, soft and crooked. "Told you. You've got fans."

I nod, still holding Lucy and trying to discreetly dab my eye on my sleeve. "Yeah. Think I might just frame this."

And honestly? I mean it.

A little later, after Theo's left for work with a quick kiss to Lucy's head and a lopsided smile in my direction, Lu and I settle at the kitchen table for a highly important morning activity: clay gnomes.

We've covered the surface in newspaper, rolled out a slab of air-dry clay, and are now wrapping it round one of the wonky Styrofoam cones like we're dressing a tiny, lumpy wizard. I'm showing Lucy how to smooth the edges with a bit of water when she speaks—completely casual, like she's commenting on the weather.

"Yasmin from yoga doesn't have a daddy," she says, pressing her little fingers into the base of her gnome. "So I told her she can share mine."

I pause, fingers halfway through smoothing a seam, but I don't look up just yet. "That's very kind of you," I say gently, keeping my tone light.

Lucy nods, still focused. "She said she didn't know you could do that. But I said, 'It's fine. I know what it's like not to have a mummy.' So, it's fair."

I look at her then. Her expression is calm, matter-of-fact, like she's just explained the rules of a very reasonable swap system. Her hands are covered in grey clay and glitter from the craft box. There's a streak of it on her cheek too.

I feel something lodge itself in my chest—tight and warm and achingly soft.

"That's a lovely thing to do," I say, my voice quieter now. "You've got a big heart, you know."

She shrugs, then leans over to inspect my gnome. "Yours has a wonky hat," she informs me.

I grin, blinking away the sting behind my eyes. "He's whimsical. It's his thing."

She giggles and goes back to working on her own. I sit there for a moment longer, looking at her little hands, the way she frowns in concentration, and I wonder how someone so small can carry so much understanding.

Then she glances up, grinning. "Can we give them beards?"

"Obviously," I say. "No gnome is complete without a dramatic beard."

We start rolling out little sausage-shaped pieces of clay, and I'm halfway through sticking a particularly curly one onto my gnome's chin when Lucy says, casually, "Sometimes I wish I had a mum."

The air shifts, just slightly. Like the room's holding its breath.

I keep my fingers busy with the clay, not wanting to make a big deal of it, not wanting her to feel examined.

"Oh, sweetheart," I say, gently. "That makes sense. But you've got your dad, and he's... well, he's brilliant."

She nods instantly. "He is. He always hugs me. Even when I've been really, really naughty."

I smile at that. "Sounds like the best kind of dad."

She smooths down the clay on her gnome's face. "If I had a mum," she says, voice softer now, "I'd want her to do stuff with me. Not just say nice things. Like... make gnomes. Or help with the glitter. Or eat cereal for dinner sometimes."

I laugh, but it catches slightly. My heart feels too big for my chest all of a sudden. Like I might spill over if I move the wrong way.

I half expect her to look up at me, to ask something—something big and terrifying and far too lovely to be safe—but she doesn't.

She just shrugs and starts shaping a hat for her gnome, like she's planted a little thought in the middle of the table and that's enough.

I breathe slowly and say, as lightly as I can manage, "Well, just so you know, as your friend—and fellow gnome enthusiast—if you ever want to talk about something and you don't want to tell your dad straight away... I'm here."

She looks up at me and grins. "Okay." Then she leans in, conspiratorially. "But you *have* to promise not to tell him about the peanut butter and the trousers."

"What peanut butter and which trousers?"

She grabs my hand. "Come and see," she says, tugging me down the hallway.

In her bedroom, she drops to her knees and wriggles under the bed like she's done this before. She pulls something out with both hands—a scrunched-up pair of purple boxer shorts. And they're... well, they're definitely not clean. There's a smear of peanut butter across the front like a very unfortunate accident.

I look at her. She looks at me. It's not clear who's more horrified.

"I was trying to get a little bit of peanut butter with a spoon," she says, very fast. "Just a little bit! But I dropped it on the floor and I didn't want Daddy to see."

"Right," I say, slowly. "Understandable."

"So I grabbed some trousers from the basket and cleaned it up, really quick. Then I heard Daddy coming, so I hid them."

"Under your bed?"

She nods. "Good hiding, yeah?"

I press my hand to my mouth to stop myself laughing. "Very... creative."

She shifts from foot to foot. "I didn't mean to be naughty."

"I know, Lu," I say gently. "Let's sort it, yeah?"

We sneak off to the washing machine like we're on some top-secret mission. I help her throw the peanut butter boxers in with a couple of jumpers and a tea towel, just to make it look respectable. She pours in enough detergent to clean all the linen at Buckingham Place but I don't stop her.

"We'll just tell Daddy we did some washing to help," she says brightly.

"Exactly," I nod. "We're very helpful."

She presses the start button like she's launching a spaceship. The machine starts whirring. She beams up at me, proud as anything.

I smile back, because honestly? I've just become an accomplice to peanut butter laundry fraud. And weirdly, I don't mind one bit.

23

Crazy Frog Secrets

Theo

THE CAR HUMS STEADILY along the motorway, the landscape blurring in shades of green and brown as we head towards Dorset. The "Crazy Frog" song blares through the speakers, and I glance over at Ivy, who's laughing along with Lucy, their voices bouncing off the car's interior. Lucy's giggling so hard that she almost forgets the lyrics, but it doesn't matter—she's having the time of her life, and Ivy's right there with her, her voice rising in perfect harmony with the ridiculousness of it all.

I can't help but chuckle, shaking my head at the two of them. I never thought I'd see the day when "Crazy Frog" became an anthem for road trips, but here we are.

Lucy, in the backseat, sings the high-pitched 'ring-ring' part like she's auditioning for a role in some cartoon. It's hilarious, it's chaotic, and it's completely perfect. Ivy's laughter fills the space beside me.

"You've got the moves down," I tease, glancing at Ivy, who's playfully bobbing her head to the beat.

"Oh, you have no idea," she grins. "I'm practically a backup dancer."

"You're definitely a crazy frog," I quip back, making her laugh harder.

But then Lucy suddenly pipes up, her voice a little too serious for the song. "I need the toilet."

I wince, glancing at the rearview mirror to meet her wide, pleading eyes. "You think you can hold it, Ladybug?" I ask, hoping she's not on the verge of bursting.

"I don't know," she whines.

"Alright," I say, trying to stifle a smile. "Well, we'll pull over at the next motorway services. You think you can wait that long?"

"I'll wait!" Lucy says, her tone a bit too sure of herself, but I nod, trusting her.

Ivy turns around to face Lucy, "We can use that stop for lunch too. What do you want to eat, Lu?"

Lucy's eyes brighten, the topic change immediately grabbing her attention. "Chicken nuggets! With chips! And ketchup! And a juice!"

I smile at her enthusiasm, glancing over at Ivy. "Looks like we've got our lunch sorted."

Ivy grins. "Fast food it is."

We pull into the services, the car slowing to a stop. Before I've even switched off the engine, I hear Lucy's voice from the backseat, practically panicked.

"Ivy! Ivy! I need the loo! Now!"

THE DATING BAN

I glance in the rearview mirror to see her squirming as she unbuckles herself, eyes wide with urgency.

Ivy, already reaching for the door, says "I'll take her," before I can even respond.

The minute Ivy opens the door for her, Lu sprints off.

"Slow down!" Ivy calls after her, half-laughing, half-stressed as she hurries to catch up.

I chuckle under my breath as I step through the sliding doors of the motorway services, scanning for the golden arches. Inside, it's a wall of noise and movement—buggies, groups of people, someone's child mid-tantrum over apple slices. By the time I've wrestled my way through the queue and emerged with a tray balanced on my arm, fifteen minutes have vanished.

Outside, the sun's glaring off the tarmac, and I spot them easily. Lucy's on the swing, legs pumping like she's aiming for orbit, while Ivy sits on the bench nearby, half-watching, half-wincing every time Lucy goes particularly high.

"Lunch is served," I announce.

Lucy flings herself off the swing and barrels into me, arms outstretched. "Thanks, Daddy!" She grabs her Happy Meal like it contains a buried treasure and immediately starts rustling through it for chips.

I hand Ivy her burger. She gives me a look that's half smile, half relief.

"Perfect timing," she says, picking up a chip before even sitting down.

"I figured you'd be starving after chasing her around," I reply, nodding towards Lucy, now sitting cross-legged on the bench, already three nuggets in.

"Chasing might be generous," Ivy says, sinking into the bench with a sigh. "I mostly just issued warnings from a safe distance."

We eat in companionable quiet, the kind that doesn't need filling. Lucy finishes first, naturally, and hops up, crumbs on her chin, eyes bright.

"Daddy, can I go back on the swings?"

I glance at Ivy, still mid-burger. "Go on then. I'll push you. Ivy's earned a minute of peace."

Lucy grins and darts ahead. I follow her over, give the swing a gentle push. She kicks her legs and lets out that high, clear squeal that only kids can manage—full of delight, free of self-consciousness.

"Faster, Daddy!" she shouts between giggles.

I can't help but smile. It's infectious.

A few minutes later, when she's soaring high and entirely in her own world, I stroll back to the bench and drop down beside Ivy, stretching my legs with a quiet grunt.

"You feeling ready for the big camping adventure?" I ask, casting her a sideways glance.

She lets out a soft laugh. "As ready as I'll ever be. I've packed everything, I think. Unless I've forgotten something really crucial. Like matches. Or my sanity."

"I thought you had it all under control," I tease, nudging her gently.

"I *thought* I did," she says, rolling her eyes. "But now I'm wondering if I should've packed more chocolate. You know, emergency rations."

"You'll be fine," I say, chuckling. "You're more prepared than you think." And even if she isn't, I'll be close enough to help. No need to say that out loud—not yet.

She glances at me, and her smile softens. "Thanks for letting me come with you two. Makes it feel a bit less... like I'm doing it on my own."

"You're not," I say quietly. I hadn't planned to say it, but the words come out anyway—firm, certain. And maybe a little more than I meant to reveal.

We sit with that for a moment.

Then I clear my throat, nodding towards the building. "We should hit the loos before we get back on the road."

"Good shout," she says, standing with a stretch.

It takes a minute to pry Lucy away from the swings, but eventually she lets me scoop her into my arms, resting her head on my shoulder as we head toward the parent-and-baby toilets.

Just before we reach the door, she leans in and whispers, "Daddy, I wanna get a surprise for Ivy. For the camping. To help her."

I glance at her, surprised, then smile. "That's very sweet, Lu. Alright—we'll find something good."

She nods solemnly. "But shh! It's a secret. Don't tell her!"

"Cross my heart," I whisper back.

Inside, she chatters away, brainstorming gift ideas with the enthusiasm of someone planning a heist. When we come out, Ivy's waiting just outside the toilet block, her arms folded, amusement written all over her face.

"What are you two up to?" she asks, cocking an eyebrow.

"Can't say," I reply smoothly. "Classified."

Lucy beams. "It's a secret!"

Ivy laughs softly. "Oh, I see. One of *those* secrets."

She and Lucy share a look—one of those little wordless exchanges they've started having—and something tightens in my chest. Not in a bad way. Just… in a way.

I should probably be worried. But I'm not.

Not even a bit.

24

Somewhere in Dorset

Ivy

THEO PULLS THE CAR to a stop at the edge of a wide, open field, right next to what can only be described as a large shed with a weathered sign shouting CAMP-SIDE in big, bold letters. The shed's surrounded by a wide wooden patio with a roof and a few picnic benches scattered about, presumably so campers can enjoy their baked beans in comfort, come rain or shine.

"Are you sure you're going to be alright here?" Theo asks, giving the so-called campsite a thorough once-over. His raised eyebrows are doing a lot of heavy lifting.

To be honest, I'm not entirely sure what I expected from a campsite, but it wasn't... this. I thought there'd be more, I don't know, basic conveniences? Maybe something that felt less like the start of a survival documentary. But then again, roughing it was the plan, wasn't it? Back to nature. Proper camping. No glamping nonsense.

"It looks... lovely," I say with a cheery smile that's all teeth and no sincerity.

"Are you sleeping with the sheep?" Lucy pipes up from the back seat. She's wriggled free of her car seat and is now perched between the front seats, pointing at a group of sheep grazing peacefully near the edge of the field.

"I hope not," I mutter under my breath, the cracks in my resolve starting to show. Don't get me wrong, the location is stunning. Rolling green hills stretch out in every direction, the Dorset countryside looking like something off a postcard. But it's also painfully clear how far away the nearest civilisation is. The tiny houses dotted across the landscape look charming... and utterly unreachable.

"Want me to help you with the tent?" Theo offers, though the crease in his forehead suggests he is worried about more than just my shelter.

"No, that's fine. I've got this," I lie with the confidence of someone who absolutely hasn't got this. "Don't you need to get to your cottage?" I throw in an extra-wide smile for reassurance.

"Okay... if you're sure," he says, not sounding convinced.

"Absolutely," I reply with a chirp, turning to Lucy. "Right, Squirt, have a fab time with your dad." I give her button nose a playful squeeze, earning a delighted giggle.

Theo's mid-unloading my backpack and tent from the boot when a stocky man emerges from the shed, waving.

"You alright there, folks?" he calls out in a thick Irish accent.

"I've got a pitch booking for a week," I reply, shielding my eyes from the sun.

"Grand," he nods, stroking his ginger beard like it's his pet cat. "Ivy Gillman, yeah?" He gives Theo a quick once-over and glances at the car.

"That's right," I confirm.

"I'm Mick. Welcome to Creggy Hill Campside. Your pitch is over there by the trees, but honestly, no one else is booked tonight, so take your pick. We are not that well known yet. Showers are over there," he points to the small shack nearby, "and the toilet's the same way. If you need anything after I leave, just use the phone by the door there." He gestures to an ancient-looking handset hanging outside the shed.

Theo frowns at this. "Is that it?"

"Aye," Mick replies with a shrug. "Most guests we've had so far came in campervans. Don't get many with just a tent." His eyes drop to my rolled-up shelter, which suddenly looks about as durable as a plastic carrier bag.

"I'll be fine. I've got a cooker," I say, clinging to my one bit of semi-reliable kit. Thank fuck for that sales assistant who convinced me to buy the gas cooker. Let's just hope I can figure out how to use it.

Theo doesn't look convinced. "Ivy, are you sure—"

"Absolutely, I've got it all under control," I interrupt, letting out an awkward laugh. I steer him towards the car before I lose my nerve. If he lingers much longer, I'll end up begging him to take me with him.

Mick grins at me, clearly amused. "Love, let me give you a hand with your bags." He grabs the tent and my backpack, carrying them towards the trees.

"Right," Theo says hesitantly.

I give him a reassuring pat on the chest, careful not to meet his eyes in case he spots the wobble in mine. "This is exactly what I need. You and Lucy go have a great time, and I'll see you in a week when you pick me up."

Theo studies me, then pulls out his phone. "There's no reception here, Ivy. What are you going to do if something happens?"

I wave dismissively towards the phone by the shed. "I'll use that. Stop worrying, Theo."

"Promise me you'll call if you need anything?" His voice is gentle now, almost pleading.

"Stop worrying," I say again, more firmly this time, and wink before scooping up the sleeping mat. I twirl dramatically, waving at Lucy. "Have a fabulous time, you two!"

Lucy waves back, beaming. Theo just shoves his hands into his pockets, his expression like I'm marching off to war.

I can't let him rattle me. I'm not the first woman to go camping alone. Look at that woman who walked that massive mountain trail in America—what's-her-name? If she can do that, I can handle a week in Dorset.

"Need help with the tent, love?" Mick calls as Theo reverses the car onto the road.

"Nah, I'm good," I reply with a grin I hope looks confident. "I practiced."

"Fair play to ya'," he chuckles, heading back towards the shed.

I take a deep breath, looking out at the rolling hills and feeling the sun on my face. The breeze is cool, carrying the fresh smell of grass and sheep.

"Let's do this," I mutter, hoping I believe it.

"What the fuck!" I hiss through gritted teeth. This is officially getting ridiculous. Back in my flat, it took me fifteen minutes to put this bloody tent up. Fifteen minutes. What I hadn't accounted for, however, was the sheer force of nature out here in the wild. Namely, the wind, which has turned my tent into a flailing sail and me into an unwilling circus act.

First, the wind decided to snatch my tent bag and send it cartwheeling across the field, so I had to sprint after it like an idiot. Then, while I was wrestling with one end of the tent, the other end flapped up and smacked me in the face. I tried pinning it down with my backpack, only to realise I'd left the pegs in my backpack. Somewhere in all this chaos, a vicious wasp—bee? Whatever it was, it had wings and a vendetta—buzzed right into my personal space, nearly flying into my ear. I shrieked, flailed, and ran around the field like a maniac, arms flapping like I was signalling for rescue.

By the time I calmed down, Mick had thankfully buggered off back to his farm, leaving the sheep as my only witnesses. They've shuffled further away, probably deciding I'm too much of a liability to be anywhere near them.

Finally, after what feels like a lifetime, I manage to click the second pole into place and pull the frame up, coaxing it into something resembling a tent. I tie the sides to the poles and voila, my new home is standing proud in the Dorset countryside.

"Aha!" I cheer triumphantly. It's a two-man tent, but with my massive arse and my overpacked backpack, I need every square inch of space.

"Oh shit." A strong breeze catches the tent, lifting it off the ground. I lunge to press it back down without destroying what I built. I should have done the pegs first! The tent flaps angrily in the wind, mocking me, and I swear I hear the sheep chuckling from a distance.

Desperately, I hold it in place with one hand while unzipping the entrance with the other. Another gust nearly takes me with it, and I swear under my breath. Autumn's definitely on its way, and this wind is its sassy little herald.

Still holding the tent down, I stretch towards my backpack, which is agonisingly just out of reach. I can't let go of the tent or it'll end up in the next field, but I need the bloody bag to weigh it down while I pitch the pegs. "Come on," I mutter, stretching so hard my muscles start to cramp. The strap is right there, so close, just an inch from my fingertips.

And then, because I am a genius, I lose my balance. With a yelp, I topple over, dragging the tent with me. Brilliant. Just brilliant. For a second, I just lie there, staring up at the inside of the tent and letting my idiocy wash over me. Why didn't I just carry the tent over to the bag? It's not pitched yet! I'm such a numpty.

I can't help it, I start laughing. Proper, uncontrollable, belly-aching laughter. I'm sprawled on the ground, holding up the tent like I want to juggle with it, and it's all so ridiculous I can't stop. The sheep look on in judgmental silence as I crawl out from under the mess, still giggling.

Scrambling to my feet, I grab the tent and my backpack and lug them back to the flat patch of ground I'd chosen earlier. This time, I shove the backpack into the tent's entrance with a triumphant grunt and zip it up tight. There. The tent is finally weighted down, and I can take my time putting the pegs in without the wind staging another coup.

I straighten up, wipe the dirt off my jeans, and glare at the tent like it's a naughty child. "Right," I say to no one but the sheep. "Let's finish this."

25

Hopalong and the Queen

Theo

I'VE BEEN LOOKING FORWARD to this week away from work, but now, instead of enjoying a few days of just me and Lucy, I'm worrying about Ivy.

My eyes drift to the kitchen window as I unpack the food into the fridge. Dark clouds are gathering in the distance.

She'll be fine. The trouble with Ivy is that she never says when she's not fine. I know she was putting on a brave face when I dropped her off at the campsite but I could see the doubt in her eyes. As much as she protests, she's not exactly the outdoorsy type. She grew up in London, and I've no doubt she can handle whatever the city throws at her, but alone in a little tent? That's different.

"Daddy, I found a new friend!"

Lucy's voice pipes up behind me. I turn to see her standing in the doorway, her small hand stretched out, palm flat. A tiny, unsteady moth clings to her skin.

"I think it's ill," she frowns.

I don't need to be an expert to see that one of its wings is broken.

"Ladybug, I think its wing is hurt." I kneel beside her, watching the little creature hobble about on her hand.

"Oh. I'll call him Hopalong," she grins, and I don't have the heart to tell her that Hopalong won't be hopping for long.

"That's a lovely name. Maybe take him outside and put him next to the roses in the flower box," I suggest gently.

"Okay," she says and skips off.

Through the window, I watch as she carefully places the moth on the soil, her lips moving in quiet conversation. I can't hear what she's saying, but knowing Lucy, she's probably reassuring him that everything will be alright.

I love how peaceful it is out here, just farmland and open space. No roads, no traffic, no other people. The only way in is a long gravel path leading from the farm that manages the cottage.

Up here, Lucy can play outside without me having to worry. There's nothing around that could harm her.

"Madam Lucy, how about some afternoon tea?" I say in my best posh voice as I step onto the patio.

"Yes!" she shouts, then quickly adds, "please," when I raise an eyebrow.

"Good manners," I nod approvingly. "Strawberry or raspberry tea?"

Lucy loves a proper afternoon tea, so I made sure to bring some cakes from the shop, and I'll put together a few sandwiches in a minute.

"Strawberry, please!" she squeals, running up the steps after me.

She climbs onto the bar stool by the kitchen island.

"Is Ivy coming over for tea?" she asks, snatching a piece of ham from the open packed I was just about to use for our sandwiches.

"No, Ladybug, she'll be having dinner in her tent, remember?"

"Oh." Lucy looks disappointed, then brightens. "Can we save her some cake? This one has strawberries. Ivy likes strawberries. Maybe she'll visit us."

I look from the tiny cream cake with a few strawberries perched on it to Lucy and back at the cake. *How could I say no to that?* Under Lu's watchful eyes, I place the little round cake into a plastic pot and store it in the fridge. Lucy beams at me before tucking into her own cake, humming happily between bites.

I take a sip of my tea, putting on my most serious voice. "Ah yes, a fine vintage. The delicate notes of... strawberry and... very serious sweetness."

Lucy giggles. "Mine tastes like yummy!"

"Ah, the finest flavour," I nod. "And what do you think of the cake, madam?"

She takes an exaggerated bite, chewing thoughtfully. "Hmm... it's good. But it needs more..." She taps her chin like she's thinking very hard. "More cream. And more strawberries. And more cake."

I gasp. "More cake? But then we'd have too much cake!"

Lucy shakes her head, looking at me like I'm completely ridiculous. "Daddy, there's no such thing as too much cake."

I sit back, pretending to be shocked. "No such thing? My whole life has been a lie!"

She bursts into giggles, nearly spilling her tea. Wiping her chin with the back of her hand, she sits up straighter and sticks out her pinky, grinning.

"Look, Daddy! Fancy!"

I nod solemnly. "Very fancy. You, madam, are the fanciest lady in all the land."

She beams. "I am Queen Lucy of Cake Land."

"Well then, Queen Lucy," I bow my head. "Would Your Majesty like a ham and cheese sandwich and maybe another cup of tea?"

"Yes, please!" She slides her cup over to me. "And make it extra fun."

"Ah, extra fun tea, coming right up." I drop the tea bag with some added drama into the mug and then pour water over it with an exaggerated flourish, making her giggle again.

As I pass Lucy her tea, a low rumble rolls through the sky. Distant but heavy, the kind that lingers in the air.

I glance towards the window. The dark clouds that had been gathering earlier have thickened, swallowing what's left of the blue sky. The wind stirs the trees at the edge of the field, their branches swaying. It's coming in fast.

Lucy doesn't notice at first. She's too busy dunking a biscuit into her tea, watching as it soaks up the liquid before quickly popping it into her mouth. But when another rumble follows, louder this time, she pauses.

I try to ignore the uneasy feeling creeping up my spine.

I picture her out there, alone in that tiny tent that didn't look like the sturdiest model on the market. I quite like thunderstorms but not when I am camping in a field and I doubt Ivy will enjoy it much. I just wish there was reception at the camping ground so I could check in with her.

The wind suddenly picks up, whistling around the cottage. The door to the patio rattles in its frame, making Lucy jump.

I stand up, crossing the room to shut it properly. As I slide it closed, a flash of lightning flickers in the distance, illuminating the storm clouds for a split second before plunging everything back into grey. The air feels thick, charged.

Lucy has gone quiet.

"Daddy?" Her voice is small. "Is it gonna be a big storm?"

I turn back to her, forcing an easy smile. "Might be, Lu. But we're all cosy in here, aren't we?"

She nods, but her fingers tighten around her tea cup. Another clap of thunder rumbles through the sky, and she flinches.

Time for a distraction.

"You know," I say, settling back into my seat, "when I was little, I used to think thunder was just the clouds playing a big game of bowling."

Lucy blinks at me. "Bowling?"

"Yep. Every time you hear thunder, that's a cloud getting a strike."

She looks out the window, considering this. Another deep, rolling boom shakes the air.

"Oh," she says, eyes wide. "That was a big one. Do you think the clouds are really good at bowling?"

"Definitely. I reckon that one just won the championship."

She giggles, some of the tension in her shoulders easing. I drum my fingers on the table like a little drumroll. "And now, let's see if they can do it again…"

We sit for a moment, listening. The wind howls, the trees rustle, and then—another crack of thunder, closer this time.

Lucy gasps. "They did it!"

I grin. "Told you. Best bowlers in the sky."

She still glances at the window, but at least now there's a hint of excitement behind her nerves. I place some of the small ham sandwiches I made on her plate, keeping my voice light.

"Shall we have a competition? You guess how many more strikes they'll get before bedtime."

She nods eagerly. "Five!"

"Five? That's a bold bet, Your Majesty," I tease, tapping my chin. "I say three."

Lucy picks up a sandwich, but before taking a bite, she looks up at me with wide, serious eyes.

"Daddy... does Ivy have an umbrella?"

I pause, caught off guard by the question. "An umbrella?"

She nods, glancing out at the rain that's now pattering against the windows. The storm is rolling in quickly, the sky darkening even more.

I smile, keeping my voice steady. "She's got her tent to keep her dry, sweetheart. And I'm sure she packed her wellies and her rain jacket. She'll be nice and snug."

Lucy still looks doubtful. "But what if the rain gets in the tent?"

I lean forward, lowering my voice like I'm telling her a big secret. "Did you know tents are like giant raincoats for camping? They're made to keep the rain out. And Ivy's a very clever woman—if a little bit stubborn. She'll have made sure everything is safe and dry."

Lucy considers this, her little nose scrunching as she thinks it over. "Hmm. Okay," she says at last. But she still doesn't look entirely convinced.

Another roll of thunder shakes the sky, and she quickly shoves the rest of her sandwich into her mouth, as if the act of chewing might help her feel braver. I reach for my own sandwich and take an exaggerated bite, making a big deal out of chewing thoughtfully.

"Mmm," I say, smacking my lips. "This might just be the finest ham and cheese sandwich in all the land. Fit for a queen, even."

Lucy swallows and grins, playing along. "That's because Queen Lucy only eats the best food."

"Of course," I nod seriously. "How silly of me to forget."

She giggles, and just like that, the worry in her eyes fades—at least for now.

I glance at the window again, watching the wind whip across the fields. The storm is well and truly here now. The flashes of lightning are getting closer, the thunder rolling louder. And somewhere out there, Ivy is sitting in her little tent, braving it alone.

I really hope she's dry.

26

Emergency Jammie Dodgers

Ivy

"Well, would you look at that," I say to absolutely no one as I sit cross-legged inside my newly assembled tent. "A structurally sound, waterproof, sheep-proof—probably—tent, put up entirely by yours truly. Who says city girls can't survive in the wild?"

I clap my hands together, victorious. It only took me, what, an hour? Two? A minor wrestling match with a pole that refused to slot into place? But here I am. Tent up, dignity mostly intact, and no major injuries apart from that one incident where I tripped over.

I glance at the little camping cooker in front of me. Right. Time for the next challenge.

I pick up the instructions, squinting at them.

Step one: attach the gas canister. I look at the canister. Then at the cooker. Then back at the canister. "Okay, that seems easy enough."

I twist it one way. Nothing.

I twist it the other way. Nothing.

I push. I pull. I wiggle it aggressively.

It does not attach.

"Right, cool. Love this for me," I mutter, shaking it like that might magically fix the problem. "Really thriving out here."

I set it down, taking a deep breath. It's fine. I have time. The storm clouds rolling in aren't a concern. Nope. Not at all. Just a bit of drizzle on the way, a light sprinkling of nature. I'm an outdoorswoman now. I can handle a little rain.

Thunder rumbles in the distance.

I freeze. "That was far away. Definitely far away. No need to panic."

To prove my own point, I casually lean out of the tent and check the pegs holding everything in place. The inner and outer layers seem fine—nice and sturdy, no obvious disasters waiting to happen.

I sit back inside, feeling smug. Maybe I should start a survival blog. "How to Conquer the Outdoors: A Beginner's Guide to Being an Absolute Legend." I'd have tips like:

1. Do not trip over your own tent.

2. Do not kick your mallet into the bushes and spend twenty minutes looking for it.

3. Do not spend an alarming amount of time talking to yourself like a lunatic.

Another deep rumble shakes the air. I glance outside. The sky is getting darker by the second, thick clouds swallowing up the last bit of daylight. The wind tugs at the sides of the tent, making the fabric ripple.

I frown. "Did it say how much wind these things can handle?" I flip through the instruction booklet but, annoyingly, there's no section titled "How Not to End Up in Oz When Camping in a Gale."

One of the strings hanging from the outer tent, the ones I didn't bother doing anything with, flaps against the tent fabric in the wind. Hmm. With me in the tent, there is no way the tent will fly away so I'm sure it's fine I didn't peg the guy ropes.

Another gust of wind flaps the fabric violently.

"...Nah, it's fine."

I shove the thought away and return to the gas cooker, determined. "Right, listen here, you stubborn little—" I grip the canister with both hands and twist as hard as I can.

Click.

I freeze. "Oh." I poke it gingerly. It's actually attached.

I straighten my back, victorious once more. "Ladies and gentlemen, we have fire."

I turn the knob, and with a satisfying whoosh, a little blue flame appears.

Immediately, I realise two things.

One: the inside of my tent is, in fact, a tent—a small, enclosed, very flammable space. Two: outside is not an option, because the wind is currently auditioning for a role in Twister.

I stare at the flame. The flame stares back.

"Nope."

I twist the knob, snuffing out the flame before I manage to set myself—or my tent—on fire. Not today, death. Not today.

Leaning back, I assess my supplies. Right. What gourmet meal am I working with tonight?

Item one: A bottle of water. Useful, yes. Delicious? Not exactly.

Item two: Instant noodles, instant soup, and instant porridge—all requiring hot water that I do not have. Excellent.

Item three: One slightly bruised apple. Not exactly filling, but hey, it's got vitamins.

Item four: The pack of Jammie Dodgers, courtesy of Lucy, who had solemnly pressed them into my hands at the motor services, telling me, "These are emergency biscuits, Ivy. In case you get hungry or sad."

I pick up the biscuit packet, staring at it.

Well, Lucy, my love, I am both.

With a sigh, I tear it open and pull out a biscuit, biting into it as the wind howls outside. The tent flaps violently, and I flinch.

"Could you not?" I say to the weather, as if that might make a difference.

Thunder cracks overhead, loud enough to make my heart jump. The fabric of the tent shudders under the force of the wind, and I do a quick scan of the seams. Still holding. For now.

I crunch on the biscuit, chewing slowly. I should probably be more concerned about this storm.

The rain starts to hammer down properly now, the sound a relentless drumbeat against the tent. I adjust my sleeping bag around my shoulders, cocooning myself in what little warmth I can find.

I could go out and check the tent pegs again, but honestly? I don't fancy getting drenched, and I'm not entirely convinced I wouldn't just end up flying away like a very ungraceful human kite.

I take a sip of water, staring at my sad little pile of food. Well, this is bleak.

Another gust of wind rattles the whole tent, and I instinctively grip the edges of my sleeping bag tighter. But I shake off the moment of unease, forcing a smirk.

"Come on, Ivy," I mutter to myself. "You survived your first flat in London with no heating, dodgy electrics, and a neighbour who used to watch TV at full volume at three in the morning. You can survive one night in a tent."

I bite into my apple for good measure, pretending it's a meal and not just an appetiser to my inevitable biscuit binge.

I settle back, stretching out inside my sleeping bag, and listen to the storm raging outside. The thunder rolls on, deep and steady, like a giant clearing its throat. The rain pounds against the tent, a relentless *tap-tap-tap* that, if I weren't currently in the middle of the wilderness, might actually be quite soothing.

For a moment, I let myself believe this is nice. Cosy, even. Like nature's own white noise machine.

Then—plop.

Something cold and wet lands right on my forehead.

I freeze.

Did... did my tent just spit on me?

I swipe at my face. Yep. Definitely water.

Frowning, I sit up and squint at the tent's roof. The dim light from my torch catches a small, suspiciously dark patch just above me.

Another plop.

I slap my shoulder where the water just hit. What the—

I run my hand along the inside of the tent and—oh, fantastic. The fabric feels damp. Not just in one spot, either. I shuffle sideways, patting around, and—yep. There's another wet patch. And another. My sleeping bag? Damp. My backpack? Damp.

Oh, that's just bloody great.

"Are you kidding me?" I grumble, shifting onto my knees.

I squint harder at the ceiling. Is this tent leaking?

I haven't even been out here that long! I spent ages putting this thing up! I even double-checked the seams! Sort of. Maybe. Okay, briefly, but still!

Another drop of water lands on my wrist, followed by a very unwelcome drip-drip sound coming from the far end of the tent.

Oh, no. No, no, no.

I grab my torch and shine it around, properly inspecting the damage. The fabric of the inner tent is visibly damp in several places. My sleeping bag is officially soggy. And now that I think about it, the outer tent was flapping suspiciously close to the inner one earlier.

Did I... set this up wrong?

Another gust of wind shakes the whole thing, and I sigh, rubbing my face. Right. That's it. I am not sleeping in a leaking tent.

Decision made, I yank my backpack toward me and start stuffing everything inside. Clothes? In. Phone? In. Emergency biscuits? Definitely in. My sleeping bag is too damp to pack away properly, so I roll it up and leave it in the tent, hoping it'll stay semi-dry for the next few minutes.

I wriggle into my rain jacket, yank my hood up, and take a deep breath.

Time to evacuate.

With the rain still hammering down, I unzip the tent, squeeze out, and immediately get smacked in the face by the wind.

"Oh, brilliant," I mutter, blinking against the downpour.

The tent flaps wildly beside me as I reach down, fumbling with the pegs. The ground is muddy, making them slick, but I tug them free one by one, nearly losing my balance in the process.

The moment the last peg is out, the tent moves dramatically, like it's personally offended by me. I don't even have the energy to argue. Luckily the sleeping bag and backpack I left in the semi-dry tent are weighing it down enough that it can't take off.

Grabbing fistfuls of damp fabric, I half-lift, half-drag the entire tent toward the only bit of shelter I know exists—the small, roofed patio next to the shower shed.

My boots squelch in the mud, my soaked hair sticks to my face, and my arms ache from the effort. But at this point? Dignity is dead. Survival mode is on.

By the time I reach the patio, I am drenched, panting, and thoroughly questioning every single decision that led me here.

But at least, finally, I am out of the rain.

27

Exile in the Shower Shed

Ivy

Eight o'clock. It is only eight o'clock.

I stare at the time on my phone, willing the numbers to move faster. No signal. Still. Of course.

I tried the landline on the wall of the shower shed earlier, but naturally, that wasn't working either. I pressed the receiver to my ear, listened to the deafening silence, and then hung it back up with a *thunk* that probably conveyed more frustration than necessary.

So, no phone. No internet. No way to check the weather forecast. No way to call the campsite owner and say, *Hey, remember me? The clueless city woman pretending she knows how to camp? Yeah, well, I'm currently squatting in your shower shed like a cold, damp gremlin, so if you could pop by with a cuppa, that'd be great.*

I sigh and push the mobile back into my pocket.

At least my situation has somewhat improved. My tent is no longer a miserable pile of wet fabric; it's now propped up inside the shower block, where it can dry without the risk of turning into a makeshift kite. My sleeping bag is draped over one of the cubicle doors, hopefully drying out as well.

And, most importantly, I am dry.

Well, mostly.

After stripping off my wet clothes, I'd thrown on dry hiking trousers, thick socks, a fleece jumper, and my jacket—bless my overpacking habits. For once, my tendency to bring three times the amount of clothes I actually need has worked in my favour. Theo laughed at me when I told him that I am bringing a fleece jumper in August but who is laughing now?

I sit on a picnic bench I've shoved up against the shed wall, my back pressed against the rough wood, bracing myself for a long, cold night.

The wind howls, rattling the wooden beams above me. Every so often, a particularly strong gust sprays a fine mist of rain into my face, because of course it does. I sigh and wipe my cheek with my sleeve, scowling at the weather as if that might convince it to behave.

It does not.

I glance at my torch, which is resting beside me, casting a dim glow over the small space. The battery is still good, but I know I'll have to be careful with it if I want it to last through the night. The idea of sitting here in total darkness does not appeal.

Another violent gust of wind tears through the trees, sending an eerie creak through the shower shed's structure. The sound makes my skin prickle.

I cross my arms, tucking my fingers into my armpits to warm them. I am fine. This is fine.

I try to think of something—anything—to distract myself.

Food.

Not a great topic, considering my options are still limited.

I fish out the Jammie Dodgers from my bag and rip the packet open. "Emergency biscuits," I murmur, remembering Lucy's solemn little face as she handed them over.

I take a small bite, trying to make them last longer. They're slightly crushed from being shoved into my bag, but they still taste good. Comforting. A small victory in an otherwise spectacular failure of an evening.

The rain continues to lash down, the wind roaring through the trees. I let my head fall back against the shed wall, chewing slowly, staring up at the rafters.

Tomorrow—sod camping: I'm finding the campsite owner first thing and getting a lift into the next village. There's bound to be a B&B with a warm bed, hot food, and—if the gods have any mercy—a strong cup of tea.

And honestly? That sounds like a much better way to enjoy the countryside. I can take long walks, breathe in the fresh air, maybe even find some inner peace before heading back to a place with walls, a proper roof, and zero risk of waking up in a puddle.

Yes. That's the plan. Camping isn't for everyone, and that's fine. It's definitely not for me.

I sigh, nibbling on my biscuit, already feeling relieved at the idea of not spending another night like this.

And then—something moves on my shoulder.

Something large.

I freeze.

A slow, horrible tickling sensation skitters along my upper arm.

I glance down.

It's a spider. A big one. A horrifyingly large one.

For half a second, I am paralysed, my brain short-circuiting as I process the actual nightmare scenario happening in real-time.

And then—pure, unfiltered panic.

I yelp, flailing so violently that I nearly fall off the bench, my biscuit packet flying out of my hand. I swipe frantically at my shoulder, sending the spider somewhere (I do not care where as long as it's not on me). My heart is hammering, my breathing rapid, my entire body doing that horrible, involuntary full-body shudder that comes from the deep, primal part of the brain that really, really hates spiders.

I stand there for a second, arms still half-raised, heart racing.

Then comes the wave of deep, burning shame.

"Oh, for fuck's sake," I mutter, brushing aggressively at my jacket, just in case. "It was just a spider, you absolute wimp."

I take a steadying breath, shake out my arms, and attempt to reclaim some dignity. No one saw that. It didn't happen.

...Still.

I thoroughly inspect the shed wall, scanning every single crevice, crack, and shadow for any other unwelcome eight-legged visitors. I do not find any, which should be reassuring, but instead just makes me wonder where the first one actually went.

I glance at the rafters.

Nope.

I absolutely do not check the rafters. Because I know there are probably about fifty spiders up there, lurking, waiting, watching. I am not emotionally prepared for that reality.

With a final glance around, I cautiously settle back onto the bench, hugging my arms around myself. My biscuits are somewhere out in the soggy grass, and I'm not about to get soaked chasing after them. The wind's howling, the rain hasn't let up, and I've come to a firm conclusion: camping is not for me. Absolutely not.

Tomorrow. Tomorrow I'll be in a warm, dry room with zero spiders, and this entire evening will just be a ridiculous story to tell later.

The thunder may have passed, but the rain is relentless. The damp clings to my skin, settling deep in my bones. I shift on the bench, pulling my extra jumper tighter around my legs in a sad attempt at warmth. My sleeping bag is still too wet to use, and my body aches from the cold. *This is fine. Just a few more hours, and then I am finding the nearest B&B and reclaiming my humanity.*

Then—headlights.

Bright, cutting through the rain, bouncing off the puddles, lighting up the gravel path leading to the shed. A car rolls slowly towards me, its tires crunching over the wet stones before coming to a stop just outside.

I sit up, my heart immediately hammering.

Who the hell—

I grab my torch and flick it on, pointing the beam at the car. The light bounces off the wet windscreen, turning it into a useless, glowing blur. I can't see anything inside.

My stomach clenches.

The driver's door opens.

The interior light flicks on, and in an instant, I see her—Lucy, her small face squashed against the back window, eyes wide.

Theo.

A rush of relief floods me so hard that my legs nearly give out.

Theo sprints through the rain, barely pausing before reaching the shelter. He's soaked in seconds, water dripping from his jacket as he ducks under the patio roof.

He studies me for a second. "What are you doing here?"

I huff out a breath, shoving my damp fringe out of my face. "Oh, you know. Just embracing my new life as a shower-shed gremlin. Thought I'd really lean into the whole outdoor experience."

Theo raises an eyebrow. "Right."

I sigh, shaking my head. "Long story short? My tent betrayed me. It rained, the inside got wet, my sleeping bag got soggy, and instead of drowning in my own terrible choices, I dragged everything here." I gesture to the shed dramatically. "Welcome to Ivy's Emergency Shelter for the Woefully Unprepared."

Theo snorts and shakes his head, sending a few raindrops flying. Then, without a word, he drops onto the bench beside me.

For a moment, we just sit there, listening to the rain pounding around us. Then he tilts his head toward me, smirking.

"So… did you pitch the outer tent properly?"

I narrow my eyes at him. "Excuse me?"

"You know," he continues, far too casually. "Because if the inner and outer tent touch, the rain can seep through. So if you didn't leave enough space—"

I throw my hands in the air. "Oh, fantastic! Where were you with this wisdom before I became a human rain sponge?"

Theo laughs. "I did offer to help."

I glare at him, but I'm too cold and tired to put real effort into it. Instead, I slump back against the shed wall, pulling my jumper-blanket tighter around me and leaning my head against his shoulder. I just need this tiny bit of human connection in this moment.

"Great. So, not only am I failing at camping, but I've also failed at basic tent logic." I sigh dramatically. "I am never living this down, am I?"

Theo chuckles. "Nope."

"You want to hear the worst part?"

Theo tilts his head toward me, smirking. "Oh, absolutely."

I exhale dramatically. "I lost my emergency biscuit."

"Your what?"

"My emergency biscuit. The ones you and Lucy got me at the motor services. For, and I quote, 'if I get hungry or sad.'"

Theo snorts. "And how exactly does one lose an emergency biscuit?"

I glare at him. "A spider attacked me."

That's it. That's all it takes. He throws his head back and laughs, a proper, belly-deep laugh.

I scowl. "I'm glad my suffering amuses you."

But then—midway through his laughter—I suddenly sit up straighter, my eyes widening.

"Oh, for crying out loud!"

Theo wipes his eyes, still grinning. "What now?"

I stare at the small, covered space around us. The solid concrete floor. The roof that, despite letting a little spray in, is definitely not flapping around like a soggy disaster.

"I could have used the gas cooker in here."

"You only just realised that?" Theo chuckles.

I groan, dropping my head into my hands. "I ate a cold, sad apple and three biscuits while shivering in my misery when I could have made tea."

Theo shakes his head. "Yep. I definitely won't let you forget this."

I groan again and let my head fall back against the wall with a thud.

After a moment, I turn my head toward him. "Anyway," I say, voice still muffled with regret. "What are you doing here?"

Theo leans back against the shed wall, stretching his legs out in front of him like he's getting comfortable. "Well," he says casually, "the queen was very worried about you. And so was I."

I snort, caught off guard. "The queen?"

He smirks. "Yes. Queen Lucy."

"Queen... she doesn't rule over me," I grin.

"Tell her that." Theo shrugs. "She runs a tight kingdom. And right now, her royal decree is that you come to the cottage, because—" he gestures toward me, my damp jumper-blanket, and the general misery of my current situation, "—let's be honest, this is bleak."

I narrow my eyes at him. "You're not wrong, but I don't appreciate how fast you came to that conclusion."

"We have a spare room. And beef stew waiting. And tea that doesn't require a gas cooker."

I let out an exaggerated sigh. "Ah, I see. You think, as a knight, it is your duty to rescue a damsel in distress."

Theo scoffs. "You? A damsel?" He shakes his head. "I don't think so." His tone softens. "Look, I know things didn't go to plan, but you put the tent up. You figured out how to move to safety. You've got a plan to dry everything out. You don't need to put yourself down."

I glance at him, a little taken aback by the sincerity in his voice.

He shrugs. "You're capable. You don't need rescuing." He gives me a small smile. "But as a friend, I'd like to offer you a warm place to stay. If you want it."

I stare at him for a second, hesitating—not because I don't want to go, but because, despite everything, some stubborn part of me still feels like I should stick this out. Like I need to prove something to myself.

Then Theo adds, "Oh. And the queen saved you a strawberry cream cake."

I'm already standing before I realise I've moved.

Theo smirks. "That was fast."

I grab my backpack. "Listen. I have my limits."

Theo and I gather my things under the shelter, taking a final moment to brace ourselves before making a break for it. The rain is still coming down in thick sheets, but at this point, I'm beyond caring. Dry clothes and hot food are waiting, and that's all the motivation I need.

"Ready?" Theo asks, gripping the straps of my backpack.

"As I'll ever be," I mutter.

"On three. One... two... go!"

We sprint into the downpour, splashing through puddles as we race to the car. Theo yanks open the boot, and we shove my damp belongings inside as fast as humanly possible. I roll my tent in on top of my backpack and slam the boot shut just as another gust of wind sends rain pelting sideways.

"Go, go, go!" Theo shouts, and we both make a run for the doors.

I wrench mine open and slide inside, finally out of the rain.

"Ivy!"

Before I can even get my seatbelt on, Lucy launches herself forward from the backseat, wrapping her arms around my neck in a fierce hug. "You're here! You're not in the storm anymore! I saved you a cake!"

I laugh, squeezing her back. "You, my Queen, are a hero."

She pulls back, beaming. "And Daddy made stew! And we have blankets! And you can stay forever!"

I glance over at Theo, who shakes his head fondly as he reaches for the ignition button.

I smile, settling into the seat. "Tell you what—I'll take it one night at a time."

As the car hums to life and the heater starts to kick in, I lean back, already planning to ask Theo for a lift to a B&B in the morning.

But for now? With warmth seeping into my fingers, Lucy practically bouncing in excitement, and the storm safely shut outside?

For now, this is exactly where I want to be.

28
Great Survival Adventure

Theo

THE RAIN STILL POURS relentlessly as I pull into the garage beside the cottage, the steady drumming against the roof a reminder that the storm isn't letting up anytime soon. At least we don't have to make a mad dash through it this time.

I switch off the engine and glance back at Lucy, who's already kicking her feet excitedly against the seat. "Alright, my queen," I say, reaching back to unbuckle her. "Let's get you inside."

She grins as I lift her out, her little arms winding around my neck for a second before she wiggles free, landing lightly on the ground. The second her feet touch the concrete, she's off towards the door, coat flapping, ready to be the first inside.

"You're taking my room tonight," I say before Ivy can get a word out.

She frowns immediately. "What? No, I'm not."

"Yes, you are." I pop the boot open and start pulling out her stuff. "It's got an ensuite. The guest room doesn't."

"I can use the other bathroom, Theo," she says, exasperated.

I sling her backpack over my shoulder. "Yeah, but then you'd have to share with Lucy. And I love her dearly, but she treats the sink like a potions lab and the bathmat as a permanent puddle storage system."

Ivy presses her lips together. "I can handle that."

"But why would you, when you could have a perfectly good ensuite, instead of stepping on a mystery wet patch in the morning?"

She exhales sharply, giving me a flat look. "You're very annoying."

I smirk. "Go on, admit it. You want the ensuite."

She sighs, defeated. "Fine. But only because I'm too tired to fight you on this."

"Smart choice." I nod towards the door. "Ladybug, why don't you show Ivy my room?"

Lucy gasps as if I've just given her the most sacred of duties. "Yes! Come on, Ivy, it's this way!"

Ivy throws me a look that says "I see what you did there," but she lets herself be dragged inside.

I watch them disappear before turning back to the boot. Her tent is still damp, and the last thing she needs is for it to turn into a mouldy disaster. I grab it and carry it to the small utility room by the side of the cottage. It's nothing fancy—just a washer, dryer, and some space to hang damp clothes—but it'll do the job.

Unrolling the tent, I drape it over the drying rack and step back, hands on my hips. "You better dry out properly," I mutter at it, before heading back into the warmth of the cottage.

In the kitchen, I ladle some stew into a bowl and set it on the table. Ivy's definitely not eaten a proper meal today, and I have a strong suspicion she was planning to survive on rainwater and stubbornness. Not on my watch.

Lucy appears in the doorway, her pink bunny pyjamas peeking out from under her jacket I put on her when we went on our mission to rescue Ivy. She is still way too awake for this time of night.

"Alright, my queen," I say, placing a spoon next to the bowl. "It is definitely time for bed."

She pouts. "Daaaddddyyy!" *Oh, I get the daddy with five Ds today.* "But I wanna stay up with Ivy!"

Ivy steps into the kitchen just in time to hear Lucy's dramatic plea. She raises an eyebrow at me, then looks down at Lu with a thoughtful tilt of her head.

"What if I read you a bedtime story?" Ivy offers, crouching slightly to be on Lucy's level.

Lucy's face lights up instantly. "Really?"

Ivy nods solemnly. "But only if you're in bed within five minutes. No dawdling."

Lucy gasps, clearly taking this as a challenge. "I promise!" she says, already half-turning toward the hallway.

I smirk as Ivy straightens up, shaking her head fondly. "Well played," I mouth.

She flashes me a quick grin before following Lucy down the hall. And just like that, something shifts in my chest—something warm, something that makes me want to keep looking at her even when she's already turned away.

I trail after them, leaning against the doorframe as Ivy tucks Lucy under her duvet. The little lamp by the bed casts a soft glow over the room, making the space feel smaller, cozier. Lucy is practically vibrating with excitement, already holding out a book, but at the last second, she clutches it to her chest and looks up at Ivy with a mischievous glint in her eye.

"Wait," she whispers. "Can you tell me what happened this afternoon first?"

Ivy presses a hand to her heart, feigning shock. "You mean my great survival adventure?"

Lucy giggles and nods rapidly.

I bite back a laugh, folding my arms as I listen.

"Well," Ivy begins, sitting on the edge of the bed. "It all started when I bravely set up my tent. It was perfect—until the storm decided to test me." She leans in, her voice conspiratorial. "Did you know that rain can attack?"

Lucy giggles, eyes wide. "It can?"

"Oh, absolutely," Ivy says gravely. "One moment, I was dry and happy. The next? Drip, drip, drip—ambushed! I was practically swimming in there."

Lucy bursts into laughter, clutching her stuffed rabbit.

"And then," Ivy continues, "just when I thought I had things under control—*bam*! A giant, fearsome beast launched itself at me!"

Lucy gasps. "A bear?!"

"Worse." Ivy pauses dramatically. "A spider."

Lucy shrieks with laughter, kicking her legs under the duvet. My own grin slips out before I can stop it.

Ivy keeps going, describing her panicked reaction in exaggerated detail, complete with wild gestures and sound effects. I watch her, the way she completely loses herself in making Lucy laugh, how animated her face gets, how her eyes sparkle when she sees she has her full attention.

I feel that pull in my chest again, stronger this time.

I clear my throat, stepping inside. "Alright, bedtime comedian, that's enough."

Lucy whines, but I give her a look, and she sighs dramatically. Ivy just smirks at me over her shoulder, like she knows exactly what she's done.

I flip off the lamp, letting the small nightlight take over. "Lights out, Queen Lucy. You can hear more stories in the morning."

Lucy sighs but cuddles under her duvet. Ivy brushes a loose curl from her forehead before standing up.

As she walks past me, I catch the faintest scent of something—rain, warmth, something undeniably her. It lingers as she moves, and before I can stop myself, my fingers twitch at my side, like they have half a mind to reach for her.

I don't.

Instead, I step aside, letting her pass.

But the feeling stays.

"Night, Ladybug," I whisper before placing a kiss on Lu's forehead.

"Night, love you." Lu mumbles.

"Love you too." I say those words every night but somehow it never feels enough.

Ivy is waiting for me in the corridor and follows me back to the kitchen, her socked feet quiet against the wooden floor. The house feels still now, the storm still grumbling outside, but softer, distant. I grab the bowl of stew and put it back in the microwave to warm up.

"You don't have to do that," Ivy says, leaning against the counter. "I'll eat it cold. I'm not fussy."

I glance over my shoulder. "You say that, but may I remind you of your cold apple and three biscuits earlier." I shake my head. "I'm not letting you add cold stew to your list of poor life choices today."

She snorts but doesn't argue.

A few minutes later, I set the steaming bowl in front of her. She wastes zero time before diving in, wolfing down the first few bites like someone who hasn't had a hot meal in days.

I lean against the counter, watching in amusement. "Should I be worried for my fingers? You're eating like I might take it away from you."

She pauses only to send me a flat look. "If you do try to take it, just know I will fight you."

I hold up my hands. "Duly noted."

She keeps going, clearing the bowl so fast I barely have time to offer her more before she's already pushing it towards me. "Would it be terrible if I'd ask for seconds, please."

I smirk, taking the bowl and ladling out another helping. "Seconds, thirds... plenty here for you."

She grins. "Turns out being rained on and emotionally terrorised by spiders really builds up an appetite."

I chuckle, crossing my arms as I watch her polish off the second portion. When she finally leans back with a satisfied sigh, I grab the small plastic container from the fridge and place it in front of her.

"Your strawberry cream cake," I say, tapping the lid.

Ivy eyes it, then shakes her head. "I'm too full. Besides, I know Lucy will want to give it to me herself tomorrow, and I'm not about to rob her of that joy."

"Good thinking." I nod. "I'd hate to be the target of her wrath if she thought I betrayed her cake-saving mission."

"Oh, she'd exile you," Ivy agrees, then smirks. "Maybe even have you executed."

I play along. "I did tell you she runs a tight kingdom."

She laughs, but it softens into something quieter, something warmer. We're still standing close, the kitchen a little too small, or maybe we just feel too big for the space.

Ivy shifts slightly, her shoulder brushing against mine. I glance down, and she's already looking up at me.

The teasing fades into something else, something heavier, like a charged wire strung between us. My eyes flick down, just for a second, just enough to notice the way her lips part slightly, the way she tilts her chin up the tiniest bit—

And then she steps back.

I barely stop myself from following.

"Well," she says, clearing her throat. "I should probably head to bed. Fighting with the elements also makes one tired."

I exhale, forcing a small smirk. "Yeah. Good plan."

She hesitates just a second longer, then offers me a small, knowing smile. "Goodnight, Theo."

I nod. "Night, Ivy."

And just like that, she slips away down the hall, leaving me standing in the kitchen, feeling restless, like I almost had something I wasn't sure I was even allowed to want.

29
Someone's Packing

Ivy

THE SECOND I STEP into the ensuite and lock the door behind me, I let out a long breath. The cottage is quiet, except for the rain still tapping against the window. No wind shaking a tent, no thunder rumbling overhead, no spiders launching themselves at me like tiny assassins. Just warmth, calm, and a real bathroom.

I turn on the shower, and the moment the hot water bursts from the nozzle, I could weep.

Stripping off my clothes, I step under the spray, and a deep groan escapes me as the heat sinks into my skin. The muscles in my shoulders slowly loosen, the chill in my bones finally fading.

This. This is what I needed.

I close my eyes, letting the water stream over me, my mind drifting whether I want it to or not.

Theo.

Theo and his stupid wet hair. How can he even look cover-page-worthy when other people would look like drowned rats.

I exhale sharply, but it doesn't stop the images flashing through my brain—the way his damp hair clung to his forehead, the way he'd run a hand through it, ruffling it absentmindedly, making it look even better. The way his T-shirt stretched across his shoulders, slightly damp from carrying my rain-soaked tent inside. The smirk he gave me when I devoured that stew like a half-starved goblin.

And then—that moment.

The air between us in the kitchen had changed. It had thickened, stretched tight, charged.

I'd seen the way his gaze flicked to my mouth. I know he'd noticed the way I leaned in slightly before I came to my senses.

I groan again, pressing my hands to my face.

This is exactly why I needed the dating ban.

I know that. I know that.

Three months. No dating, no relationships, no rebounds. Time to find myself—or whatever Pee-Pee had said when she convinced me to do this.

And I've stuck to it. For nearly quarter of a year, I've resisted bad decisions, ignored temptation, and reminded myself that I don't need to be with someone to be happy.

I have three weeks left. Just three weeks. I know Pee-Pee said to find out what this is and that I can date him, but not before the ban is over. For once I'd like to finish something and I am so close.

I will not break my ban for Theo.

Even if he smells stupidly good. Even if his voice went all low and rough when he said goodnight. Even if, for half a second, I really thought he was going to kiss me—and I wanted him to.

No.

THE DATING BAN

No, no, no.

I stand there for another long moment, letting the water run over me, breathing through the ridiculous tangle of thoughts in my head.

Tomorrow, I'll thank him properly, figure out my next steps, and get out of his way.

That's the smart choice. The right choice.

So why does part of me really not want to make it?

I wake to the sound of giggling.

Soft, mischievous, the kind of giggle that usually means someone is up to no good.

I frown, still half-asleep, shifting slightly under the covers. Before I can fully register what's happening, I turn my head—and nearly jump when I come face-to-face with Lucy, who is grinning at me from the side of the bed, her little chin propped up on her hands.

I blink, my brain struggling to catch up. "Lucy?"

She lets out another giggle, practically vibrating with excitement.

Before I can ask what she's doing, a whisper-shouted "Lucy!" comes from just outside the door.

My stomach tightens slightly.

Theo.

I barely have a second to process that before the door creaks open, and Theo sneaks into the room, clearly trying to retrieve his daughter before she causes any early-morning chaos.

His focus is completely on her at first, his face set somewhere between amused and exasperated. But then—he looks up.

And his eyes meet mine.

We both freeze.

Because oh God.

Theo is in his pyjamas.

And not like the sensible, respectable kind. No, of course not. The universe wouldn't be that kind to me.

He's in a loose, slightly crumpled T-shirt and a pair of boxer briefs that leave very little to the imagination.

Boy, oh boy, someone's packing.

My entire body goes hot.

Theo's ears go bright red.

I suddenly become painfully aware of my own state—dressed in an oversized T-shirt, but without a bra. My breasts are not meant for public appearances without some very serious structural support. Yet here they are, the outline very clearly visible under the thin fabric, drooping unapologetically toward my belly button.

I cross my arms immediately, locking them in place like a human barricade.

Theo is still standing there, like his brain has momentarily short-circuited, and I know I should be playing it cool, should be saying something, but my mouth is refusing to cooperate because I am so wildly aware of the fact that he's standing in my borrowed bedroom in his boxer briefs.

Lucy, entirely oblivious to the silent meltdown happening between the adults, claps her hands together and announces, "We should all have breakfast in Ivy's bed!"

Both Theo and I snap our heads toward her at the same time.

"No," we say in unison.

Lucy frowns, clearly unimpressed with our lack of enthusiasm. "Why not?"

I shift under the blankets, now clutching the duvet defensively over my chest, because there are already too many things happening that I did not emotionally prepare for this morning. "Because," I say, grasping at any reason, "breakfast in bed is messy."

Lucy gasps like I've just insulted the very foundation of her beliefs. "No, it's cosy."

Theo, finally regaining his ability to function, folds his arms over his chest. "Lucy, we eat at the table."

"But Ivy is the guest! We have to do special things!" she argues, already burrowing herself further into the duvet like she's settling in for the long haul.

Theo lets out a long breath, clearly trying to pick his battles. "Tell you what," he says, crouching beside the bed, his voice lowering to that calm, reasonable dad tone that clearly has years of practice behind it. "Remember how you saved Ivy a cake?"

Lucy's eyes widen. "The strawberry one?"

Theo nods. "Yep. And if you get up right now, you can be the one to give it to her first thing after breakfast. But only if you come to the kitchen like a civilised person."

Lucy gasps dramatically, throwing off the covers like this is a great and noble mission.

"I forgot about the cake!" She scrambles off the bed with newfound purpose, already halfway to the door. "I have to check if it's still okay!"

Theo, still crouched beside the bed, exhales in pure relief as Lucy disappears down the hall.

I snort. "You bribed her."

"Parenting," he says, "is 75% bribery and 25% bluffing."

I raise an eyebrow. "And what happens when they call your bluff?"

He rubs a hand over his jaw, smirk widening. "Pray they don't."

Theo stands, stretching his arms over his head—and I make the colossal mistake of looking.

Because the movement makes his T-shirt ride up, just enough to reveal a sliver of toned stomach, the defined cut of his hip, and—oh hell—that dark trail of hair disappearing into the waistband of his boxer briefs.

Oh no.

Oh no no no.

A very inappropriate thought pops into my head, followed by about six more, and I must make some kind of involuntary noise because Theo glances at me, eyebrows raised.

I snap my gaze violently toward the ceiling, praying that I don't look as flustered as I feel.

"Right." He clears his throat, taking a half-step back. "I, uh—should probably get dressed."

"Great idea," I say far too quickly, already trying to extract myself from the blankets. "Same. Also. Clothes. Big fan of them."

Theo blinks at me, and I want to die.

He huffs a laugh, rubs one of the tips of his red ears, shakes his head, and backs out of the room without another word.

I let out a breath and immediately fling myself out of bed, marching toward the bathroom.

I so have to move to a B&B.

30

Unbalanced

Theo

BY THE TIME BREAKFAST is finished, Lucy is practically buzzing. She keeps glancing at the fridge like it holds some kind of sacred treasure, which, in her mind, it probably does.

I lean back in my chair, watching as she finally can't take it anymore and jumps off her seat, clapping her hands together. "It's time!"

Ivy looks at her, amused. "Time for what exactly?"

"For your cake, obviously!"

She dashes to the fridge, carefully retrieving the little plastic container like it's made of pure gold. Then, with exaggerated importance, she carries it to the table and places it directly in front of Ivy, standing back with her hands on her hips.

Ivy blinks down at it. "Wow. A royal presentation."

Lucy nods seriously. "It's very special."

Ivy presses a hand to her chest. "I'm honoured."

I chuckle to myself, carrying the empty plates to the sink as Lucy watches Ivy with great anticipation.

Ivy peels off the lid and stares down at the little strawberry cream cake. "This looks amazing."

"It is," Lucy says knowingly.

Ivy picks up a fork, about to take a bite, but then—she pauses. "Actually, you know what? I think I'd like to share it."

"You will?" Lucy asks with a big smile on her face.

"Of course." Ivy grins, cutting the cake in half and pushing a piece toward her. "I can't possibly eat something this special all by myself."

Lucy looks at Ivy like she's just become her absolute favourite person in the universe.

And, honestly? Watching the two of them grin at each other over their shared cake? I'm not far behind.

I shake my head, turning back to the dishes before I start thinking too much about how stupidly good Ivy looks when she smiles.

As I rinse the plates, I glance over my shoulder casually. "So," I say, keeping my voice easy, "what's your plan, then?"

Ivy, mid-bite, raises an eyebrow. "Plan?"

"Yeah." I turn back to the sink. "For today. For the rest of your trip. You sticking it out at the campsite or are you thinking of... reevaluating your life choices?"

There's a beat of silence behind me before I hear her scoff.

"You're enjoying this, aren't you?"

I smirk to myself, scrubbing a plate. "Maybe a little."

Ivy huffs, setting her fork down. "Well, since you ask so nicely, I was thinking of heading into the next village today. Maybe find a B&B."

I glance over my shoulder again. "Giving up on camping already?"

She levels me with a look. "I spent a night in a shower shed, Theo."

I let out a quiet chuckle, placing the last plate in the drying rack. "Fair point."

But even as I turn off the tap and shake the water from my hands, my mind is already somewhere else.

She's planning to leave.

Which is fine. It's smart. Logical. She never planned to stay here, and I know Ivy—she doesn't like feeling like she's imposing. She'd rather check into a B&B and deal with it herself. That's who she is.

But I'd be lying if I said I liked the option of her leaving.

Truthfully, I'd love to have her around.

Even if it isn't the best idea.

Even if yesterday there was that almost-moment in the kitchen, thick with something neither of us acknowledged.

Even if she's on this ridiculous dating ban and I have no business thinking about what would happen after it ends.

None of that changes the fact that I want her here.

Just for a little while longer.

I turn, about to say something—anything that might nudge her in the direction of staying—when Lucy suddenly gasps dramatically, nearly knocking over her juice.

"Ivy should stay here!" she declares, like she's just had the most brilliant idea in the world.

Ivy laughs, but shakes her head. "Oh, Lucy, I—"

"No, listen!" Lucy hops out of her chair and rushes over to Ivy, gripping her arm with both tiny hands. "You like it here! And I like you being here! And you don't have to sleep in a scary shower!"

Ivy glances at me, looking amused but also a little uncertain. "Lucy, that's really sweet, but I—"

Lucy turns to me, eyes huge. "Daddy! Tell her she can stay!"

Ivy gives me a wary look, clearly expecting me to swoop in and diffuse the situation, back up her reasoning, give her an easy out.

But I don't.

Instead, I lean casually against the counter, arms crossed, and say, "Well, she's got a point."

Ivy blinks. "Wait, what?"

I shrug. "We've got the space. You'd be more than welcome to stay."

Ivy's eyes narrow slightly, like she's waiting for me to follow up with some kind of teasing remark.

I don't.

Because for once, I'm being completely serious.

She hesitates, fiddling with her fork. "Theo, I don't want to intrude."

"You wouldn't be," I say easily. "It makes sense. You get a dry, warm bed. Lucy gets her new favourite person around for a little longer." I smirk. "And I get the pure joy of reminding you that I was right about the whole 'camping being a bad idea' thing."

She rolls her eyes, but there's something else in her expression. She's considering it, but something's holding her back.

I see it—the hesitation, the conflict.

But I also see the way her fingers still rest on the table, tapping lightly, like she's talking herself out of something she wants.

So I make it easy for her.

"No pressure," I say lightly, pushing off the counter. "It's just an offer. If you'd rather get a B&B, I'll still give you a lift."

Lucy tugs on Ivy's arm again. "Pleeeeease?"

Ivy lets out a long sigh, shaking her head—but she's smiling.

"You guys are relentless," she mutters.

I lean in slightly, dropping my voice to a conspiratorial tone. "And if you stay..." I pause for dramatic effect. "I'll make homemade pizza."

Ivy gives me a *so what* look, pretending to be unimpressed. "Oh, now you're bribing *me*?"

"Absolutely." I cross my arms. "I make a mean pizza."

"What kind of toppings are we talking?"

I smirk. "Whatever your heart desires."

Ivy huffs, shaking her head, but there's a small, reluctant smile tugging at her lips. "You really aren't making it easy to say no."

"Then don't," I reply.

"Say yes," Lucy chimes in, practically bouncing with excitement.

Ivy exhales, eyes flicking between me and the hopeful little girl beside her. I decide to seal the deal.

I lean forward, resting my arms on the table, my voice dropping just slightly. "Most importantly," I say, locking eyes with her, "I'm a first-class spider catcher."

A spark of amusement flickers across her face, but she doesn't look away. "Well, now I have to say yes," she murmurs.

Still, neither of us moves.

Then—bam. Lucy launches herself between us, wrapping Ivy in a fierce hug.

Ivy lets out a small *Oof!* but laughs, hugging her back.

I push away from the table, turning back toward the sink, exhaling slowly as I pick up the tea towel.

This feels like the best decision in the world.

And maybe also the worst.

The sun is warm, the grass soft underfoot, and the air has that perfect early-morning stillness. It's the kind of day that makes yoga outside feel like a great idea. We have done yoga every day this week but always indoors because the weather hasn't been very kind. Today, however, the sun is out, and so Ivy suggested to move it to the garden.

And to be fair—it was a great idea.

Except now, standing in Tree Pose, I'm far too aware of Ivy balancing beside me.

She's steadier than she was during our last lesson, but she still wobbles now and then, her foot pressing a little too hard into her thigh, her arms shifting ever so slightly as she works to keep her balance.

It's distracting.

Not because she's bad at it but because she bites her lip when she concentrates, and it's making it very hard to focus on my own pose.

Lucy, standing between us, is completely in her element. She's balancing effortlessly, her little hands pressed together, her eyes closed like she's some kind of tiny yoga master.

"Ivy, you're doing better!" she announces happily.

Ivy exhales, adjusting her stance. "I feel better. I mean, my legs still hate me, but I haven't fallen yet, so I'm calling that a win."

I smirk. "See? Told you you'd improve."

"Yes, yes. Theo is always right. What a shocking revelation."

"Glad you're catching on."

She gives me a look that promises payback, but she's still smiling.

"Okay," I say, shifting into Warrior. "Let's move into the next pose."

Lucy follows instantly, lifting one leg behind her and stretching her arms forward, her tiny frame perfectly aligned.

Ivy hesitates, then moves into position, lifting her leg and stretching forward—only slightly wobbly this time.

"Look at that," I murmur, tilting my head toward her. "No dramatic flailing."

She huffs, focusing on keeping steady. "Oh, I'm sorry, did you want me to fall?"

"No, I'm just—"

But then—she wobbles.

Just a little. Just enough that she reaches out without thinking—

And her fingers brush against my arm.

It's a light touch, barely there, but I feel it everywhere.

Her breath catches, and for a second, she looks up at me—

The moment is broken when Lucy groans loudly and flops dramatically onto the grass.

"My tummy is angry!" she declares. "It needs food!"

Ivy lets out a soft laugh, stepping back from me—too quickly, if you ask me.

"Oh no," she says, crouching beside Lucy. "That sounds serious. What does it need? Toast? Cereal?"

Lucy shakes her head very solemnly. "Something cold."

Ivy hums, pretending to think. "Well, lucky for you, I bought ice lollies yesterday in town."

Lucy's eyes widen with joy. "Can I have one now?"

Ivy looks at me, eyebrows raised. "What do you think, Dad? Ice lollies before lunch?"

Lucy turns to me, clasping her hands dramatically. "Pleeeease?"

I sigh, knowing I've already lost this battle.

"Fine," I give in. "But only one."

Lucy cheers, already sprinting toward the house, yelling, "I want the red one!"

Ivy grins as she follows her, tossing a look over her shoulder. "How about you?"

I exhale. "Nah, I'll stay out here a bit longer. Finish up properly."

She shrugs, still smiling. "Suit yourself."

Then she disappears inside, leaving me standing in the middle of the field, very much not as relaxed as I was five minutes ago.

I inhale deeply, shifting into a slow stretch, trying to get my head back into yoga mode.

Breathe in. Breathe out.
Find balance.
Find focus.
Find—
...Ivy.

Her smile, the way it tugs just slightly higher on the left. The way her eyes crinkle when she laughs. The way she rolls them at me constantly but never actually walks away.

I exhale sharply, moving into a side bend, determined to push the thoughts away.

Nope. Not doing this.

But it's too late.

Because I'm not just thinking about her laugh.

I'm thinking about the way her T-shirt clung to her back when she stretched earlier. The curve of her hips in those leggings. The way her hair looked loose and messy this morning, like she'd just woken up and—

Nope.

I squeeze my eyes shut, shifting into Firefly Pose.

This is not yoga. This is not balance.

This is me in the middle of a field, thinking entirely inappropriate thoughts about my house guest. My friend. Who, if she knew where my mind had just been, would probably throw her ice lolly at my head.

I exhale slowly, but my heart is still pounding in a way that has nothing to do with exercise.

Maybe I should've said yes to that ice lolly.

Because I need to cool the hell down.

31

Level Up

Ivy

LUCY'S SOFT, EVEN BREATHING fills the dim bedroom as her little fingers still cling to the edge of her duvet. I smile, tucking a stray curl out of her face before carefully slipping off the bed.

Another bedtime story down.

Another night when my heart feels far too full for something that I thought I would never experience.

I brush the thought aside and quietly head into the hallway, closing the door softly behind me. As I make my way towards the living room, I spot Theo sprawled out on the sofa, his long legs outstretched, busy flipping through something on his laptop.

He glances up when he hears me and nods towards the space next to him. "She's out?" he asks.

"Completely," I reply with a sigh, stretching my arms above my head. "Didn't even get past the big reveal."

Theo smirks. "Amateur."

I settle on the other end of the sofa, curling my feet underneath me. "What about you? Got any exciting plans tonight?"

"Well..." He tilts the laptop screen towards me. "I was thinking of watching something. Fancy it?"

I snort, spreading my arms wide, as if to take in the whole room. "There's no TV here, Theo."

He raises an eyebrow. "And?"

I frown in confusion. "And how do you plan on watching anything then?"

A playful smirk tugs at his lips, as though he's about to let slip an important secret. Then he taps the laptop. "I've got *Line of Duty* downloaded."

I gasp. "You're into *Line of Duty*?"

"Obviously," he replies with a scoff. "What kind of person do you take me for?"

I laugh softly, feigning disbelief. "The kind of person who should have mentioned that three nights ago."

"Fair point." Theo shrugs, scrolling through his files. "So, which season are we watching? Picking up where you left off or starting from the beginning?"

"You mean you're up for a full rewatch from season one?"

Theo nods, mockingly serious this time. "I'm dedicated to the craft."

"I reckon you're just saying that because you're a fan of Keeley Hawes," I tease him.

"Okay, first of all—" he says, placing a hand on his chest in mock offence, "that's season two."

I snort.

"Secondly," he continues, clicking on the first episode, "if we're rewatching, we do it properly."

I settle in as the opening credits roll. "I think this is the most attractive thing you've done all week."

Theo chuckles as he adjusts the laptop on his lap. "You really have low standards."

And that's when I realise I've made a mistake.

I hadn't thought about the logistics of watching a show like this.

Theo's warm presence beside me is almost too much—his arm brushes against mine as he shifts the laptop, and I feel his nearness everywhere. The clean, warm, and delightfully pleasant scent of him swirls around me, completely messing with my focus.

I swallow hard.

This is fine.

It's just a show. Just the two of us watching *Line of Duty*.

Not a big deal.

Except my heart's doing somersaults every time he moves, every time his arm grazes mine, every time I catch even a faint whiff of him, soapy and warm and unmistakably Theo.

I press my lips together, forcing my focus back to the screen.

Because this? This is exactly the danger that will cause me to break my ban.

I exhale slowly, keeping my gaze fixed on the laptop.

I can do this.

I just have to ignore the way his arm keeps brushing mine, and the way he smells, and the fact that I kind of, sort of, don't ever want to move.

The first episode ends, the screen fading to black before the credits roll. I stretch my arms above my head and glance over at Theo.

"Well," I say, tilting my head, "still think starting from season one was a good idea?"

Theo smirks, shifting slightly as he sets the laptop on the coffee table. "Obviously. I enjoy watching you watch it."

I scoff. "Oh, what, because I'm so expressive?"

He nods. "Exactly."

Theo lets out a laugh, but before I know it, his hand darts out and pokes me right in the ribs.

I squeak.

Oh no.

His grin widens. "Oh."

I shake my head. "Theo, don't—"

But it's too late.

His fingers dig into my sides, and I shriek, twisting away from him.

"No, no, no—" I protest, trying to wriggle free, but he's relentless, laughing as I squirm. "I hate you!"

"You keep saying that," he teases, continuing his playful assault, "yet here you are."

I grab one of his wrists, trying to shove him away, but in the tussle, he loses his balance.

And suddenly—

He lands on top of me.

The atmosphere shifts.

His weight gently pins me against the sofa, his hands braced on either side of my head. My breath catches.

His expression softens—the smile fading into something quieter, heavier.

Neither of us moves.

My fingers, still curled around his wrist, stop pushing. His body is so close I can feel his warmth and the steady rhythm of his breathing.

His eyes drift to my mouth again.

I swallow hard.

There's a long, charged pause.

And then—slowly, almost unbearably—he lowers his head.

My heart pounds. I could stop this. I should.

But I don't.

His nose brushes against mine, and I forget to breathe.

Then, finally—finally—his lips meet mine.

And I melt.

The first kiss is tentative, as if he's waiting for me to pull away. But when I don't, when I can't, he deepens the kiss, his lips firm and searching.

I sigh into him, my fingers sliding up his arms, my body instinctively leaning into his warmth.

It's slow, deep, intoxicating.

And completely against every rule I've been trying to stick to.

But at this moment?

I couldn't care less.

The kiss grows so deep it pulls me under like a riptide.

I can't say how long it lasts—seconds or minutes—but then, as if a switch has been flipped, reality crashes back.

I freeze.

Theo must feel it too because he immediately pulls back, his breathing uneven, his forehead barely not touching mine.

His eyes are wide, searching mine, and I know—he's thinking exactly what I am.

We shouldn't have done that.

We can't have done that.

I scramble upright, trying to create some space between us. My skin burns, my heart races, and Theo—Theo runs a hand through his tousled hair and exhales sharply.

"Shit." His voice is rough. "I—I just broke your dating ban."

I groan, leaning back against the sofa. "I swore to my therapist I'd stick to it. I promised."

He rubs the back of his neck, looking half-apologetic, half-something else. "I, uh... technically I don't think a kiss was part of your therapist's official ban, right? Just, you know... dating?"

I shoot him a dry look. "Oh, I'm sure that's exactly what she meant. 'Go ahead and make out with random men, as long as you don't have dinner with them.'"

Theo winces. "Ouch."

I sigh, shaking my head. "Not you. Sorry. It's just... me. My whole pattern." I wave vaguely. "The very reason I even set up this fucking ban in the first place."

He hesitates, then, in the sweetest, most tentative way, asks, "What about after the dating ban?"

I turn my head, blinking in surprise.

His fingers tap once on his knee, as if he's nervous but determined. "I mean..." He clears his throat. "Would a date after the ban still count as breaking the rules?"

My stomach flips.

I open my mouth, then close it, before exhaling a laugh and shaking my head. "You're asking if I'd go on a date with you in a few weeks?"

His lips twitch. "I could set a reminder. Keep everything very official."

I giggle like a naughty school girl. "You're impossible."

But my heart is still pounding.

Because the truth is—I want to say yes. And I guess this is my answer. This is what Pee-Pee told me. When it's right, I'll know.

"Alright. Ask me again when the ban's over," I say confidently.

Theo studies me carefully before shifting to pull his phone from his pocket.

"What are you doing?"

"Setting a reminder." He scrolls through his phone like it's the most natural thing.

Again, I let out a laugh. "You're not serious."

"Completely serious," he assures me, tapping away on his calendar. "So… when's the big day?"

I press my lips together, suddenly feeling far too warm.

I shouldn't encourage this. I should laugh it off, change the subject, pretend it isn't making my stomach do backflips.

Instead, I sigh dramatically, resting my chin on my hand. "The first of September."

Theo nods, keying something into his phone. "Alright. Three weeks from today."

I lean in slightly, squinting. "What exactly are you putting in there?"

He angles his screen so I can see, and he's typed:

"Level up! Quest to call Ivy."

I stare at it, something oddly warm curling through my chest.

He meets my gaze, his smirk softening just slightly. "Satisfied?"

I roll my eyes, but my smile betrays me. "You're such a dork."

"Yep," he agrees easily, locking his phone and slipping it back into his pocket. "But now it's official."

I shake my head, settling back against the sofa. "What if I change my mind?"

Theo shrugs, completely unbothered. "Then I'll pretend I set the reminder for something else. Like... reminding you to top up your Oyster card or submit your meter reading."

I snort. "Oh, romantic."

He grins. "I try."

There's a pause, the easy teasing settling into something more intimate.

His arm is still stretched along the back of the sofa, close enough that I can feel his warmth, and I know if I leaned just a little, I'd be right up against him.

Three weeks.

That's not long. That's not long at all.

But right now it feels like forever.

I exhale sharply, forcing a light tone. "Alright, Casanova. Press play before I start reconsidering."

Theo chuckles, but there's something in his expression—something knowing—as he reaches for the laptop and does exactly that.

And as the episode starts, I find myself trying to work out how many minutes there are in three weeks.

32

Overthinking Drama Queen

Ivy

I SIT ACROSS FROM Pee-Pee, the familiar calm of her office doing little to settle the nerves buzzing in my chest. The end of the dating ban is just days away, and I can't help but feel like I'm about to be shoved out of a safe little bubble.

"So, Ivy," Phyllis says, her voice soft but steady, "the dating ban is almost over. How are you feeling about that?"

I let out a long sigh, folding my arms across my chest. "Honestly? It all went wrong. Every part of it."

Pee-Pee raises an eyebrow, not buying it for a second. "Really? All of it? Sounds a bit dramatic to me. I wouldn't be so quick to call it a disaster."

I'm about to protest, but she holds up a hand, clearly ready to continue. "You've told me about the yoga and the clay. Those didn't go perfectly, but they also didn't go as badly as you're making them sound. You've made progress."

I roll my eyes but can't help the small smile that tugs at my lips. "Yeah, I guess yoga was a bit better than I thought. I still look like a drunk flamingo, but I'm... okay with it. And the gnome army? Well, it's growing, and I'm kind of proud of them."

Pee-Pee nods approvingly. "Your gnome army sounds like a victory in itself. And yoga, even with the stumbling, is a win. You're allowing yourself to try, Ivy. You're getting to know your limits."

I let out a small, reluctant chuckle, my shoulders loosening just a fraction. "I guess that's true. And the gnome army is definitely a force to be reckoned with now." I pause, staring down at my hands. "But none of that changes the fact that I feel like I've spent three months in a holding pattern. And now, I'm about to step back into a world I was trying to avoid."

Pee-Pee studies me for a moment, her eyes gentle but knowing. "You've spent three months working on you, Ivy. Not avoiding anything but learning how to face it. You don't have to throw yourself back into dating just because the ban's over. What you choose to do next is still up to you."

The weight of that statement sinks in, heavy and oddly comforting. I know she's right, but still...

"But the whole point was to get back into it, right? Not just sit here making gnomes and doing tree pose in my living room."

"Not exactly," she says, leaning back in her chair. "The point was for you to reconnect with yourself first. To unlearn some of those habits that keep you stuck in patterns that aren't working for you. Whether that means diving back into dating or not, that's up to you."

My brain races. Do I dive back in? Do I even want to? The thought of Theo pops into my mind, but I shake it off quickly. It's still fresh. Too fresh. "I don't know if I'm ready. I've gone this long without it. And honestly, every time I even think about Theo, it's like... a big mess of feelings that make zero sense."

"So, what's stopping you from feeling those feelings and letting them just be?"

I lean forward in my chair, frustrated. "Because what if I am wrong and I ruin a good thing we are having?"

She nods, her expression soft. "Ivy, sometimes it's not about having it all figured out. Sometimes it's about being with the uncertainty and letting it guide you, not control you. You don't have to make a decision today. Just... let yourself be where you are."

"Ugh," I groan, slumping back in the chair. "Why is it that every time I talk to you, I feel like I'm a drama queen? You make things sound so simple."

Pee-Pee laughs softly, a sound full of warmth and understanding. "It's not simple, Ivy. It's just uncomplicated. We make it harder than it needs to be by overthinking everything."

I bite my lip, mulling over her words. "Maybe that's part of the problem. I've been thinking about it all. Every moment, every possibility, every outcome. The future, the past, what I'm supposed to do next. It's exhausting."

"That's why you took the ban, remember?" Phyllis says gently. "To stop the spiral, to create space for you to breathe without all that pressure."

I nod slowly, feeling the weight of it all settle into my bones. "Yeah, I remember. I just... I guess I didn't expect it to be this hard to know what is me and what is me going down the wrong path again."

"And that's okay," she says. "It's okay to not have everything figured out, Ivy. But you've made more progress than you realize. You're here. You're aware of your feelings, and you're willing to look at them. That's the work."

I close my eyes, taking in her words, but they don't quite sink in yet. "I just wish I could just flip a switch and everything makes sense."

She smiles softly. "But you don't need to flip any switches. You're already doing the hard work. And sometimes the most important thing you can do is let the answers come to you, instead of chasing them."

I let out a breath, feeling a little lighter. "So, what, you're saying I should just... let things unfold?"

"Exactly," she says. "And if Theo is part of that unfolding, let it happen. But don't force anything. Let yourself just be, Ivy. That's where the real growth happens."

I nod, the idea of just being a little more foreign to me than I care to admit. But before I can say anything, I blurt out, "Theo said he'll ask me out proper when the ban is over."

Pee-Pee gives me that same calm look, waiting for me to continue. I'm suddenly nervous, like I've said too much too soon. But it's already out there.

Pee-Pee raises an eyebrow. "That's... a good thing, right?"

I chew on the inside of my cheek, unsure where to start. "It is, but..." I hesitate. "I don't know. I want to say yes. I really want to say yes. But part of me is scared that I'm just about to fall right back into the same pattern I've always had with guys. I don't want to be the kind of person

THE DATING BAN

who dates for the sake of dating, you know? I don't want to fall into that serial dating thing where I'm always just bouncing between guys, never really having anything real. I want a relationship. I don't want to waste my time with someone who isn't looking for the same thing. And what if Theo... what if he's not a relationship guy?"

Pee-Pee silence stretches for a few beats, and I feel my heart thudding in my chest. It's the first time I've really said it out loud. The fear that maybe I'm not just overthinking this—I'm overprotecting myself from something I actually want, because I'm terrified I'll end up alone again if I don't keep my walls up.

Pee-Pee looks at me with an expression that's equal parts understanding and challenge. "So, you're afraid of the possibility that Theo might not be the one, and you're thinking that means you should avoid even trying."

I nod, unable to stop the frown forming on my face. "Exactly. I don't want to waste time. I'm not in a place to just date around anymore. I'm not looking for flings. I want something real, something that has the potential to last."

Phyllis crosses her arms, settling back in her chair as she considers me. "Ivy, it's okay to want a relationship. But you can't control whether or not it happens with someone. Not even with Theo. All you can control is how you show up to it. What kind of relationship are you willing to build, and how much are you willing to let go of the fear that it might not look the way you expect?"

I stare at her, processing what she's saying. "But what if I let myself go for it and he doesn't want what I want? What if I get invested and then end up with nothing?"

"Then you'll have learned something," Pee-Pee says. "You'll have learned something about yourself, about him, about what you truly need. And you'll have grown. But you can't sit on the sidelines forever waiting for the perfect person to fall into your lap. Relationships—real ones—take risks. But you don't have to go in blind. You can be honest with Theo. Talk about what you both want, what you're both ready for. And the fact that you are even thinking about all of this, Ivy, I am very proud of you because you have come a very long way. Three months ago, you wouldn't have worried about any of this."

I let her words sink in, and the quiet ache in my chest grows a little less sharp. "I don't want to keep holding myself back from something real, just because I'm scared of it not working out."

"No one wants to be disappointed, Ivy. But disappointment doesn't always mean failure," Pee-Pee says gently. "Sometimes it just means you were brave enough to try. It doesn't mean the story is over. It just means you've learned something, and you can carry that with you moving forward. How do you know what he wants if you don't ask him? A lot of miscommunication happens when we make assumptions about what another person feels or thinks without giving them a chance to express themselves."

I nod slowly, the idea of being vulnerable with Theo still making my stomach twist, but less terrifying than before. "Yeah. I guess I'm not really giving him a chance to tell me what he wants if I don't let him in."

Pee-Pee smiles, standing as the session comes to a close. "Exactly. You won't know what's possible until you let it happen. Trust yourself, Ivy. Trust that you'll make the right decision. And if it doesn't work out, you'll be okay.

If you have an open conversation and he doesn't feel the same way, it doesn't mean you have to lose him as a friend."

She is right. In my heads it's been all or nothing, but we can handle this like adults.

As I leave her office, I feel lighter, even though the uncertainty is still there. But maybe that's the point. Maybe the fear of falling into old patterns isn't something to avoid, but something to face head-on. I need to trust myself enough to see where this could go with Theo—without letting fear decide for me.

A bra flies across the room and lands on the lamp. The lamp doesn't deserve this, but I'm past caring.

My wardrobe's been ransacked. It looks like a stylist had a tantrum and stormed off halfway through a styling session. There's a silk blouse crumpled in defeat on the floor, two dresses that scream "please take me seriously", and one particularly dangerous jumpsuit I only wore once, when I briefly lost touch with reality.

I'm down to the leather trousers.

They gleam up at me from the bed with the smug confidence of clothing that knows it's a poor choice. Still, I tug them on, one determined hop at a time. They make a noise like cling film and immediately begin the slow, hungry crawl north. I wiggle. They wiggle back. My arse is now in a fight for dominance and losing.

"Perfect," I mutter. "Very subtle. Nothing says romance like synthetic thigh friction."

Top next. I try on one that feels a bit too low-cut, but I catch my reflection and pause. The neckline is... working. There's cleavage, yes, but tasteful cleavage. Cleavage with purpose. I stand sideways and try to decide if I look effortlessly cool or like I've been vacuum-sealed.

In the mirror, I adjust a strand of hair, then pause again. *What if he kisses me?*

The thought appears out of nowhere and sends a ridiculous thrill through my chest. I grin—actually *grin*—at myself like a teenager with a crush. What if this is it? What if it goes brilliantly? We laugh, we eat, we kiss, I somehow don't spill wine on anything, and he looks at me like I'm not just Lucy's babysitter or the woman who baked cat vomit.

I pin my hair up—loosely, with one of those clips that makes it look like I didn't try, when really it took me three attempts and mild swearing. Then makeup: a bit of eyeliner, mascara, that lipstick Christa said makes me look "dangerously capable". Whatever *that* means.

I step back from the mirror again, catch a glimpse of myself with flushed cheeks, slightly glossy lips, hair up just so—and for a second, I feel it.

That buzz. That ridiculous, fizzy kind of excitement I haven't had in years. The good kind. The *what if this is the start of something* kind.

What if the date is perfect? What if he kisses me and it's everything I hoped? What if this isn't just a nice night out, but the first line in a completely new chapter?

What if I finally get it right?

I press my palms to my cheeks to cool them down, still grinning like a lunatic. My heart's pounding. In a good way. I feel electric. Alive.

And then, because my brain is *me*, the doubts start to creep in.

What if it's awkward? What if we run out of things to say? What if I get spinach in my teeth or laugh-snort in that unfortunate way I do when I get nervous and then try to cover it up by over-explaining and oh God—

I suddenly can't remember how to walk in the trousers. The fabric is climbing again, heading somewhere no synthetic blend should go. I tug at it, unsuccessfully, and glance at the clock.

Still just enough time to cancel.

No, I tell myself. Don't be ridiculous. You've got this.

But my chest's gone tight. My stomach's staging a protest. My hair suddenly looks too "done". My top feels too tight. My cleavage is trying to make a statement I'm no longer sure I believe in.

I grab my phone, scroll to Christa, and hit call.

Voicemail.

Of course.

I take a shaky breath and launch into it.

"Christa, it's me. I'm dressed. I look—honestly, I look sort of amazing, but also possibly like I'm going clubbing in 2013, and I'm officially freaking out."

I start pacing.

"I'm going on an actual date. With Theo. The trousers are at war with my arse, the top is making bold choices with my boobs, and I've just realised I have absolutely no idea how to behave like a calm, collected adult woman who goes on dates without saying things like 'Did you know sloths can hold their breath longer than dolphins?' in moments of silence."

I stop in front of the mirror again, trying not to hyperventilate.

"Anyway, if you get this and you hear I've fled the country, you'll know why. I'm wearing the cursed trousers. Please call me back and talk me down."

I hang up.

Silence.

Well.

No more stalling.

I grab my bag, dab the tiniest bit of sweat from the back of my neck, give the trousers one last tug of decency, and open the door.

Fine. I'm going.

Probably to my doom.

But also, maybe to something wonderful.

And either way—I've got lip gloss, a debit card, and emergency chocolate in my bag. That's enough to survive anything.

Probably.

33
The Green Lamp Conspiracy

Theo

I STAND IN FRONT of the mirror, adjusting the collar of my white shirt for the third time. The suit trousers feel slightly too formal for a Saturday night, but the jumper takes the edge off. Hopefully.

I don't usually dress like this outside of work—not anymore—but tonight's not just any night. Tonight's *our* first proper date. No child in the next room, no takeaway on the sofa, no pretending we are just friends.

I reach for the cologne I bought in duty free four years ago and have barely used since. One spray. Then another. I pause. Then a third, for good measure. I cough… maybe it was a bit much.

From the living room comes the clink of plastic cups and the unmistakable sound of Lucy hosting a tea party in full dramatic voice. I follow the noise.

Jasper and Geoff are sitting on the rug like overgrown toddlers, cross-legged and pretending to sip invisible tea.

Lucy beams at me from behind a toy teapot, apron tied crookedly over her dress.

"Daddy!" she calls. "You're just in time. Uncle Jasper's the dog."

"I said *I was bringing* the dog," Jasper grumbles, not moving from his spot.

Geoff squints at me over the rim of a pink cup. "Blimey. Look at you. Someone's dressed to impress."

Lucy stares at me intently for a second, her head tilted. "You look nice," she says, very seriously. Then she wrinkles her nose. "But you smell a bit weird."

"Thanks?" I say.

"It's like soap and flowers. But loud."

Jasper snorts. Geoff grins. "Well, you heard the expert."

"She's not wrong," Jasper adds, waving a hand in front of his nose. "Bit much. You smell like a posh hotel lobby."

"Brilliant," I mutter, tugging at my jumper. "Exactly the vibe I was going for."

Geoff sets down his plastic cup with all the care of someone holding posh crockery. "Right, well, before you embarrass yourself entirely... I booked you a table at *The Green Lamp*."

I blink. "You what?"

"The Green Lamp," he repeats. "Michelin-starred. Fancy, but not stiff. Romantic without being cheesy. Perfect for a first date where you want to impress her."

I pause. "Geoff, that place is booked out for months."

He shrugs, smug. "I know someone who knows someone. You're welcome."

I glance between them, suddenly less sure. "I don't know... is that too much? She's not— we're not—"

"You *are*," Jasper cuts in. "You *are* going on a date, and for once in your life, you need to stop overthinking it and just go."

Geoff nods. "Yeah. Stop being Theo the Sensible, Theo the organised coffee guy, Theo the responsible single dad who always carries spare tissues. Tonight, just be the bloke who wants to take a woman out and show her a good time."

"You make that sound... easy."

"It *is* easy," Jasper says. "You're the only one making it hard."

I take a breath, glancing at Lucy, who's now trying to balance a biscuit on Geoff's head. "She's just... different."

Geoff's grin softens. "Exactly. Which is why you don't take her to that local Italian where they know your order and always give you extra pity garlic bread because you are single."

I groan. "Alright, message received." *Come on, Theo. You are forty-three years old, not a teenager on the way to his first ever date!*

Geoff stands, stretching. "Green Lamp's booked for seven. Go. Enjoy yourself. And for God's sake, don't start talking about coffee bean origins unless she brings it up first."

I snort. "Noted. No monologues about roasting profiles."

"Unless it ends with *you* getting roasted," Jasper mutters, ducking before I can slap him on the head.

Ivy's already waiting outside when I get there, leaning against the doorframe like she does this sort of thing all the time—cool, composed, and completely unaware she's currently short-circuiting my brain.

Her leather trousers are doing things to my self-control. So is the top—fitted, confident, possibly designed in a lab to challenge single fathers trying to behave themselves.

"Hey," she says, smile easy, as she joins me and places a kiss on my cheek.

"Hi." My voice cracks slightly. *Brilliant start.*

We walk to the curb where the Uber's waiting, and I open the door for her—a rare, possibly extinct bit of chivalry I dusted off for the occasion.

Once we're inside and moving, the awkward hits in full force. Ivy looks effortlessly glamorous. I'm sweating lightly under my jumper and trying to remember how to sit like a relaxed, confident man instead of someone waiting for exam results.

"You look..." I begin, then instantly regret not workshopping the sentence in advance. "...structured."

She turns her head slowly. "Structured?"

I nod. "Yeah. You know... put together. In a really... architecturally strong sort of way."

She lets out a laugh. "So I look like a building."

"Not a *building*," I say, flailing gently. "Just... something with lines. And intention. Like—" I cut myself off. "You know what? You look amazing. Let's leave it at that."

She raises an eyebrow, clearly trying not to grin. "I'll take amazing. But I might put 'structurally sound' on my dating profile."

I stare straight ahead. The driver turns up the radio slightly, as if even *he* can feel the second-hand embarrassment rolling off me in waves.

Right. New strategy. Assertiveness. I can do assertiveness.

"So, I booked us a table at The Green Lamp," I say, sitting up slightly.

She leans back in her seat, tilting her head to look at me. "Wait, is this *that* place? The one where the WAGs always hang out?"

I try to play it cool. "Might be."

"The place with the cocktails that come in a cloud of dry ice and cost more than a weekly shop?"

"That's the one."

She raises an eyebrow. "And you got a table?"

I shrug, aiming for nonchalant but I'm not sure if I succeed. "I know a guy who knows a guy."

She stares at me, clearly trying to decide whether I'm full of it. "You're a man of mystery, aren't you?"

I give her what I hope is a suave, knowing look, but it probably lands somewhere between smug and slightly constipated. She smirks and looks out the window, and I swear I catch the faintest hint of a blush on her cheeks.

The rest of the journey is... quiet. Not in a bad way, but definitely in a *we are both trying very hard not to be weird and failing slightly* way. Ivy keeps tugging at the hem of her top and shifting awkwardly in her seat like she's trying to subtly negotiate a peace treaty with her trousers.

I sneak a glance at her—flushed cheeks, hair pinned just-so, lips glossed and slightly pursed in thought. She looks incredible. Also mildly afraid to bend at the waist.

I should say something cool. Confident. Low-key flirtatious.

"You look like a woman with very powerful ankles," I say instead.

She blinks, turns her head slowly. "Sorry, what?"

What the hell, Theo? Powerful ankles? Powerful ankles?!

That's not a compliment. That's... that's something your nan might say about a prize sheep.

"I meant the heels," I say quickly, hands up like I've walked into a hostage negotiation. "The way you walked in them. With conviction. Poise. Stability. Not—not like a horse. God. That's not—what I mean is—"

I glance over.

She's looking at me now the way you might look at a man who just complimented your elbows with a straight face. A bit wary. A bit amused. Possibly wondering if I've been left unsupervised for too long.

And maybe I have. Honestly, maybe this is who I am now. A man who ruins compliments and smells faintly of overconfident aftershave and stress.

"I'm going to stop talking now," I mutter.

"You probably should," she says, biting back a smile.

"Yep."

Silence. The car hums along, the driver mercifully ignoring us while some melancholy acoustic cover of a pop song plays quietly over the speakers.

I stare straight ahead, hands clasped in my lap like a man waiting for his performance review.

I can feel her still watching me out of the corner of her eye. I want to look. I *don't* look. I'm afraid I'll see confirmation of what I already suspect: that she's realised this was a mistake. That she's reconsidering the date. That she's mentally drafting a polite excuse to leave after the starters.

Or maybe that's just my brain trying to sabotage me. Again.

Out of sheer survival instinct, I clear my throat and try again—carefully, slowly, like someone diffusing a bomb. "You look great, by the way. Really great. The kind of great that probably makes other people consider breaking up with whoever they're dating."

She turns her head toward me, one brow raised. "Better."

"Only took me three attempts."

"Well," she says, settling back in her seat, "you're trending upwards. Keep going and by dessert you might manage an actual compliment without referencing livestock."

I chuckle—mostly out of relief. Maybe I haven't completely tanked this. Yet.

The Uber pulls up outside the restaurant, and I make a noble attempt to get out smoothly. My leg catches the door, I grunt softly, and then do that thing where you pretend it didn't happen and carry on as if your shin isn't throbbing.

I go around and open Ivy's door like some strange cross between a gentleman and a concierge with boundary issues. She takes my hand as she steps out—steadying herself more than anything else—and I'm fairly certain I hear the leather trousers emit a warning creak.

Inside, the restaurant is all low lighting, starched linens and that kind of expensive hush that makes you instinctively lower your voice and regret your footwear.

The maître d' greets us with a professional nod, clipboard in hand, posture so perfect it makes my spine feel self-conscious.

"Name?" he asks, expression unreadable.

"Theo Corbin," I say.

Then—because apparently I have verbal diarrhea—I add, "Table for two. Just us two. On a date."

"Right," he sneers. "Follow me."

Behind me, I feel Ivy's confusion radiating like a polite heatwave. She says nothing, which honestly makes it worse.

The maître d' leads us through the restaurant with gliding precision, every step somehow silently judging our entire lives. Ivy walks like she belongs here. I walk like someone trying to remember how knees work.

At our table, Ivy lowers herself slowly into the chair with the measured control of someone managing high-stakes leather trousers. I do my best not to knock over anything as I sit.

Then we both just... stop.

Silence.

The sort of silence where napkins suddenly become very interesting.

I try to smile. Ivy gives me one back—polite, patient. Encouraging, maybe. Or pitying.

Say something, Theo. Something charming. Light. Interesting.

"Did you know that after the Siege of Vienna in 1683, the Ottoman army left behind sacks of green coffee beans, and that's how Viennese café culture started?"

She gives me a puzzled look.

"Um... no?"

I nod like I've just shared an exciting personal triumph. "Yep. They filtered it with muslin and added milk and sugar to make it taste better. To the locals, I mean. And then coffeehouses started becoming social hubs—places for conversation and community—"

Stop talking, Theo. They told you not to do this. No bean chat. No brewing history. No bloody café trivia before the starters.

I take a sip of water and pretend I didn't just monologue my way into the nerd quadrant before we've even looked at the menu.

Ivy's watching me now with a look I can't quite read—halfway between *mild fascination* and *is this man okay?*

"I really liked your ankles comment better," she says at last, dry as toast.

I bury my face in the drinks list.

This date is going just about exactly as expected.

34

The Siege of Vienna

Ivy

WHAT IS HAPPENING?

He's attractive. Smart. Lovely with Lucy. Capable of forming full sentences in most situations. And yet here we are, three minutes into dinner, and he's delivered a lecture on the Siege of Vienna like this is some sort of historically-themed speed date and I'm about to be tested on key dates and bean filtration methods.

Is it me?

Am I radiating *Please talk about early coffee culture at length* energy?

I shift in my seat and immediately regret it. The trousers have ridden even further up than before, and I swear if I breathe too deeply, I'll have to get them surgically removed. My knickers are no longer involved in the evening. They've been left behind. Lost in action.

I try to subtly adjust myself. There's no way to do it gracefully. I nudge, twist, clench slightly, then give up and take a sip of water while pretending I'm just terribly, *terribly* interested in the candle.

Across from me, Theo is staring down at the menu like it's written in Morse code. He still looks handsome, in that nervous, floppy-haired way. But he also looks like he might bolt at any moment or begin reciting the *History of Cutlery in Western Europe*.

He wasn't like this before.

For three months, we've been full of banter and cake and the kind of easy chemistry that made me think maybe, just maybe, this could turn into something. I've laughed more with him in the past ninety days than I have in the past two years combined. He made me feel... seen. Wanted. Like maybe being a bit of a mess with strong opinions and complicated feelings didn't automatically put me in the 'lovely but not relationship material' box.

But now? Now he's barely looked at me.

Maybe I pushed this. Maybe I misread everything.

Maybe I was just convenient—a friend, a babysitter, someone who got a bit too comfortable and mistook kindness for something else.

And, of course, I chose *tonight* to wedge myself into trousers that feel like an emotional support compression garment. I can't sit properly. I'm terrified to stand. My thighs are trapped in a slow, squeaky death grip. Even my napkin is judging me.

Theo's still staring at the menu like he's about to draft legal amendments to it.

I clear my throat and try to sound breezy. "Thinking of suing the chef, or...?"

He blinks up, startled. "What? No. Sorry. I was just—trying to decode the 'beetroot textures.' Is that a sauce? A sculpture? A warning?"

I smile, but it feels tight. I want to ask *What's going on?* but instead I say, "You know, if I spontaneously combust, I'd like you to tell people it was the trousers."

He chuckles softly, but it fades fast. He's clearly trying, and that almost makes it worse. I can feel the weight of both of us overcompensating—like we're tiptoeing around something neither of us wants to admit out loud: that this... isn't working.

Not tonight.

I sip my water. Somewhere behind us, someone's laughing—actual, carefree laughter—and I want to throw my bread roll at them.

This isn't what I pictured. I thought our first date would be all spark and banter and knees bumping under the table. But instead, we're here in this stiff curated restaurant, both choking on nerves and unmet expectations.

The waiter arrives to take our order. Theo panics and points at the tasting menu. I do the same, because it's easier than deciding whether I want duck or a beef dish I can't even pronounce.

We both smile at the waiter like everything's fine.

It's not fine.

I think we're both realising it at the same time.

Theo clears his throat and says, "Oh... Lucy told me to say hi. She's having a tea party with Geoff and Jasper. I think Geoff was a fairy princess. Jasper was... unwilling."

I smile, automatically. "That sounds about right."

But then the smile doesn't quite stick.

Because suddenly, my brain's at it again.

Maybe he brought her up on purpose.

Maybe he thinks that's why I'm here. Why I'm *into* him. Because of Lucy. Because I've wormed my way into their little unit and now he feels like he has to give me a proper dinner before letting me down gently.

Maybe I'm not a potential girlfriend. Maybe I'm just the convenient, child-friendly woman upstairs who bakes and helps out with his daughter.

My stomach turns, and not from hunger.

I think about Lucy, all glitter and peanut butter crimes and unsolicited honesty. I think about her curling up beside me on the sofa and saying she sometimes wishes she had a mum. And about the tiny, sticky cardboard medal she gave me, like it was a treasure.

And for a terrifying, vivid second, I let my brain run wild. I imagine what it would be like if she was mine. If bedtime stories were my job. If I picked her up from school. If she looked for me in the audience during assembly. If she called me Mummy and meant it.

My throat tightens.

Is that what this is about? I think, panicking. *Have I just been using him as a gateway to a life I can't have on my own?*

What if this whole thing is backwards? What if it's Lucy I've fallen for—that version of life, that dream—and Theo's just the packaging it came in?

And what if he knows that?

What if he's sitting across from me thinking s*he's sweet, but she doesn't want me. She wants a family, and I'm the delivery method.*

I blink, hard.

And realise the waiter is gone, Theo's sipping his wine, and there's a plate of food in front of me—something delicate and green and artistically drizzled with too much olive oil—and I have absolutely no idea how long I've been sitting here in total silence.

I glance up.

Theo's watching me. Not unkindly. Not impatiently. Just... with that same quiet, confused smile.

And all I can think is: *Abort mission. Abort mission now.*

Dinner lasted approximately six years.

We spent a portion of it discussing beetroot. A solid twenty minutes on whether the warm weather would hold through September. And an inexplicable ten minutes on composting—not in a fun way. In a *council bin collection* way.

If romance had been invited, it left somewhere around the first course.

By dessert— which was technically a foam—I was actively praying for the fire alarm to go off. Or a blackout. Or a spontaneous sinkhole. Anything with dramatic exit potential.

Now we're in an Uber again, and I'm pretending to be absorbed in the streetlights.

Theo sits beside me, arms neatly folded, like a man who's being perfectly polite but would rather be anywhere else. The driver hums along to the radio. I don't hum. I think about how it's possible to be so close to someone and still feel like they're miles away.

When we pull up outside my building, Theo gets out too. He says it's just to stretch his legs before heading around the corner to his place, but we both know it's also the proper, gentlemanly thing to do.

Which is very Theo.

I lead us from the curb to my door, and we stop. There's a soft glow from the stairwell light and the faint smell of someone's slightly burnt toast from upstairs. It's a quiet night. The kind of night that might've ended with a kiss, if this were a different story.

We both stand there. Not speaking.

I shift awkwardly, and the trousers remind me of their ongoing assault.

Theo scratches the back of his neck.

Then, simultaneously:

"I guess—""So maybe—"

We stop. Awkward laugh. Silence again.

He tries first. "I mean, maybe it's just... one of those things."

"Yeah," I say quickly, "like, not everything needs to turn into something, right?"

"Exactly," he says. "Sometimes it's just—nice to know."

"To try," I add. "To rule it out."

We nod. Too much.

A pause.

Neither of us looks directly at the other.

I want to say *This wasn't what I hoped*, but instead I say, "Thanks for dinner."

He smiles. "Thanks for letting me talk about coffee. And... 17th-century history. And clouds."

"Very educational evening," I say, mouth dry.

He chuckles, almost embarrassed. "Yeah. I should... probably go. Let you get out of those trousers."

My eyebrows shoot up.

"I mean—" He grimaces. "That came out wrong."

I burst out laughing. It's the first real one I've had all night. "Go, Theo. Save yourself."

He grins, backing away. "Night, Ivy."

"Night."

And just like that, he turns and disappears around the corner. No kiss. No lingering look. Just a faint whiff of aftershave and the sound of retreating footsteps.

I unlock the door, step inside, and lean against it once it clicks shut.

Well.

That could've gone worse.

Technically.

But in the pit of my stomach, there's a hollow sort of ache. The quiet, resigned kind. The one that comes when something you really wanted... doesn't want you back in quite the same way.

And now I've got to get out of these trousers before they become part of my skeletal system.

35

Austen-esque

Ivy

I WAKE UP TO the sound of my phone buzzing from a notification, a low, juddery hum that rattles against a book and makes it sound far more urgent than it is.

But it's not the buzzing that jolts me upright—it's the sharp, strange little pop in my chest. Like a balloon that's been slowly deflating all night and finally gave up.

I sit in bed, blinking into the murky light, wrapped in the kind of stale emotional hangover that settles in your limbs like cement. And all I can think is:

Last night. The date. Oh, God.

It comes back in waves—the awkward start, the endless weather chat, the way we'd both slowly shrunk into ourselves like the world's least sexy time-lapse video.

I rub my eyes and reach for my phone.

Christa. There's no one else I'd rather confess this trainwreck to.

She picks up after two rings. Her voice is sleepy but warm. "Ivy? You're up early. What's happened?"

I groan, flopping back into the pillows. "Disaster."

She's instantly more alert. "Oh no. The date with Theo?"

"Well..." I sigh. "Yeah. Sort of. It just... it was awful, Christa. Like, impressively awful. Guinness World Record awkward."

There's a pause, then the sound of sheets shifting. "Okay, go on. What happened?"

"He picked me up. I looked great—I'll stand by that. Hair pinned, makeup decent, boobs making a strong effort. The leather trousers were... a mistake, obviously, but I was feeling brave."

Christa lets out a soft groan. "Oh God. Did they do the thing?"

"All the things. Rode up, cut off circulation, might need exorcising."

"Brave," she says again, with clear judgement.

"We got to the restaurant—and it was gorgeous, don't get me wrong, but so not us. You know when something feels too polished? Too... not pizza?"

"Michelin star vibes?"

"Exactly. Like we were auditioning to be people we're not. And the minute we sat down, he changed. Like, full-on PowerPoint Theo. We talked about autumn. For twenty minutes."

"Oh, Ivy."

"And composting. Composting." I groan, dragging the pillow over my face. "It was like the version of us that's fun and messy and *real* just... didn't turn up."

She's quiet for a beat. "Did anything happen at the end?"

"We stood outside my flat like two teens at the world's driest school disco and basically agreed—without actually agreeing—that maybe it wasn't meant to be."

"Wait—what? You both just... let it go?"

"I don't know. We didn't fight. We didn't even get emotional. It was just... tired. Like we were both hoping the spark would appear if we behaved well enough for long enough." I sigh again. "I kept thinking: *maybe it's me*. Maybe I made it weird. Maybe I've read this whole thing wrong and he's just... not that into me."

Christa scoffs. "You didn't make it weird. You wore trousers that attacked you and tried to be open to something new. That's not weird—that's optimistic."

I pause. "What if I only like him when Lucy's around?"

"Do you?"

"I don't think so. I mean, we had plenty of fun with Lucy not there. And we kissed in Dorset and that was nice. But last night I couldn't stop wondering if he thought that. Like maybe he thinks I'm just using him to get... them. A ready-made family. I'm so confused."

Christa is silent again, and when she speaks, her voice is gentler. "Oh, Babes! You don't really think you are using him? I always thought you had made your peace with—"

"I have. I really have," I say immediately. "I've accepted that I can't have children. I truly have! I've got Pee-Pee's bills to prove it. But... I do love Lucy. And it's terrifying, because I didn't mean to. She's not mine. She never will be. But I love her." I breathe in.

"What about Theo." My heart starts beating faster when I think on how he makes me laugh, how he helps me without making me feel silly or helpless. How I feel like me when I am around him.

"I think I may be falling in love with him as well."

"And he might love you back," she says quietly. "Just maybe not in that restaurant, or in those trousers, or on that particular day."

I laugh, then sniff. "I don't know what went wrong. It's like we tried to be something else and forgot how to be us."

"Probably because you were both trying so hard," she says. "You're not auditioning for a romcom. You already had the magic—and then you went and put it in a place with amuse-bouches and stuffy twats."

I sit up a little. "You think there's still a chance?"

"I think," she says carefully, "that what you had was rare. And if there's even the smallest part of you that still wants it... the real thing.... then you owe it to yourself to be honest."

I don't respond. Not right away. Because part of me wants to crawl back into bed and forget the whole thing. But another part is still wondering if maybe what we had isn't gone. Just... buried under one very weird night and a lot of unspoken things.

"I'll think about it," I say, quietly.

"I root for you both." She pauses, then adds, "Also, the next time you try to reinvent yourself, can we maybe ease into it with a skirt?"

I laugh. "Deal."

As I hang up, I settle back into my pillows, staring at the ceiling, lost in thought. It's clear that I'm not done with this—whatever this is between me and Theo. I'm not ready to call it over.

Ten minutes later, when hiding under my duvet is no longer an option, I pull on my hoodie and head downstairs, the weight of the morning still hanging over me. I need a distraction, so I decide to get some coffee. But not from Theo's café. I can't bring myself to go there—not yet. I might just cheat on him with a cheeky Starbucks.

As I reach the bottom of the stairs, something catches my eye. The letterbox in the door has an envelope lying on the floor beneath it. As I pick it up, I recognise the handwriting. I freeze, my heart thudding in my chest. It's from Theo. I stand still for a moment, just staring at the envelope. It feels like the world has shifted in some strange way, like it's suddenly become a little smaller, and a lot heavier.

Why is he sending me something? He could have just texted me... or called me... or I don't know. My stomach twists, but I know I can't just leave it there. I can feel the flutter in my chest as I tear it open. It feels like an eternity before I pull out the single sheet of paper inside.

I unfold it, running my fingers over the edges, holding my breath.

> *Dear Ivy,*
> *Yes, I'm writing a letter. I realise that makes me sound like I've wandered out of a period drama by Jane Austen, but I couldn't quite bring myself to text you after yesterday. Texts don't carry the weight I need them to. And I owe you more than a blinking cursor and a half-thought-out emoji.*
> *I messed up.*
> *Not in a catastrophic, scandal-worthy way, but in that quiet, clumsy, soul-sinking way where you realise you've taken something good and made it... weird. I wanted the dinner to be special, and instead I made it awkward. That's on me. Entirely.*

I tried to turn something simple and real into a performance. I overthought it. I picked a restaurant that didn't suit us. I wore way too much cologne. And worst of all, I turned into a version of myself I barely recognised. Uptight. Tongue-tied. Talking about Viennese coffee like I was doing a dissertation.

You didn't do anything wrong. You showed up. You were stunning, thoughtful, generous as ever, and I made you feel like a stranger. I don't know how I managed that, but I felt the shift as much as you did. We lost the thread. The spark. The us.

And that was my fault.

For three months, I've had the enormous privilege of knowing you. And I liked you from the start. Then I started to care about you. And then, somewhere between glue sticks and flour explosions, I realised I was in love with you.

Friday night, I let all that go quiet because I got scared. I thought I had to show you something more. That maybe being a single dad, a bit chaotic, not wildly glamorous or interesting, wasn't enough. So, I overcompensated. I tried to be someone else. Someone who wouldn't let you down. But in doing that, I let you down.

I didn't need to impress you. I just needed to be present. And myself. The man who laughs at your drama and loves how you light up when Lucy says something completely bonkers. The man who feels calmer when you're in the room. Who misses you when you're not.

So here's me, owning it. All of it.

And here's what I'm asking, if you can bear to read this without throwing it dramatically into your recy-

> *cling bin: let me try again. Not to impress you. Just to be with you. To show up honestly, and ask if maybe, despite the very beige weather conversation and talk about composting (I AM SORRY!!), you'd consider a second date.*
>
> *Nothing fancy. No reservations, no maître d', no culinary foam. Just me and you and whatever food doesn't require a glossary.*
>
> *Say yes, and I'll be at your door Friday at seven. I promise not to mention coffee. Unless you bring it up first.*
>
> *Yours, completely*
> *Theo*

I drop onto the stairs like my legs have given out beneath me.

Not dramatically. Not *deliberately*. Just one of those soft, stunned collapses where your whole body says, *Right, we're doing feelings now. Sit down.*

The letter's still in my hand, shaking slightly.

My throat's tight. My eyes sting. And then, just like that, a stupid, ridiculous little sniffle escapes me.

It's not even a sad cry. It's that quiet, overwhelming kind of joy that sneaks up on you when you've been bracing for disappointment and get hit with something tender instead.

He loves me.

Not in some hypothetical, *she's nice to have around* kind of way. Not because I'm good with Lucy or handy with biscuits. But because I'm *me*.

Flawed. Fumbling. Flour-covered and far too emotionally invested in small clay gnomes.

I wipe my eyes with the sleeve of the hoodie and pull out my phone with shaky fingers. Christa picks up on the second ring.

"I'm guessing this is either a life emergency or you need chocolate," she says. "Which is it?"

"He wrote me a letter," I say, my voice high and wobbly and absolutely not normal.

There's a pause. "A what?"

"A letter. An actual, handwritten, sincere, heart-melting, *Theo letter*."

I hear bedsheets rustling. "Wait. Is this a 'declaration of feelings' letter or a 'please return my soup ladle' kind of letter?"

"The first one," I whisper. "He took all the blame. Like, all of it. He said he tried too hard and turned into a stranger and that I didn't do anything wrong. He said I've always been enough."

"Oh my God," Christa breathes. "You're crying, aren't you?"

"I'm fine," I sniff. "It's just a normal physiological reaction to someone writing something *devastatingly perfect* and saying they love me."

"Oh babe. Now I'm tearing up."

I laugh and cry at the same time. "He even promised not to talk about coffee unless I bring it up first."

"Well, that's commitment," she snorts.

"I think I'm in love with him," I say, finally admitting it out loud. "Like. Actually."

Christa makes a noise somewhere between a squeal and a celebratory sigh. "I knew it. I *knew it*. So, what are you going to do?"

I look down at the letter again. His handwriting's a little crooked. He crossed out a word in the middle and rewrote it above like a nervous schoolboy. It's so him, it aches.

"I'm going to say yes."

36
Three Tubs of Ice Cream

Theo

I'M HUNCHED OVER THE kitchen table, half-drunk coffee at my side, trying to help Lucy with her writing. She's focused like a little artist with a grand vision—only her "masterpieces" look like scribbled attempts at something very abstract. But to her, they're perfect, and that's all that matters.

"You're doing great, Ladybug," I say, guiding her tiny hand to get the wobbly letter A a bit smoother.

"Look, Daddy! So pretty!" she says, holding it up proudly. It's more like a triangle with a line in the middle, but I'm not about to crush her spirit. "I'm a master!"

"Perfect. Soon you won't need me to help you anymore," I grin, ruffling her hair. "Now try a D. Remember, it's like a big curve, then a straight line down."

Lucy's so intent on her work that she doesn't notice me sneak a glance at my phone sitting beside me. The screen lights up, and I see a text from Ivy.

My heart skips a beat before I even read it. I grab my phone, fingers shaking just slightly as I unlock it.

The message is short. Simple.

Ivy

> Turns out I'm free Friday at 7.
>
> No trousers with a vendetta this time.
>
> Love to have dinner with my dorky Theo.
>
> (Preferably in jeans.)
>
> x

I feel a strange mix of relief and something else, something deeper—hope, maybe. *My dorky Theo.* I clutch the phone tightly. She is willing to give us another chance. I want to scream it from the hills—well, in the streets of Shoreditch more like.

Lucy looks up, noticing the sudden change in my expression. "What's wrong, Daddy?" she asks, her little face scrunched with concern.

I force a smile, slipping the phone back into my pocket. "Nothing, Lu. Just... something good."

Her face lights up, clearly not needing any further explanation. "Is it ice cream?"

I laugh, shaking my head. "No ice cream just yet, but I'll tell you what. Let's finish up these letters, and then maybe we'll see about that later, yeah?"

Lucy's grin spreads across her face as she gets back to her work, and I take a moment to breathe before texting my brothers.

"Lu, how about a sleepover at Uncle Jasper or Uncle Geoff on Friday?" I ask.

"Uncle Geoff. He dresses up as a princess with me," she giggles.

"Sounds like a plan," I laugh. Now I just need to come up with a plan on what Ivy and I can do, that is us.

Shifting the shopping bag from my right to my left, where I'm already juggling a second tote and what feels like a small corner shop's backroom, I jab the intercom.

"Coming," Ivy says.

"No, wait—let me up," I blurt, already regretting not explaining this in advance.

A beat of silence crackles back.

"Why?" Suspicion. Deserved.

"Just let me up, Ivy." I try to laugh, keep it light.

Another pause, then the door buzzes open. I exhale through the nerves I didn't realise I'd been holding in.

By the time I get to the top of the stairs, I'm slightly out of breath and deeply regretting the extra tub of ice cream. Ivy's standing in the doorway, arms folded, one brow raised, expression somewhere between curious and mildly unimpressed.

Then I see her properly, and everything slows.

Not in a dramatic film-score kind of way. Just quietly. Naturally. Like someone's turned the volume down on the world and left me standing here, watching her.

She's wearing a black skirt that flutters slightly around her knees and a soft blue top that dips just enough to be dangerous. Her hair's down. There's the faintest shimmer on her cheeks.

And my brain, usually decent at basic human functions, forgets what to do with that.

"Wow."

It slips out low and honest, and I instantly wish I'd saved it, bottled it somehow, just so she'd know I meant it in the absolute best way.

Her cheeks flush. "Wow?"

"Yeah." I shift the bags awkwardly to one arm. "A good wow. Like... a really good wow."

She squints slightly, not buying it yet. "You're not just saying that because your brain's oxygen-starved from carrying forty-seven pounds of groceries up the stairs?"

I grin. "Forty-five, tops. But no. I'd say wow even if I was completely empty-handed."

Her lips twitch like she's trying not to smile. "You're such a dork."

"An honest one," I say, and then because I'm an idiot, I add, "Also, you smell amazing."

Oh God. Abort.

To my relief, she lets it slide with only the faintest eyebrow raise. "So.. What's with the bags?"

"Dinner."

"You brought dinner?"

I walk past her into the flat before she can argue, dropping the bags on the kitchen counter like I do this all the time. "Lasagna. Homemade. Three-hour sauce. The works."

There's a pause. I can feel her looking at me. I keep my back to her while I pretend to be busy emptying the bags.

"You made lasagna?" she asks, voice just a little too even.

I turn around slowly, holding up an oven safe dish like a sacred artefact. "I did. I'm not saying it'll change your life, but... well. Actually, I *am* saying that."

She walks over, hands on her hips. "Do I get a menu, or is it just lasagna and promises?"

"Lasagna, salad, bread, and ice cream," I say smugly. "And not just *any* ice cream."

I reach into the bag and dramatically reveal three tubs like they're a royal flush. "Coffee and walnut, salted caramel, and classic vanilla. Choose wisely."

She stares at me for a beat, then grabs the salted caramel and clutches it to her chest. "You absolute hero."

"Glad to be of service," I say, and try not to look too pleased when she starts digging out two spoons from a drawer.

"Hang on," she says around a mouthful of ice cream. "Where's Lucy?"

"Sleepover at Geoff's."

Her eyes widen. "Does Geoff know he's hosting a royal guest?"

"She brought three tiaras and a wand. She called him 'Your Glittery Majesty' as I was leaving."

Ivy snorts into her spoon. "Oh no. Did he cry?"

"He texted me a crown emoji and a threat."

She shakes her head, still laughing, and something shifts in the air—softens. There's no pressure. No looming silence. Just the two of us, standing in her kitchen, trying to remember how to be... us.

I hand her a tomato and a knife. "You're on salad duty."

She raises an eyebrow. "That feels dangerously close to a power move."

"My kitchen, my rules."

"We're in my kitchen."

I ignore that small detail. "I'm still the head chef. Don't challenge me."

She slices the tomatoes carefully, but there's a smile at the corners of her mouth. I can feel it blooming in the room, that slow, quiet return to something that almost slipped away.

And maybe this time, we'll get it right.

37
Most Handsome Channel Islander

Ivy

THE LASAGNE IS DELICIOUS—RICH, cheesy, perfectly layered—but I barely manage half a portion. It's not that I'm not hungry. It's just... him.

Unlike our last date, tonight is good. Comfortable. Familiar. Like we've done this a hundred times before. Like it's not just dinner—it's foreplay.

I know it. He knows it.

Every glance, every accidental brush of hands, every low murmur of conversation is laced with tension, and it's making my stomach do ridiculous flips.

After we finish eating—well, after Theo finishes eating, because I spend most of dinner trying to pretend I'm not hopelessly distracted—we take our drinks into the living room. The sofa is deep and ridiculously comfortable, and I sink into it, tucking my legs beneath me. Theo settles beside me, stretching out in that lazy way of his, arm slung over the back of the sofa.

Too close. Not close enough.

We chat easily, laughter slipping between us as effortlessly as the wine in my glass. And then, between sips, I tilt my head at him, something suddenly clicking in my mind.

"You know, I've been meaning to ask..." I gesture at him. "You, Jasper, Geoff—what's with the old-fashioned names?"

He sighs dramatically, swirling his drink. "Theodor and Geoffrey, oh how we hated it."

"Fitting." I start laughing, covering my mouth with my hand. "You all have an air of poshness around you."

Theo rolls his eyes, but he's grinning. "Yeah, yeah. Meanwhile, Jasper gets off easy—he's just Jasper."

I shake my head, still giggling. "So what, were your parents obsessed with history or something?"

He exhales. "My mum. She's got some kind of old English upper-class blood, very remotely related to Edward II or something. Not that it means anything." He rolls his eyes. "But she likes to pretend it does."

I raise a brow. "Oh?"

He smirks. "Put it this way—she's your typical eccentric middle-class housewife who somehow thinks she's royalty. She basically rules the 'high society' of Guernsey."

I stare at him for a second. "You're telling me... your mum is the Queen of Guernsey?"

Theo bursts out laughing. "Something like that. She insists on calling us by our full names. Theodor, Geoffrey, Jasper—like we're characters in a Brontë novel. Needless to say, none of us go home often."

I let out a laugh, already picturing some grand, overly decorated house with an eccentric, pearls-and-cashmere-clad woman barking orders at her formally named sons. "I have to meet her one day."

Theo arches a brow. "Are you mad?"

I grin. "A little."

He chuckles, taking a sip of his drink, but before the moment can stretch, something clicks in my brain, and I sit up straighter, suddenly very excited.

"Wait, wait, wait." I point at him, eyes wide. "You grew up on Guernsey?"

He nods, amused by my sudden enthusiasm. "Yes...?"

I gasp. "Like Henry Cavill?!"

Theo freezes for half a second, then groans, rolling his eyes so hard I'm surprised they don't fall out of his head. "Oh my God."

I lean in, practically bouncing. "Do you know him?"

He lets his head fall back against the sofa. "Right. That's it. Date's over. Get out... I mean, I'll leave." He tries to get up, but I burst out laughing, and I stop him placing a hand on his arm.

"Come on! You both lived on a tiny island—you must have crossed paths at some point!"

Theo narrows his eyes at me, lips twitching. "First of all, no, I do not know everyone that lives on Guernsey. It is small but not that small. Second of all, he's from Jersey, not Guernsey."

I wave a hand dismissively. "Close enough."

"It is not close enough!" He looks deeply offended, and it just makes me laugh harder.

"I mean, it's all the Channel Islands, right?"

Theo groans again. "Okay, this is the highest level of insulting."

I clutch my stomach, absolutely delighted. "But imagine if you did! You and Superman! Just two lads growing up together on a little island, sharing your deepest dreams—"

Theo levels me with a dry look. "Yes, Ivy. That's exactly what happened. In fact, Henry and I used to have tea every Thursday. We'd sit on the cliffs and discuss our futures. He wanted to be a movie star, and I wanted to learn yoga."

I cackle, tipping my head back against the sofa.

He shakes his head in mock despair. "Unbelievable. Unbelievable."

But even as he's playing it off, there's a flicker of something else in his expression. A tiny, good-humoured flicker of jealousy.

I smirk, leaning in closer, dropping my voice into something conspiratorial. "Admit it. You're just bitter that I brought up Henry Cavill."

Theo scoffs. "Oh, absolutely. Gutted. Devastated, even."

"You are!" I tease. "You wanted me to say 'Wow, Theo, you're the most handsome Channel Islander I've ever met!'"

He leans in, close enough that I can feel the warmth of his breath. "I *am* the most handsome Channel Islander you've ever met."

My smile falters slightly. Because suddenly, we're not joking anymore.

I swallow, my throat suddenly dry. I exhale, forcing a casual tone. "Fine. You win. You're officially the hottest person to come out of the Channel Islands."

Theo grins. "I should hope so."

But my heart is still hammering. Because we're sitting here, on this sofa, joking, laughing, flirting—and underneath it all, the tension is still there.

Simmering. Waiting.

We both know where tonight is heading. The question is—who's going to make the next move?

Theo shifts on the sofa, his fingers drumming idly against his knee as he glances around the room. Then he smirks.

"Hang on." He looks at me confused. "Where's your army of gnomes gone?"

"What?"

"The gnomes." He gestures around dramatically. "The creepy little festive creatures that used to haunt this place. Did they finally rise up and overthrow you?"

I roll my eyes, but my stomach tightens just a little. He noticed.

"They're in a box," I admit, tucking my legs under me.

Theo's brows shoot up. "You boxed them up?"

I nod, chewing my bottom lip. "Yeah."

His smirk deepens. "Why? Did they become self-aware? Were they plotting something sinister?"

I let out a breathy laugh, shaking my head. "No, you dork." I hesitate, my fingers tracing patterns on the sofa fabric. Then, before I can overthink it, I say it. "I just... I wanted to make sure the place was tidy. In case you—" I swallow. "In case you wanted to come up after dinner."

Theo stills.

I feel his gaze on me, but I don't look up. Bloody hell, saying it out loud makes me feel so exposed.

I risk a glance at him.

He doesn't tease me. He doesn't smirk.

Instead, he leans in, his voice lower, rougher. "So, you were planning this."

I shrug, forcing an air of nonchalance even though my pulse is going insane. "Well, you did bring dinner to me, so I'd say we're even."

Theo studies me. Then he exhales a quiet laugh, shaking his head. "Look at us."

I arch a brow. "What about us?"

"We were both doing it." He runs a hand through his hair. "I was over here making lasagne like some sort of domestic god, hoping you'd want to spend the night, and you were boxing up your gnome army to make sure I wouldn't be scared off."

I giggle, the tension cracking just slightly. "It was a risk. They're quite intense."

"You're intense," he murmurs.

Something about the way he says it makes my breath catch.

My giggle dies in my throat, and I suddenly realise how close we are.

His arm is still resting along the back of the sofa, and if I shifted even slightly, I'd be right against him. His gaze flicks to my lips, and for a second, I think he's going to joke, make some snarky comment—

But he doesn't.

Instead, his hand lifts, fingers brushing along my jaw, tilting my chin ever so slightly.

My heart stutters.

"Theo—"

But then he kisses me.

It's not hesitant. It's not testing the waters. It's deliberate, firm—like he's wanted to do this for hours and finally decided he can't wait another second.

I melt instantly, my hands gripping the front of his shirt, pulling him closer. He makes a low sound in the back of his throat, deep and satisfied, and I feel it everywhere.

The tension that has been simmering between us all night finally ignites, and I know, without a doubt, that neither of us is stopping now.

Theo's lips move against mine, slow and sure, like he has all the time in the world. His hands settle on my waist, firm but careful, and before I can even process it, he shifts, pulling me effortlessly into his lap.

I gasp softly against his mouth, my hands landing on his shoulders as I straddle him. I can feel his hard cock pressing against my pussy. With my skirt flared out, only the material of my knickers and his jeans is between us. A delicious shiver runs through me.

His lips trail from my mouth down to my jaw, then lower, pressing slow, lingering kisses along the curve of my neck.

I exhale, tipping my head slightly to the side, giving him more space, wanting… needing him closer.

He hums softly against my skin, his hands roaming lightly over my back, fingers dipping just under the hem of my top, teasing but not pushing. His breath is warm, his lips soft, and the way he's holding me—steady, unhurried—makes my stomach flutter.

I shift against him instinctively, and his grip tightens slightly, like he's trying to keep himself in check. Like he's waiting for me to tell him exactly how far I want this to go.

And I do want this. Fuck, I want this.

But I also want him. Not just the heat, not just the way he's making my body hum with anticipation—I want everything.

As if he can sense my thoughts, Theo presses one last kiss just below my ear and murmurs against my skin, "You know... you haven't given me the full tour yet."

His voice is laced with something that causes a thousand butterflies in my stomach.

I force myself to focus, my fingers still curled into the fabric of his shirt. "The tour?"

His lips brush my skin again. "Mmhmm." He presses a kiss just beneath my jaw, then lowers his voice further. "You haven't shown me the bedroom yet."

I almost forget to breath because I know what he's asking.

He's not demanding, not assuming. He's checking in with me in the gentlest, most ridiculously perfect way.

And just like that, I know my answer.

I lean back just slightly, meeting his gaze. His eyes are dark, searching, waiting for me to decide.

I swallow, then smile softly. "Well, we can't have you missing part of the tour, can we?"

His lips curve into a slow grin, his hands tightening on my hips but I wiggle free and stand up. "No," he murmurs, as he watches me. "That would be a tragedy."

A shiver runs through me as I hold out my hand as an invitation to come with me. His fingers curl around mine, warm and steady, and without a word, I lead him towards the bedroom.

The anticipation between us is palpable.

I reach the door, pushing it open, then flick on the bedside lamp. A warm, golden glow fills the room, casting soft shadows on the walls. The light feels intimate, safe. Like a quiet invitation.

And then Theo is there, right behind me, his hand still in mine.

He turns me slowly, his other hand coming up to cup my cheek.

For a second, he just looks at me, like he's memorising this moment, this choice. And then he kisses me.

Deep, slow, devastating.

I sigh into his mouth, pressing closer, hands gripping his shirt as he tilts my head, deepening the kiss. His tongue pushes against mine with quiet certainty, like he's staking a claim without words.

Then, without breaking contact, his fingers trail down, brushing the hem of my top. He hesitates—just for a fraction of a second—giving me space to stop him if I want to.

I don't.

I lift my arms slightly in answer, and he exhales against my lips before peeling my top over my head. The fabric slides away, pooling somewhere behind me, but I barely notice. Because now his hands are on me—exploring, mapping, tracing slow, burning lines down my spine.

I gasp as his lips leave my mouth, trailing down my neck, over my collarbone.

He's taking his time. Letting me feel everything.

My hands find his T-shirt, fumbling with the hem, eager, needing to feel his skin against mine.

He lets out a low chuckle, his lips brushing against my shoulder. "Impatient?"

I don't even hesitate. "Yes."

Theo grins, a lazy, obnoxiously sexy grin, before reaching behind him, pulling the T-shirt over his head in this sexy way that I thought only happens in films.

I've seen him topless, but we were surrounded by people. Having him here, half naked, just the two of us, that is a completely new level of sexy as hell.

Strong shoulders, toned arms, the kind of stomach that makes my fingers itch to explore.

I trail my hands over his chest, feeling the warmth of his skin beneath my palms, the steady rise and fall of his breath.

His hands also start to explore my body again, finding the waistband of my skirt. He pauses, giving me another moment to change my mind, but I don't want to.

I press my lips to his, my answer clear.

Theo groans softly against my mouth as he tightens his grip before he starts to undress me properly.

And I know—tonight, I'm not holding anything back.

As my skirt pools at my feet, I step out of it, my pulse hammering. Theo's gaze drags over me, slow and deliberate, his expression dark with hunger. He looks devastated by the sight of me, like he can't quite believe I'm real.

The way he watches me sends a thrill down my spine, emboldening me.

Holding his gaze, I slip out of my knickers, then unclasp my bra, letting it fall away. His jaw tightens before he growls deeply. This man might be an adorable dorky single dad, but anyone who thinks that makes him any less a man needs their head check out. This, here, is the sexiest man I've ever had in my bedroom.

Heat coils in my stomach.

I slide backwards onto the bed, leaning back just enough to hopefully look half-sultry—while subtly adjusting my posture to make sure my boobs don't resemble sad little sacks of gravity's betrayal.

Theo exhales sharply, his eyes never leaving me.

"Ivy... the few times I let myself hope we'd get here—to this moment—I imagined what you might look like naked. But no fantasy ever came close to this."

He watches me for a beat, his chest rising and falling in slow, deliberate breaths, like he's trying to rein himself in. But the way his hands flex at his sides, the way his jaw tightens, tells me he's barely holding on.

Then, with a quiet exhale, he reaches for his belt.

The soft clink of the buckle sends a shiver down my spine.

He keeps his eyes on me as he unbuttons his jeans, pushing them down in one smooth motion. The fabric pools at his feet, leaving him in nothing but black boxer briefs that do absolutely nothing to hide how much he wants me. If I thought he was packing at the cottage, it's nothing compared to when he is hard. And this is all for me. Because of me.

Heat pulses low in my stomach.

I bite my lip, drinking him in. Every inch of him is effortless, stunning.

Theo catches my look and smirks, but there's something almost shy behind it, like he's not used to being this exposed, this vulnerable.

That thought alone makes me want him even more.

Slowly, I sit up, moving to the edge of the bed until I'm within reach. My fingers trail over the taut skin of his stomach, feeling the way his muscles tighten beneath my touch.

His breath is unsteady now, his control slipping.

Then, before I can overthink it, I hook my fingers into the waistband of his briefs and look up at him.

A silent question.

Theo swallows hard, his hands sliding into my hair, his thumbs brushing over my cheekbones as he leans down. His lips find mine again, deep and unhurried, savouring every second.

When he finally pulls back, his forehead rests against mine.

"Ivy," he murmurs, his voice thick, rough around the edges.

That's all I need to hear.

With one slow tug, I strip away the last piece of clothing between us.

Theo inhales sharply, his grip on me tightening for just a moment before he pushes me back onto the bed, following me down.

His weight, his warmth, the sheer presence of him above me—

I'm lost.

And I don't ever want to be found.

Theo hovers over me, his weight pressing me gently into the mattress, but there's no urgency in his movements.

Not yet.

Instead, he takes his time, his fingertips skimming over my skin in slow, reverent strokes, mapping every inch of me. Like he's trying to commit me to memory.

I shiver beneath him, arching into his touch, and he lets out a quiet, satisfied moan, his lips ghosting over my collarbone. He kisses his way lower, taking his time, trailing warmth wherever his mouth lands.

"You're stunning," he murmurs against my skin.

I let out a breathy laugh. "You keep saying that."

He lifts his head, his gaze locking onto mine. "Because it keeps getting truer."

The look in his eyes—the way he's staring at me like I'm something precious, something he can't quite believe is his—makes my heart ache.

I reach up, threading my fingers into his hair, pulling him back to me.

The kiss that follows is slow and deep, his body pressing flush against mine, his hard cock nestled between us. There's no hesitation anymore, no lingering uncertainty. Only heat, only need, only us.

Theo moves against me, his hands roaming, teasing, until every nerve in my body is singing. I can feel the restraint in him, the way he's holding back, waiting for me to tell him I want this just as much as he does.

So I do.

I press my lips to his ear and whisper, "Theo, condoms are in—"

His control snaps. He reaches for the drawer I had been pointing at.

A low groan rumbles in his chest as he rolls on the protection before he reaches for me, his mouth finding mine again with a new kind of urgency.

There's nothing slow about this now.

No more teasing, no more hesitation.

He pushes into me and then stills, allowing us to savour the moment. His hands roam my body like he's been starving for this—slow at first, then firmer, surer, like he needs to feel all of me. Like he needs to memorise every curve, every reaction.

I moan against his lips as he finally starts to move, his thrusts sending delicious shivers up my spine. He tilts his head, deepening the kiss, and the heat between us turns molten.

His weight presses me into the mattress, his bare skin hot against mine, and every nerve in my body is alive, aching for more.

"Theo," I breathe, nails digging lightly into his back, and the way he shudders in response sends a thrill through me.

He pulls back slightly, his lips hovering just over mine, his breath uneven. His darkened gaze meets mine, searching, checking.

"You feel like a dream, Ivy," he murmurs, voice rough, thick with something deeper than just desire. "Tell me this is not a dream! Please tell me," he begs.

I reach up, cupping his jaw, brushing my thumb over the stubble there. "Not a dream, Theo. Just the best reality ever," I whisper.

Something shifts in his expression—like he's relieved—before his lips crash into mine again, stealing the last of my breath.

His hands explore, his fingers teasing, tracing, learning exactly what makes me gasp, what makes my body arch into him. My skin burns everywhere he touches, every nerve ending sparking with anticipation.

I let go completely, giving myself to this moment, to him.

Theo groans softly against my neck as he thrust harder. Then one of his hands finds my clit and I want to scream with need. He slowly circles my bundle of nerves and I can feel the first signs of an impending orgasm.

"Ivy," he murmurs, voice strained, desperate.

I smile against his skin. "Hmm?"

He pulls back just enough to meet my gaze, his fingers stopping for a moment.

"I need you," he rasps.

I forget to breath because I know he doesn't just mean now.

He means completely.

I press my lips to his, answering him without words, and in the next moment, there's nothing left between us.

And when he finally moves again, I know, I'm gone.

38

Cuddles, Kisses & Ice Cream

Theo

IVY IS UNDERNEATH ME.

Naked. Flushed. Beautiful.

I brace myself above her, trying to breathe, trying to hold onto some scrap of control, but it's slipping fast. She's warm and soft, her hands roaming over my back, her nails trailing down my spine in a way that sends heat straight through me.

She just said my name—breathless, needy—and I swear to God, I nearly lost it right then.

I rest my forehead against hers, trying to steady myself, trying to take this slow, but she shifts beneath me, pressing closer, and a sharp exhale escapes me.

Her lips brush mine, light, teasing, knowing, before she whispers, "Theo, I need—"

I don't let her finish.

I kiss her like I need her to survive, like she's the essence of my life.

She melts into me, her fingers tightening in my hair, and any remaining restraint I had left is gone.

I don't hold back anymore. I thrust into her with all my need. My cock is hard, painfully hard... but it's good pain.

I let my hands roam, let my mouth explore, learning every sound she makes, every gasp, every shiver. I want to memorise her—how she reacts, how she moves, how she falls apart beneath me.

We move faster and I am sure I can't hold on any longer. My fingers find her clit again and when I start circling it, she digs her fingernails into my back.

"This feels so good, Theo. Don't stop. Don't bloody stop," she demands. Not even the end of the world could get me to stop. Here, now, this is why I knew we needed a second chance. We are perfect as friends and we are even better as lovers.

Ivy's body is warm and yielding, her hands roaming over my skin, pulling me closer, urging me deeper. And God, she feels incredible.

I press my forehead against hers, swallowing hard, trying to ground myself, but it's impossible. Every breath, every sigh, every quiet sound she makes drives me closer to the edge.

Her fingers tighten in my hair, and I groan, my grip on her waist firming.

"Ivy," I murmur, voice rough, desperate.

She tilts her head, brushing her lips against mine in the softest, laziest kiss—like she's savouring this, like she's savouring me.

It undoes me completely.

I shift, angling myself just right, and Ivy lets out a sharp gasp, her back arching.

Fuck.

I press my lips to her shoulder, my breathing uneven. Ivy calls out and I can feel her pussy fluttering around me as her orgasm hits. That's enough to set me off as well. For a moment I see stars and I stop breathing before I half collapse on top of her, mumbling her name like it's a prayer.

Nothing will ever feel this good. Nothing will ever feel this right.

Neither of us moves for a while. I rest my forehead against her collarbone, still catching my breath. I half-expect her to shift, to pull away, to crack some joke to ease the intensity of what just happened.

But she doesn't.

Instead, she lets out a soft, satisfied hum, running her fingers lazily through my hair, her nails scraping gently against my scalp.

My eyes flutter shut.

I could stay like this forever. But I can't. I roll off her to take care of the condom, still trying to catch my breath.

After a moment, I shift onto my side, pulling her with me, not wanting to lose the warmth of her. She comes easily, tucking herself against my chest, her leg sliding over mine, her skin still flushed and warm.

I press a kiss to the top of her head, and she sighs, her breath fanning against my skin.

"That," she murmurs, voice thick with sleep, "was worth boxing up the gnomes for."

A low chuckle rumbles through me. "High praise."

She lifts her head slightly, meeting my gaze. "You're still thinking about it."

I blink, caught off guard. "Thinking about what?"

She smiles, small but knowing. "This. Us."

I exhale, brushing a strand of hair from her face. "Yeah," I admit, voice quieter. "I am. Glad I asked for a second chance?"

Ivy studies me for a moment, her fingers absently tracing along my chest. "More than glad."

Then she leans in, pressing a kiss just above my heart before settling back down.

I tighten my arms around her, holding her close, and for the first time in a long time, everything feels exactly as it should.

I wake to warmth. Solid, steady warmth pressed against my chest, my arm draped over her waist, fingers lazily tracing soft circles against her skin.

I blink sleepily, stretching just a little, and the movement makes Ivy shift against me. Instinctively, I tighten my hold, pulling her closer, burying my face in the crook of her neck so I can breathe her in.

"Good morning," she mumbles, voice thick with sleep.

I hum against her skin. "Hmm. Good morning."

Her voice does something to me. That soft, sleepy rasp pulls at something deep inside me, making me want to stay here forever.

She shifts in my arms, turning to face me, and when I open my eyes, she's already watching me. Her hair is wild, curling in every direction, and her eyes are still heavy with sleep. She's never looked more beautiful.

She reaches up, running her fingers through my hair, trying to smooth it down.

I smirk. "Am I a mess?"

"The messiest," she says with a grin, tugging lightly at a strand.

I shift, leaning over her with a slow, satisfied smile. "Well, whose fault is that?"

She giggles, and I catch that little flicker in her eyes—the one that makes my stomach flip.

"Oh, I don't know…" she says, voice playful. "I seem to recall *you* being very determined last night."

I lower my head until my lips just barely brush against hers. "Determined, huh?"

"Mmhmm."

I kiss her deeper, slow and unhurried, like we've got all the time in the world. And maybe we do.

She sighs into my mouth, her fingers sliding down my back, leaving goosebumps in their wake. The feel of her beneath me—soft, warm, *home*—makes me want to hold on tighter.

Suddenly, she pulls back, grinning like she's up to something.

I blink, slightly dazed. "What?"

She presses a quick, teasing kiss to my lips before wriggling out from under me and sprinting out of the bedroom.

"What the—? Ivy!"

I groan and fall back onto the pillows, listening to her laughter echo down the hall.

A minute later, she comes back clutching something, her grin wide with triumph.

I sit up, raising a brow as my eyes drop to the tub in her hands. And then I see it. Ice cream. A flash of pure delight sparks in my chest.

"Ice cream?" I ask, smirking.

She plops down beside me on the bed, holding up a single spoon. "For breakfast."

I let out a low chuckle, shaking my head. "You are chaos."

"I am," she agrees proudly, popping off the lid and scooping out a generous bite of salted caramel. She holds the spoon out to me. "But you love it."

I eye the spoon for a second before leaning in and taking the bite. The cold hits my tongue in the best way—and the way her eyes darken when I wrap my lips around the utensil? Yeah, that does things too.

I lick my lips. "Blimey. That's good."

"Right?" She scoops another bite for herself, her satisfaction clear as she lets the cold hit her tongue.

I watch her, smirking. "So this is your idea of a perfect morning?"

She grins. "Cuddles, kisses, ice cream? Pretty much."

I shake my head, amused, and steal the spoon from her hand, scooping a bite for her this time. "Alright, but we need to lay down some ground rules."

She raises an eyebrow. "Rules?"

"Well, one rule really. You can never, under any circumstances, let Lucy know I had ice cream for breakfast."

She snorts. "Why?"

I sigh dramatically. "Because I've forbidden her from doing it, and if she found out, she'd never forgive me."

She gasps in mock horror. "Theo! You hypocrite!"

I level her with a serious look. "I know. She would *end* me."

She bursts into laughter, collapsing against me. "Okay, okay! I promise I won't tell your tiny overlord."

I exhale in relief. "Good. You might have just saved my life."

She shakes her head, taking the spoon back from me and scooping another bite. "You're a terrible influence."

I smirk, pulling her into my lap. "Yet, you seem to love it. Besides I'm not the one that brought ice cream to the bedroom."

She hums in agreement, letting me kiss the lingering taste of caramel from her lips.

Yeah. This is the perfect morning.

39

Bracing for Impact

Ivy

WE'RE STILL TANGLED UP in each other, the ice cream tub nestled between us, trading bites in lazy contentment. Theo's arms are loose around me, his fingers idly tracing patterns along my bare back, his warmth keeping me cocooned in this perfect little bubble.

But then...

"And yet, you seem to love it."

His words hang between us, light, teasing—just part of the banter.

But it's the way he suddenly freezes that makes my stomach dip.

His fingers stop moving. His body tenses.

And when I glance up at him, I see it—the flicker of uncertainty in his eyes.

A beat of silence.

Then, quietly, he says, "Was the letter too much?"

I try to breath calmly. "What?"

He exhales, rubbing the back of his neck. "The letter I sent you. My very outdated declaration. Was it... too much?"

I frown slightly, caught off guard by the sudden change in mood. "Of course not," I say, shaking my head. "If it had been, I wouldn't have agreed to meet you again, would I?"

Theo searches my face, like he's still not entirely convinced.

I soften, setting the ice cream aside before shifting fully to face him. My fingers find his, lacing them together as I choose my next words carefully.

"But," I continue, voice steady, "you did say in the letter that you loved me."

His throat bobs as he swallows, his grip on my hand tightening slightly.

"Yeah," he admits, low and rough.

I nod, keeping my expression open, my tone light despite the way my heart is suddenly pounding. "Did you mean... as a friend? Or...?"

I hesitate, then add with a small, wry smile, "I'm not fishing, I just figured I should ask. You know, so there are no confusions or miscommunications."

Theo's jaw tightens, his fingers flexing in mine.

I hold my breath, waiting.

Then, finally, he exhales, his thumb brushing absentmindedly over my knuckles.

"I meant," he says slowly, carefully, "that I love you."

My stomach flips.

His eyes are locked on mine, steady and serious, as if he's making sure I hear him properly, making sure there's no room for doubt.

"Not as a friend," he continues, his voice quieter now. "Not as anything casual or complicated." A dry laugh escapes him. "I mean, it has been all so different, complicated, I know that. But that doesn't change the fact that I love you, Ivy."

He means it.

It's real.

And I have no idea how to breathe.

My heart stumbles over itself.

He loves me.

Not as a friend. Not as something casual. Not as a maybe or a possibility.

He just does.

Theo watches me, his breath uneven—like he's bracing for impact, like he's terrified of whatever I'm about to say next.

I don't make him wait.

I reach up, cupping his face between my hands, my thumbs brushing lightly over the stubble on his jaw. His skin is warm beneath my fingertips, his pulse steady but fast.

He swallows hard. "Ivy—"

"I love you too," I whisper.

For a moment, he just looks at me, his expression unreadable, like he's trying to process the words, make sure he's heard them right.

Then, all at once, something in him breaks.

His lips crash into mine. It's not slow. Not careful. It's deep, urgent—like he needs to kiss me, like he's making up for every moment he's ever wanted to and couldn't.

I gasp against his mouth, and he groans, pulling me closer, his hands sliding over my waist, gripping me tightly like he's afraid I'll slip away.

I tilt my head, deepening the kiss, my fingers tangling in his hair. He makes a low, needy sound in the back of his throat, and heat spreads through me like wildfire.

His hands roam, familiar but hungry, learning my body all over again.

I press myself against him, sighing into his mouth as he rolls us over, pinning me beneath him.

I can feel his heartbeat, his love, in every touch, every kiss, every whisper of breath between us.

And this time, when we lose ourselves in each other, it's not just about need.

It's about us.

About everything we are.

"I love you," I whisper, my voice steady. "Not too. Just—I love you. Not because you said it first. Not because I feel like I should. I'm not giving you what I think you want from me."

I take a breath, feeling his skin warm beneath my palms, his breath uneven against my lips.

"I. Love. You," I repeat, letting the words sink between us. "Regardless of whether you love me back or not. Although, the fact that you do is—well, great."

A slow, disbelieving smile spreads across his face.

For a second, he just stares at me, like he's committing this—me—to memory.

Then he groans, his grip tightening on my waist. "You ruin me," he mutters, before crashing his lips to mine.

I laugh into the kiss, but it quickly dissolves into something deeper. Something more.

Theo presses me back into the pillows, his body covering mine, his warmth seeping into my skin, his hands roaming like he needs to feel every inch of me.

I sigh into his mouth, fingers twisting into his hair, pulling him closer, wanting all of him.

And then—

Thud.

We both freeze.

Theo pulls back, eyes hazy, lips kiss-swollen. "What was that?"

I blink, momentarily lost, before I glance sideways.

The tub of ice cream.

It's rolled onto its side on the floor, melting into a sad puddle of caramel disaster.

I gasp. "The ice cream!"

Theo groans, dropping his head to my shoulder. "Unbelievable."

I bite my lip, trying not to laugh as I gently push him off me. "We have to save it."

He flops onto his back dramatically. "I can't believe this. I just told you I love you and now you're abandoning me for ice cream."

I grab the tub, inspecting the damage. "You knew who I was when you got into this relationship."

Theo turns his head, watching me with amusement as I pluck the spoon from the sheets and scoop up a bite before shoving it into my mouth.

He shakes his head, sitting up, completely naked, but somehow looking like he belongs exactly here. Like we belong exactly here.

"Give me a bite, then," he says, reaching for me.

I smirk, pulling the spoon back. "Didn't you just call me *unbelievable*?" I mock his tone.

Theo narrows his eyes. "I take it back. Now give me the ice cream."

I consider this. "Hmm. I could. Or... I could make you work for it."

His eyes darken instantly. "Oh?"

I grin. "Kiss me first."

He lets out a low chuckle. "Easiest deal I've ever made."

And then his mouth is on mine again. He kisses me like he's making a promise.

Like he's claiming this moment—not just for now, but for always.

His lips are warm, tasting of caramel and something undeniable. His hands slide into my hair, angling my head just right, deepening the kiss until I'm completely lost in it.

I forget about the ice cream.

I forget about everything except the way he's touching me, the way he's pressing me back onto the mattress, shifting to cover my body with his. His hands roam, slow and deliberate, exploring every inch of me. There's no rush this time. No frantic need to close the distance between us.

We know what this is now.

This isn't just heat.

This is love.

I sigh against his lips, my fingers gliding over his bare skin, feeling the steady rise and fall of his breath, the warmth of him beneath my touch.

He exhales a quiet groan as I skim my hands lower, over the taut muscles of his back, pulling him impossibly closer.

"Fuck, Ivy," he mutters against my skin, his breath warm against my neck.

I smile, threading my fingers through his hair, tilting my head to give him more access as he trails soft, lingering kisses along my throat.

Theo lifts his head, his dark gaze locking onto mine. His thumb brushes against my cheek, tracing the curve of my face with a tenderness that makes my chest ache.

"I love you," he murmurs again, like he needs to say it, needs to hear it.

I swallow hard, my fingers tightening on his shoulders. "I love you."

And then there's no more talking.

He moves with quiet reverence, savouring every touch, every gasp, every sigh. His body fits against mine perfectly, like we were meant for this.

Meant for each other.

I wrap my legs around him, my breath hitching as he presses his cock deeper, his forehead resting against mine.

Neither of us rushes.

We linger, lost in the warmth, in the way we move together so easily. Like this is home.

Like we've been waiting for this exact moment all along.

And when we finally fall together, when he buries his face against my neck with a quiet groan, and my name spills from his lips... I know.

This isn't just something fleeting.

This is everything.

40

Nervous Bugs in my Tummy

Epilogue

Theo

IT'S A QUIET EVENING, the kind that settles in so naturally it feels like it's always been this way.

I'm stretched out on the sofa, a book open in my hands, but I haven't turned a page in the last five minutes. Because instead of reading, I'm watching them.

Ivy and Lucy are sitting on the floor, surrounded by a rainbow explosion of coloured pencils, markers, and glitter glue. Ivy is carefully shading in a section of Lucy's drawing, while Lucy chatters away, waving her crayon like a conductor's baton.

Tomorrow is her sixth birthday, and she's creating a very detailed picture of all the things she hopes to get.

So far, there's a scooter, a mountain of presents, a suspiciously large cake, and—

I squint. "Is that a pony?"

Lucy looks up at me, all wide-eyed innocence. "Yes."

I raise a brow. "And where, exactly, are we keeping this pony?"

Lucy beams. "In Uncle Jasper's garden, of course."

I blink. "Oh. Of course."

Ivy snorts, trying (and failing) to cover her laugh with a cough.

"Lucy," I say, leaning forward, trying to find the gentlest way to break this to her, "I don't think Uncle Jasper wants a pony in his garden."

Lucy frowns like I've just suggested something outrageous. "But he has loads of space! And he doesn't use the garden."

I sigh, rubbing a hand over my face. "I'm not sure that's how it works, Ladybug."

Lucy crosses her arms. "I bet if Ivy asked, he'd say yes."

I whip my head toward Ivy, who is suddenly very invested in shading a flower, her lips twitching.

"Oh no," I mutter, narrowing my eyes. "Don't even think about it."

Ivy finally looks up, all sweetness and innocence. "I mean... I could ask."

"No."

She grins. "But imagine how fun it would be."

I groan. "Why are you like this?"

Lucy brightens. "So that's a maybe?"

"No, that's a no."

Lucy sighs dramatically, adding more glitter glue to the pony's mane. "Fine. But if I don't get a pony, I at least want extra cake."

"Done," I say quickly, desperate to escape the pony negotiations.

Ivy nudges me playfully, shaking her head. "Caved so fast."

"You try arguing with her," I mutter.

Ivy leans in, pressing a quick kiss to my lips. "You're lucky I love you."

I smirk. "I am."

I glance at Lucy, who is now back to drawing, happily oblivious. My arm wraps around Ivy's waist, pulling her closer as she rests her head against my shoulder.

Eight months ago, I told her I loved her.

And since then, she's been in everything.

She's in the way Lucy laughs more. The way our home feels warmer. The way my world finally feels complete.

It wasn't something we rushed.

Ivy and I were careful when we told Lucy that we weren't just friends anymore—that we were together in a different way now. We sat her down, explained it in simple terms, made sure she understood that nothing was changing in a way that would worry her.

She listened, serious, like she was assessing the situation, her little brow furrowed.

Then, after a moment, she asked, "So Ivy's your girlfriend now?"

I exchanged a look with Ivy and nodded. "Yeah. She is."

Lucy considered this for another second before shrugging and saying, "Okay. But can she still be my Ivy too?"

My heart nearly cracked open on the spot.

And from then on, Lucy had thrived in her new dynamic with Ivy.

Mostly because it meant she got to team up against me.

The biggest perk? When Ivy stays over, Lucy gets breakfast in bed.

Which means I am now a sap who delivers two plates of toast, fruit, and juice to them every Saturday while they lounge in my bed, watching cartoons and giggling behind their hands at my tragic fate. I'm also the weirdo who then attacks the bed with the hoover because I can't sleep with all the crumbs they leave behind. Once a dork, always a dork.

The worst part?

I love it.

I love waking up to Ivy in my bed, love the way she and Lucy fit together so effortlessly. Love the way Lucy has started insisting that Ivy be there for bedtime stories, for school drop-offs, for lazy Sundays spent in pyjamas.

Love the way my life finally feels whole.

I glance at Ivy, who is back on the floor beside Lucy, helping her colour, their heads close together, whispering about something conspiratorial. Like they're plotting. Like I'm already doomed. But I wouldn't change a thing.

I narrow my eyes. "What are you two up to?"

They both snap their heads up like they've been caught, but Ivy just grins, far too pleased with herself.

"This moment," she declares dramatically, "calls for ice cream."

I open my mouth to protest—because we literally just had dinner—but I never get the chance.

Before I can so much as breathe a word of reason, she's already gone, sprinting to the kitchen like some sort of dessert-fuelled menace.

I sigh, scrubbing a hand over my face.

Lucy giggles. "She's fast."

"Definitely when it comes to ice cream," I laugh.

Lucy just shrugs, clearly unfazed by Ivy's unstoppable ice cream agenda. Then, without warning, she scrambles onto my lap, settling in like she has done so many times before.

She rests her little hands on my chest, looking up at me with those same big brown eyes she's had since the day she was born, and suddenly—I know.

I know something big is coming.

I swallow. "What's up, Ladybug?"

Lucy hesitates, fiddling with the hem of her T-shirt. Then she leans in, her voice a whisper against my ear.

"I'm okay if I don't get a pony," she murmurs.

I raise a brow. "Oh?"

She nods. "Or presents. Or even cake."

I blink. "That's... unexpected."

She presses her lips together, gathering her thoughts, and then—quietly, like she's testing the words—she whispers, "But can Ivy be my mum?"

My breath catches.

I lean back slightly, looking down at her small, serious face. "Why are you asking me that, Lu?"

Lucy shifts in my lap, still twirling the hem of her shirt between her fingers. "Sabrina at school," she says carefully, "her mummy and daddy sleep in the same bed. And they're mum and dad."

I nod slowly. "Right."

Lucy bites her lip. "Ivy sleeps in your bed, Daddy. And I want a mum too."

My throat tightens.

She looks up at me with quiet hope. "Can she be my mum?"

There's something so simple about the way she says it. No big declarations. No confusion. Just the innocent certainty of a six-year-old trying to put her world into order.

I take a deep breath, smoothing a hand over her hair. "We should ask her," I murmur. "Only she and you can decide that."

Lucy exhales, like she's been holding that question inside her for ages.

Then, just as quickly, she straightens, suddenly looking nervous.

"Okay," she whispers. "But you have to ask her for me."

"You don't want to ask her yourself?" I frown.

She shakes her head fiercely. "No. I have nervous bugs in my tummy."

I chuckle softly, pressing a kiss to the top of her head. "Alright, I'll ask her for you."

Lucy sighs in relief, settling back against my chest, completely at ease now that she's passed the responsibility onto me.

I tighten my arms around her, my heart filled with something big, something I don't even know how to name.

And just as Ivy's voice calls out from the kitchen—"Theo, we're out of salted caramel! Emergency decision: chocolate or vanilla?"—I realise something. Lucy isn't the only one with nervous bugs in her tummy.

Because somehow, the most important conversation of my life is about to happen between spoonful of ice cream.

I take a deep breath, pressing one last kiss to the top of Lucy's head before gently shifting her off my lap.

"Stay here, Ladybug," I murmur. "I'll be right back."

She nods, completely trusting, and picks up her colouring again, oblivious to the fact that she's just changed everything.

I push myself up and head toward the kitchen, where Ivy is rummaging through the freezer, grumbling under her breath.

"Unbelievable," she mutters, pulling out two tubs. "Who even runs out of salted caramel? This is a travesty."

I hover for a second, my chest tight with everything I need to say.

She glances over her shoulder, still completely unaware, completely Ivy. "I'm thinking chocolate, unless you're about to argue for vanilla, in which case, I don't even know who you are anymore."

I exhale a quiet laugh, stepping closer. "Ivy."

She stills at my tone, turning to face me fully. Her brows draw together slightly. "What's wrong?"

"Nothing's wrong," I say quickly. "I just—I need to tell you something."

Her expression softens with concern. She sets the ice cream aside, wiping her hands on her jeans. "Okay. What is it?"

I swallow, my pulse a little too fast. Why am I nervous?

"She—" I clear my throat, shaking my head at myself. "Lucy. She, uh, she just asked me something."

Ivy blinks, waiting.

I inhale deeply. "She told me she's okay if she doesn't get a pony. Or presents. Or even cake."

Ivy's lips twitch. "Sounds fake, but alright."

I huff a small laugh. "Yeah, well. That's because what she truly wants... is for you to be her mum."

Ivy freezes.

Completely, utterly still.

Her eyes wide, her lips slightly parted like she can't quite process what I've just said.

"She—she said that?" she whispers.

I nod, my chest tight. "Yeah. She said she knows we're together now, and she said her friend Sabrina's parents sleep in the same bed, and they're 'mum and dad,' and she... she wants that too."

Ivy presses a hand to her mouth, her whole body trembling.

I step closer, my hands resting lightly on her arms. "She didn't ask you herself because she said she has 'nervous bugs' in her tummy." I smile a little. "So she asked me to do it for her."

Ivy laughs—a watery, shaky sound—before a choked sob escapes her.

And then the tears come.

She covers her face with her hands, her shoulders shaking, and I barely have a second to react before she's launching herself at me, wrapping her arms tightly around my neck, pressing her damp face against my chest.

I hold her, my arms locking around her as she buries herself in me, whispering, "Her mum."

I press a kiss to her temple, my own throat thick. "I take it that's a yes?"

She lets out a wet laugh, pulling back just enough to look at me, her eyes shining. "That's a yes, you absolute dork... if you are okay with that, that is." She looks at me with pleading eyes and I suddenly realise that she wants this. She is not just doing this for Lu; she wants this, probably wanted this for a while.

I grin, brushing my thumb under her eye to catch a stray tear. "Of course. I couldn't wish for a better mum for Lucy."

Ivy sniffs, laughing again, then suddenly gasps as if remembering something important.

"Lucy!"

She spins, rushing out of the kitchen before I can even blink.

I follow just in time to see her drop to her knees in front of Lucy, who barely has a second to react before Ivy is crushing her in a hug.

Lucy squeaks, her little arms flailing for a moment before she clings to Ivy just as tightly.

And just like that, the last missing piece of my world clicks into place.

I lean against the doorway, watching them, my chest so full I can barely breathe.

Lucy giggles, muffled against Ivy's shoulder. "Are you crying, Ivy?"

Ivy laughs, sniffling. "Maybe a little."

"Why?"

"Because I'm so happy, Lu." Ivy pulls back just enough to cup Lucy's little face, her thumbs brushing over her cheeks. "You made me the happiest person in the world."

Lucy beams, like she just won the best present ever. "Really?"

"Really."

Lucy's eyes flick to me over Ivy's shoulder. "Daddy, did you ask her?"

I nod, my voice thick. "Yeah, Ladybug. I did."

Ivy wipes her eyes and turns back to her, smiling so big it's almost blinding.

"And I said yes."

For a second, Lucy just stares at her, as if she's making absolutely sure she heard that right.

Then, slowly, her face lights up.

"Mum," she whispers.

Ivy nods, her voice thick with emotion. "My Ladybug."

Lucy launches herself forward, wrapping her arms around Ivy's neck so tightly that Ivy nearly topples backwards.

"I knew you'd say yes!" Lucy squeals into her shoulder, her little voice full of absolute certainty.

Ivy laughs, squeezing her just as tightly. "Of course I said yes, Lu."

Lucy pulls back slightly, her face so full of joy it makes my chest ache. She studies Ivy for a moment, like she's thinking, like something is shifting in her little mind.

Then—

"Love you, Mum."

The words are soft, natural, effortless.

But everything stops.

Ivy's breath catches. Her body goes completely still.

I swear, for a second, even my heart stops.

Lucy doesn't seem to realise the weight of what she just said. She just leans into Ivy again, resting her head against her shoulder, perfectly at ease, like this has always been the way things are meant to be.

Ivy's eyes flick up to mine, wide and wrecked and shining with tears she's not even trying to stop.

I swallow past the lump in my throat and nod.

Go on. Say it back.

She presses a shaking kiss to Lucy's hair, whispering, "Love you too, Lucy."

Lucy sighs happily against her, and Ivy's eyes close, like she's holding onto this moment with everything she has.

I walk over, crouching down beside them, wrapping my arms around both of them.

My girls.

My family.

Ivy

I lie in bed, staring at the ceiling, my heart still full.

I'm a mum now. I'm Lucy's mum.

The thought makes me feel warm and gooey in a way I never expected, like melted chocolate or a perfectly toasted marshmallow. It's not like anything changed officially—there was no paperwork, no ceremony—but it doesn't matter.

Lucy called me Mum.

And I am.

I smile to myself, sinking further into the pillows. I hear the faint sound of Theo locking up, followed by the soft creak of the floorboards as he checks in on Lucy.

My heart clenches.

Because I know exactly what he's doing.

He's tucking her in.

Even though she's already asleep. Even though she won't know.

But he will.

A moment later, the bedroom door opens, and Theo steps in, rubbing a hand through his hair. He's in pyjama bottoms and a t-shirt, looking effortlessly comfortable, and God, I love him.

He shuts the door behind him, padding over to the bed with a grin. "Still awake?"

I nod, lifting the duvet so he can slide in beside me. "Barely."

He settles in, rolling onto his side, propping himself up on one elbow so he can look at me. "You're thinking about it, aren't you?"

I blink at him. "About what?"

He smirks. "About the fact that she wants to call you mum."

I let out a breathy laugh. "I mean, yeah." I turn onto my side to face him, my hand slipping over his chest. "You realise this means Lucy and I officially outnumber you now?"

Theo groans dramatically, flopping onto his back. "God help me."

I grin, shifting closer, resting my head against his shoulder. "But honestly, yeah. I can't stop thinking about it."

His fingers trail absently along my spine. "I figured."

I smile against his skin. "It's just... kind of a big deal."

"It is a big deal." He presses a kiss to the top of my head, his voice softer now. "And I'm so bloody happy for you. For us."

I exhale, feeling my heart swell. "Me too."

There's a beat of silence, warm and full.

Then, Theo hums. "You do realise, though... this also means Lucy is going to be angry with you at some point."

I pull back slightly, narrowing my eyes. "Why?"

He raises a brow. "Because you have to start saying no."

I scoff. "I do say no."

Theo chuckles. "Babe, you just let her eat ice cream before bed and encouraged her pony agenda."

I huff. "Okay, fine, but in my defence, she's adorable."

Theo smirks. "She is adorable. But trust me, one day you're going to tell her she can't do something, and she's going to storm off and slam her bedroom door and declare that you're ruining her life."

I snort. "I doubt that."

He shakes his head, looking far too amused. "You won't doubt it the first time she glares at you like you're her mortal enemy because you didn't let her stay up late to watch a film."

I pause, narrowing my eyes. "She's never going to glare at me like I'm her mortal enemy."

Theo sighs, rolling onto his back, draping an arm over his forehead like he's mourning my innocence. "Oh, Ivy," he says dramatically. "You sweet, naive woman."

I laugh, slapping his chest lightly. "Oh, shut up."

He grins, catching my hand, pressing a kiss to my knuckles. "Just remember this conversation when it happens."

I roll my eyes, but I am smiling.

I shift back into his arms, letting his warmth wrap around me as I nestle into his chest.

I know he's right. One day, Lucy will get mad at me. She will slam doors, she will give me attitude, and she will push my patience.

But she'll also come running to me when she's excited, when she's scared, when she needs a hug.

She'll curl up next to me on the sofa, she'll hold my hand when she's nervous, and she'll ask me for help when she's struggling.

She chose me to be her mum.

I'm still wrapped in that thought, feeling its warmth settle deep in my bones, when Theo shifts beside me.

"You do realise what else this means, don't you?" he murmurs, his voice low and knowing.

I blink up at him sleepily. "What else what means?"

He smirks, running his fingers lazily down my arm. "You being Lucy's mum now."

I raise an eyebrow. "Go on."

"Well," he starts, his smirk deepening, "if the rule is that mums and dads sleep in the same room…" He pauses for effect. "It's about time you officially moved in with us."

I push up onto one elbow, searching his face, trying to figure out if he's just teasing. "Theo, you don't have to offer. I'm already here most nights anyway."

He shakes his head, shifting so he's looking at me properly. "We don't want you most nights, Ivy." He tucks a strand of hair behind my ear, his touch slow, deliberate. "We want you every night."

My heart stumbles.

He's serious.

This isn't just a casual suggestion. This isn't just convenience.

He means it.

Theo is looking at me, waiting, his expression open and hopeful, like he's already decided that I belong here, with them. With him.

And the thing is—he's right.

Because I do belong here. I've belonged here for a while now, haven't I? It's just that neither of us put it into words until now. I exhale a slow breath, my heart pounding but steady, and nod.

"Yeah," I say softly. "I'll move in."

Theo's lips curve into a slow, satisfied smile. "Yeah?"

I roll my eyes at his need for confirmation, but I'm grinning. "Yes, Theo. I'll move in."

His grin turns wolfish, and before I can brace myself, he rolls us over, pressing me into the mattress, his weight settling over me in the best way.

"Well, finally," he murmurs against my skin, his lips ghosting over my jaw, my cheek, the corner of my mouth.

I laugh, threading my fingers through his hair. "Oh, I'm sorry—was I keeping you waiting?"

He chuckles, low and rough, and something about the sound sends a shiver down my spine.

"You have no idea," he mutters, before finally capturing my mouth with his.

The kiss is slow at first, teasing, full of quiet knowing. Because this is different. This isn't rushed, or uncertain, or full of the tension we used to dance around.

Theo deepens the kiss, his hands roaming, exploring, like he's trying to memorise me all over again.

I arch into him, sighing into his mouth, and he makes a low, desperate sound in response, like he can't get enough of me.

Like he never will.

I pull back slightly, my breath uneven. "You do realise that now that I live here, you're going to get sick of me?"

Theo smirks, his lips trailing down my throat, leaving soft, lazy kisses that make my stomach flip. "Not a chance."

"You say that now—"

He silences me with another kiss, this one deeper, hotter, full of something deliciously possessive.

And God, if this is what moving in means, I'm never leaving this bed.

Ivy and Theo will be back when Jasper and Geoff each find their happily-ever-after

Jasper:
The Unhinged Christmas of a Cat Lady
out on 07 November 2025

Geoff:
The Bedroom Ban
out in April 2026

Why not bake your own Austrian Cup Cake (Becherkuchen)?
Find the recipe here: www.daniebooks.com/cake
Make sure to tag me if you post about it or drop me an email!

MORE FROM
Dani Elias

More from Dani Elias

Aftermath

Mission
Escape
Rescue

Cat Ladies Rule The World

Valentine's Rebellion (Prequel Novella)
The Unnatural Habitat of a Cat Lady
The Unconventional Journey of a Cat Lady
The Unhinged Christmas of a Cat Lady

Greenview Manor Tales

Fierce Family
Alluring Adventure
Elusive Embrace
Wistful Whispers
Spellbinding Spirit

Fellside Mountain Rescue Series

Blossom with Me
Sing with Me
Paint with Me
Climb with Me
Read with Me
Build with Me
Wrap Up with Me
Ride with Me
Or binge the whole series:
Love at Fellside Vol. 1
Love at Fellside Vol. 2

The Ramblers of St Claire

Twisted Paths
Crossed Paths
Fated Paths

Standalone

Christmas Alibi
The Dating Ban – Finding myself... one clay gnome at a time
Surprise Me Tonight

www.ingramcontent.com/pod-product-compliance
Lightning Source LLC
Chambersburg PA
CBHW020339010526
44119CB00048B/529